The MAILBOX® SUPERBOOK™
KINDERGARTEN

Your complete resource for an entire year of kindergarten success!

Editor:

Ada H. Goren

Contributing Editors:

Jayne M. Gammons, Kim T. Griswell, Lori Kent, Angie Kutzer,
Mackie Rhodes, Patricia A. Staino

Contributors:

Kimberli Carrier, Rachel Castro, Bonnie Cave, Marie Cecchini, Lisa Cowman, Tricia Daughtry, Holly Dunham,
Jean Feldman, Ann Flagg, John Funk, Diane Gilliam, Linda Gordetsky, Lucia Kemp Henry, Marie Iannetti,
Barbara Spilman Lawson, Linda Ludlow, Suzanne Moore, Vicki Mockaitis Pacchetti, Betty Silkunas,
Bonnie Elizabeth Vontz, Amber Weldon-Stephens, Virginia Zeletzki

Art Coordinator:

Cathy Spangler Bruce

D1403892

Artists:

Jennifer Tipton Bennett, Cathy Spangler Bruce, Clevell Harris,
Kimberly Richard, Barry Slate, Donna K. Teal

Cover Artist:

Jim Counts

www.themailbox.com

The Education Center, Inc.
Greensboro, North Carolina

ABOUT THIS BOOK

Look through the pages of *The Mailbox® KINDERGARTEN SUPERBOOK™*, and discover a wealth of ideas and activities specifically designed for you—the kindergarten teacher! We've included tips for starting the year, managing your classroom, getting parents involved, and developing youngsters' social skills. In addition, you'll find activities for reinforcing the basic skills and concepts in the kindergarten curriculum. We've also provided reference materials, literature and music lists, arts-and-crafts projects, holiday and seasonal activities, timesaving reproducibles, and bulletin-board ideas and patterns. *The Mailbox® KINDERGARTEN SUPERBOOK™* is your complete resource for an entire year of kindergarten success!

Library of Congress Cataloging-in-Publication Data

The mailbox superbook , kindergarten : your complete resource for an
    entire year of kindergarten success! / editor, Ada H. Goren ;
    contributing editors, Jayne M. Gammons ... [et al.] ; contributors,
    Kimberli Carrier ... [et al.] ; art coordinator, Cathy Spangler
    Bruce ; artists, Jennifer Tipton Bennett ... [et al.].
        p.   cm.
    ISBN 1-56234-196-0 (paper)
    1. Kindergarten—Curricula.   2. Kindergarten—Activity programs.
3. Teaching—Aids and devices.   I. Goren, Ada H.   II. Carrier,
Kimberli.   III. Mailbox.
LB1180.M25 1998
372.21'8—dc21   98-9418
                                                         CIP

Manufactured in the United States
10 9 8 7 6 5

TABLE OF CONTENTS

(Continued on next page)

PROFILE
OF A
KINDERGARTNER

DEVELOPMENTAL PROFILE OF A FIVE-YEAR-OLD

Here's a ready reference on the range of abilities of a five-year-old child.

SOCIAL-EMOTIONAL

- chooses friends
- prefers friends own age and same sex
- uses props for role-playing
- enjoys pretending in play
- directs other children in play
- understands rules of simple, competitive games
- plays cooperatively with peers without adult supervision
- expresses emotions in acceptable ways
- shows awareness and concern for others' feelings
- uses appropriate social responses

SELF-HELP

- knows street address, city, and phone number
- laces and ties shoes
- zips
- selects own clothing
- bathes and brushes teeth independently
- answers telephone appropriately and delivers message

COGNITIVE

- discriminates and names letters
- identifies own name in print
- understands *more, less,* and *same*
- can name the correct number of objects in a set from one to ten
- copies shapes, writes letters (with some errors)
- matches and identifies shapes
- sorts by more than one characteristic (size, color, or shape) at a time
- identifies left and right
- uses time concepts *yesterday* and *tomorrow*
- understands *first, middle,* and *last*
- relates clock time to daily schedule
- attention span has increased so that distractions can be ignored
- understands opposites
- knows spatial relations (far, near, on top, below, etc.)
- compares objects using "er" and "est" endings
- recognizes and continues simple patterns
- draws a person with head and eight features
- understands one-to-one correspondence
- counts ten objects
- knows and names colors

COMMUNICATION/ LANGUAGE

- retells story from a picture book
- speaks in sentences of five to seven words
- repeats longer sentences with accuracy
- takes turns talking in a conversation
- asks for definitions of words
- communicates well with family and friends
- can tell a make-believe story in own words

SPEECH MILESTONES

- has a vocabulary of over 2,000 words
- has 100% intelligible speech, although speech is not error-free
- uses pronouns
- can consistently produce m, n, ng, p, b, f, h, w, k, g, t, d, y, th, v, l, wh; as well as most vowel sounds
- uses the following grammar forms:
    -*ing* endings
    plurals
    possessives
    articles (a, the)

GROSS MOTOR

- jumps rope
- hops on one foot
- runs with arms swinging in opposition to feet
- catches a ball
- skips
- gallops
- walks backward
- aware of right and left sides

FINE MOTOR

- holds pencil correctly
- traces letters
- copies or writes own name
- holds scissors correctly
- cuts out simple shapes
- uses eating utensils correctly
- pastes and glues

Once upon a time, there was a castle. And a giant lived there. He was big and ...

HOW DOES A KINDERGARTNER GROW?

With loving care, room to spare, and the classroom described below!

The centers in our classroom provide opportunities for children to:

- develop social skills
- set goals
- make decisions
- use individual learning styles
- work at their own pace
- develop creativity and expression
- communicate ideas

Look for these centers and the learning opportunities they provide in our classroom:

DRAMATIC-PLAY CENTER

- communication skills
- life skills
- conflict resolution
- vocabulary development
- problem solving
- human equity and diversity
- understand experiences through role-playing
- classification

READING AREA

- vocabulary
- communicating
- remembering details
- reading readiness

WRITING CENTER

- sequencing
- letter recognition
- vocabulary
- fine-motor skills
- creativity
- recording ideas

BLOCKS AREA

- shape and size discrimination
- spatial relationships
- number skills
- balance
- cause and effect
- classification
- creativity
- cooperation
- measurement
- physical coordination

SAND/WATER TABLES

- exploration and discovery
- cause and effect
- measurement
- problem solving
- properties of matter

LISTENING CENTER

- following directions
- comprehension
- vocabulary

SCIENCE AREA

- observation
- exploration
- investigation
- predicting
- experimenting

ART CENTER

- fine-motor skills
- creative expression
- colors, shapes, and size relationships
- self-esteem
- exploring materials
- visual perception

GAMES/ MANIPULATIVES CENTER

- hand-eye coordination
- classification
- visual perception
- problem solving
- social skills
- counting
- patterning

MUSIC CENTER

- rhythm
- coordination
- listening skills

©1998 The Education Center, Inc. • *The Mailbox® Superbook* • *Grade K* • TEC459

Note To The Teacher: Duplicate this page for parents to explain how your classroom will meet their children's developmental needs.

HOME & SCHOOL

Parents As Partners

Parents As Partners

Develop a cooperative link between home and school with these ideas and suggestions.

ideas contributed by Marie Iannetti and Betty Silkunas

Summer News Flash

Give kindergarten families a sneak preview of upcoming class activities with this special newsletter. A few weeks before the start of school, mail each student's family a newsletter filled with information about the first-day activities, as well as some of the projects, field trips, and special events that are planned for the first weeks of school. Parents and children will eagerly anticipate these activities while you convey the message that, even before school begins, their teacher is a great communicator!

What's The Scoop?

Extra! Extra! Parents can get the scoop on upcoming events with this weekly newsletter. Reproduce page 16; then each week program the newsletter with information relevant to your class. Include the week's activities, upcoming events, class anecdotes, or requests for materials. Then duplicate a class supply of the newsletter to send home with students. Your well-informed parents will be grateful for this weekly scoop!

What's The Scoop?

We need cardboard tubes for a project. Please send in by Wednesday.

Don't forget! Field trip to the hospital on Tuesday!

This week we practiced identifying the letter Pp. Help your child circle the Ps in the comics section of the newspaper.

Kindergarten News for the week of

October 12th–16th

First-Day Postcards

I made a new friend.

Hometown School
100 Main St.
Hometown, USA

20¢

Joey Jones
220 Elm St.
Hometown USA

Your kindergarten families will cherish these official reminders of their little ones' first day of kindergarten. For each child, convert a plain 4" x 6" blank notecard into a postcard by printing his home address and the return address (your school's) on one side of the card. Before the end of the first day, invite each child to illustrate one of his first-day activities and then dictate a statement about his drawing. Have each child affix a stamp to the addressed side of his postcard. After class, rush the postcards off to the post office for a special delivery to each youngster's home.

Family Show-And-Tell

Make show-and-tell a family affair when you invite family members to share their talents with your class. Prepare an invitation explaining the steps for scheduling a class visit; then photocopy a class supply of the invitation. Ask each child to deliver an invitation to the person she wishes to be her special guest. On the day of the scheduled visit, encourage the child to introduce her guest. Then invite the guest to share her expertise, skill, or talent with the class, demonstrating related materials and equipment if she desires. Offer thanks and a round of applause to both your student and her guest for sharing their family pride!

Classroom Photo Gallery

Here's a picture-perfect way to share classroom events with your students' parents. Each month, take pictures of special events and classroom happenings. Mount the pictures on a wall or bulletin board with a brief description of each event near the corresponding photograph. Title the board "Our Classroom Gallery." Invite parents and youngsters to check out the gallery each month.

Through The Year With Picture Postcards

Keep your camera loaded and ready to capture the many memorable classroom moments throughout the year; then convert these special memories into send-home postcards. To create picture postcards, simply glue each photo onto a separate 4" x 6" blank notecard. Label the back of the card with the name and address of a student's family, and write the child's dictation about the picture. Invite the child to sign the card and attach a postage stamp. Your class-made picture postcards are ready for delivery!

We went to a pumpkin patch. I found a big pumpkin!

Cameron

To:
the family of
Cameron Littl
55

20¢

Tea, Anyone?

Make sharing children's literature with parents a special occasion with this idea. Each month organize a Parent Tea to share new and interesting titles in children's literature. During the event, display new classroom books for parents to browse through as they snack on tea and cookies. Then discuss and demonstrate a few activities that parents can do with their children when reading to them at home. Before parents leave, provide them with a suggested literature list.

Literature Make-And-Take

Roll up your sleeves, pass out the scissors and glue, and get ready for a literature make-and-take for parents. Ahead of time, invite parents to join you for a literature make-and-take workshop. On the night of the workshop, provide parents with directions and supplies that will help them create learning materials related to selected children's literature—perhaps a paper-bag puppet that resembles Corduroy or sequencing cards for retelling a favorite fairy tale. By the end of the evening, not only will parents have scads of activities to do with their children at home, but they will also have had the opportunity to mingle with other parents.

Brown-Bag It

Take the opportunity to become better acquainted with your kindergarten parents during a special brown-bag lunchtime. In advance, send each parent an invitation to bring a brown-bag lunch for herself and her child on an appointed day. During lunch, ask parents to share interesting information about themselves and their family. Then share a few things about yourself with your guests. Conclude the lunch activities with a summary of the upcoming happenings in your classroom. What a fun way to get acquainted!

Parent Appreciation Week

Show parents how much you and your class appreciate them by establishing a Parent Appreciation Week. During a designated week, plan something special to honor your parents each day of the week. For example, host a continental breakfast, have students perform special songs and fingerplays, or have youngsters present parents with special gifts. What a great way to honor hardworking moms and dads!

Family Portraits

Smile for the camera! For a very special memento, invite your students' families to school for family portraits. Duplicate the invitation on page 17 for each child; then program each child's invitation with the appropriate information, staggering the arrival times. Have each child take his invitation home. When each family arrives at the designated time, take a family photograph in a special place in your classroom or a quaint setting outdoors. Afterward encourage the student to guide his family members on a brief classroom tour before they leave. After developing the film, send each child home with his family portrait. No doubt this will be a treasured keepsake for each family.

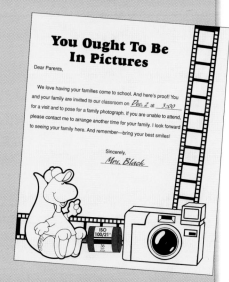

You Ought To Be In Pictures

Dear Parents,

We love having your families come to school. And here's proof! You and your family are invited to our classroom on _Dec. 2_ at _3:00_ for a visit and to pose for a family photograph. If you are unable to attend, please contact me to arrange another time for your family. I look forward to seeing your family here. And remember—bring your best smiles!

Sincerely,
Mrs. Black

What Happened Next?

If you have a class set of a particular children's book, try this idea that will keep your little ones in suspense. On an appointed day, read a section of the book to your class; then send a copy home with each child, along with a note asking parents to complete the reading to their children at home that evening. The following day, invite youngsters to discuss the surprise ending to the previous day's story.

A Family Night Out

Invite your students' families to a special night out—a family night in kindergarten! Several times during the school year send invitations to families asking them to visit your classroom for a family night out. On the designated evening, have parents and their children gather in your classroom for activities such as viewing a family movie, participating in a cookie swap, sharing a potluck dinner, or having an indoor picnic with all the trimmings. During these get-togethers, be sure to take some time just to sit and chat with parents about what's going on in your classroom. What a fun and informal way to get to know each other!

A "Bear-y" Nice Gift

If you're looking for a special way to say thanks to parents who have been helpful throughout the year, give this sweet idea a try. Send home a plastic bear container filled with honey. Tie a length of curling ribbon around the bear's neck and attach a note that reads "Thanks 'Bear-y' Much For Your Help This Year!" What a delicious way to say thank-you!

Video Portfolios

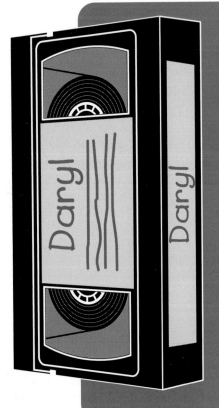

Parents can watch the development and progress of their youngsters with this idea. At the beginning of the year, ask each parent to send a blank videotape labeled with his child's name to class. Throughout the year, use each child's personalized tape to record him as he engages in a variety of class activities and special occasions. (Enlist the help of your assistant to be sure you record each child regularly.) Invite each parent to view his child's video during parent conferences. At the end of the year, return the video to the family as a special keepsake.

Sing-Alongs At Home

These personalized kindergarten sing-along tapes will quickly become home-school language links. Ask each parent to send a blank cassette labeled with her child's name to school. Then, when the class sings favorite songs or recites popular rhymes and chants, tape record their performances. After a significant number of items have been recorded, make multiple copies of the cassette, using the tapes sent by your students. Send each child's tape home with a note inviting family members to join in as they listen to it together. Remind families to replace the returned tape with another blank tape so that their children will have a continuous supply of class songs and such to share with them.

Mrs. Riley's Kindergarten Class

Scope And Scoop

Scope out the activity in your class to spot youngsters who spontaneously perform special acts of kindness. For example, a child might offer to share a snack or to help a classmate tie his shoe. Or a student might befriend a new child in the class. After praising the child for his kindness, make a quick phone call to share the scoop with his parents. Or jot down your observation on a copy of page 16 and send it home with the child. These spontaneous complimentary reports of their children will go a long way with families—and will encourage youngsters to keep up the good works!

Parent Appreciation Certificates

Certificates for parents? Why not? After all, we all enjoy recognition for our efforts! After special class events or activities that required parental input or support, present each involved parent with a personalized, programmed copy of the parent certificate on page 18. With the help of this simple—but appreciative—means of acknowledgement, your proud parents will be pleased to participate in upcoming events.

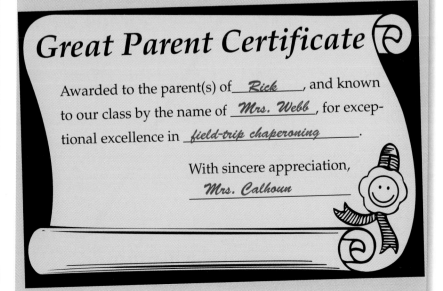

Great Parent Certificate

Awarded to the parent(s) of ___Rick___, and known to our class by the name of ___Mrs. Webb___, for exceptional excellence in ___field-trip chaperoning___.

With sincere appreciation,
Mrs. Calhoun

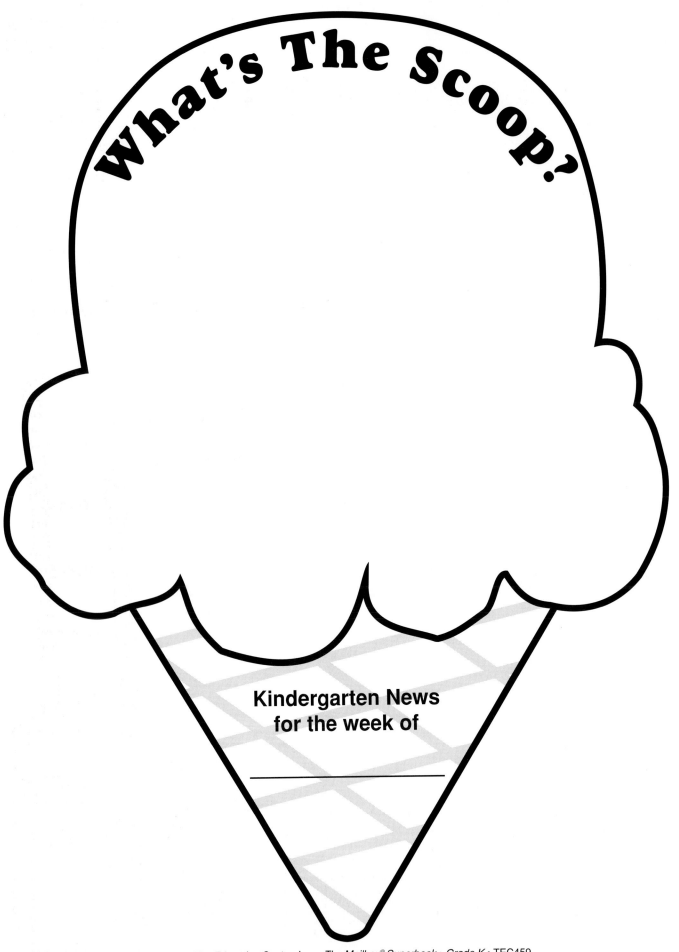

What's The Scoop?

Kindergarten News for the week of

_____

Note To The Teacher: Use with "What's The Scoop?" on page 10 and "Scope And Scoop" on page 15.

You Ought To Be In Pictures!

Dear Parents,

We love having our families come to school. And here's proof! You and your family are invited to our classroom on _____ (date) at _____ (time) for a visit and to pose for a family photograph. If you are unable to attend, please contact me to arrange another time for your family. I look forward to seeing your family here. And remember—bring your best smiles!

Sincerely,

_____
(teacher)

Parent Certificate
Use with "Parent Appreciation Certificates" on page 15.

Great Parent Certificate

Awarded to the parent(s) of _____, and known

to our class by the name of _____, for excep-

tional excellence in _____.

With sincere appreciation,

_____
(teacher)

Great Parent Certificate

Awarded to the parent(s) of _____, and known

to our class by the name of _____, for excep-

tional excellence in _____.

With sincere appreciation,

_____
(teacher)

KINDERGARTEN Conference Center

If you're looking for ideas for making the most of parent-teacher conferences, you've come to the right place. Welcome to the Kindergarten Conference Center, where you'll find recommendations for making conferences successful from start to finish.
ideas contributed by Diane Gilliam and Jayne Gammons

WANTED: PARENTS TO ATTEND CONFERENCES

This invitation is sure to lasso enthusiasm for parent conferences. Duplicate a copy of the invitation on page 21. List available conference times on the invitation; then duplicate a class supply. Personalize each invitation; then ask each child to draw a picture of his parent(s) on the corresponding invitation. Send home the invitations. When each parent returns an invitation with his conference choices listed, assign the parent a conference time. Record the assigned time on your personal calendar before sending the invitation home once more with the assigned time noted.

WANTED:

The Parent(s) Of ___Jimmy T.___ To Attend
          (child's name)
A Parent-Teacher Conference

Please choose three conference times.
Oct. 19: 3:00, 3:30, 4:00, 5:30
Oct. 20: 3:30, 4:30, 6:00

1st choice: _____

2nd choice: _____

3rd choice: _____

Homework For Parents!

Here's a great way to let your students' parents know that you value their input and that you are eager to address their concerns. For each parent, duplicate the parent homework assignment on page 21; then send them home several days prior to your conferences. When each assignment is returned, review it and make a note of comments and concerns to discuss with each parent.

Next On The Agenda...

Preparing agendas in advance and using them during conferences can help you make the most of conference times. For each conference, complete a copy of the agenda on page 22 by listing a different topic or portion of the conference in each of the train's boxcars. At the beginning of the conference, review the agenda with the parent(s); then refer to it as you continue your discussion. Finally send home the agenda with the visiting parent so that he will have a reference of your discussion for future use or when sharing with a spouse who may not have been able to attend the conference. "Yakkety" yak! This friendly agenda will help you stay on track!

Conference Agenda

John's strengths | Current Assessments | Explanation of our goals this year | Parents' Questions

HOWDY, PARTNERS!

Since most parents arrive prior to their assigned conference times, make their wait time informative and insightful. Set a table and chairs in the hall just outside your door. Try the following ideas to enhance your waiting area:

- Post your conference schedule on your door along with a note requesting that the parent knock to let you know she has arrived. When you hear the knock, you'll know it's time to finish your conversation so that you can move to the next conference in a timely manner.

- Place a basket of student-created books on the table.

- Give parents a chance to learn about your life outside the classroom by arranging pictures and brief descriptions on the table.

- Place goodies on the table with a note inviting parents to eat before you meet.

- Make copies of parenting or education-related articles. Display a note encouraging parents to take copies of articles that interest them.

- Provide an album filled with pictures of students involved in school activities.

- Display student work on the walls, making sure that each child's work is represented.

- Since it's often necessary for young children to accompany parents to conferences, consider providing age-appropriate toys and books.

Friendly Reminders

Here's a friendly list of tips that make conferences run smoothly:

- Invite parents to sit beside you rather than in front of you.

- Keep blank paper and pens handy for writing reminders and taking notes.

- Always begin a conference by discussing the child's unique strengths and qualities.

- Empower parents by asking for their input.

- Be prepared to suggest ways that a parent can work with her child at home.

- Suggest goals for the child to work toward.

A Fun Follow-Up

Follow up each conference by sending a small bag of goodies to that parent. Attach a note to let him know that you appreciate him taking time to visit and that you are available should he have additional questions.

Glad we could meet—Enjoy this treat!

Invitation

Use with "Wanted: Parents To Attend Conferences" on page 19.

WANTED:

The Parent(s) Of _____ To Attend

(child's name)

A Parent-Teacher Conference

Please choose three conference times.

1st choice: _____

2nd choice: _____

3rd choice: _____

©1998 The Education Center, Inc. • *The Mailbox® Superbook • Grade K* • TEC459

Homework For Parents

To help prepare for our upcoming conference, please jot down your questions and concerns. Return the form by _____.

(date)

©1998 The Education Center, Inc. • *The Mailbox® Superbook • Grade K* • TEC459

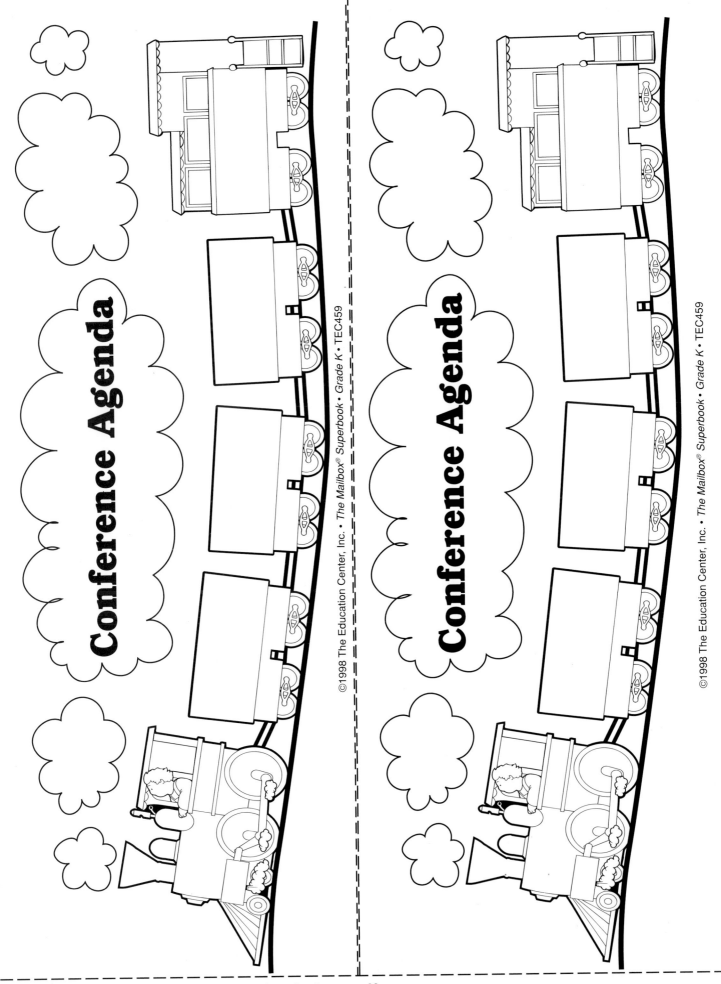

Conference Agenda

Conference Agenda

©1998 The Education Center, Inc. • *The Mailbox*® *Superbook* • *Grade K* • TEC459

©1998 The Education Center, Inc. • *The Mailbox*® *Superbook* • *Grade K* • TEC459

Note To The Teacher: Use with "Next On The Agenda…" on page 19.

GETTING READY

Setting Up Your Classroom

Start the year off right with organization tips that will put everything you need at your fingertips.

ideas contributed by Vicki Mockaitis Pacchetti

ART "ON-LINE"

A clothesline is the perfect place for gluey or painted papers to dry. Hang a clothesline in an area that your youngsters can easily reach and that will be a safe spot for drip-drying. Lay a shower curtain underneath to catch excess paint and glue. Use a permanent marker to write each child's name on a clothespin. Arrange the clothespins on the line alphabetically by first name. As a student finishes a project, he'll have a ready-made spot for his masterpiece. And at a glance, you can tell who has and who has not completed the activity.

CLOTHES "ENCOUNTERS"

Count each day of the school year with this snazzy T-shirt number line. Suspend a clothesline around your room and gather a hefty supply of clothespins. Program your school's name on the T-shirt patterns on page 27, and duplicate the page so there is one shirt for each day your little ones will be in school this year. Number the T-shirts from one through the number of school days in the year. (You may wish to color-code the shirts to show a certain pattern, such as odds versus evens, illuminating multiples of five and ten, etc.) Cut out the shirts and laminate them for durability. Each day, clip a shirt to the line to symbolize another day of class. By the end of the year, your room will be a colorful collection of calendar clothing!

SHARE CHAIR

Sharing time is a special time in the kindergarten classroom. Commemorate it with a rare chair of honor. Purchase a director's chair and some fabric paint at a variety store. Decorate the back support and seat of the chair with fancy handwriting and/or pictures. Each of your little ones will be thrilled to be seated in such a special place when it's her turn to share.

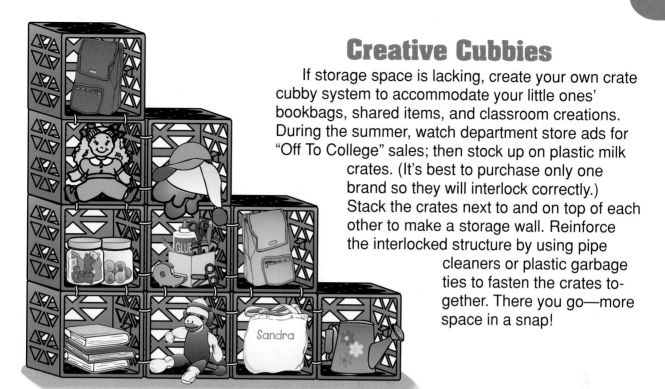

Creative Cubbies

If storage space is lacking, create your own crate cubby system to accommodate your little ones' bookbags, shared items, and classroom creations. During the summer, watch department store ads for "Off To College" sales; then stock up on plastic milk crates. (It's best to purchase only one brand so they will interlock correctly.) Stack the crates next to and on top of each other to make a storage wall. Reinforce the interlocked structure by using pipe cleaners or plastic garbage ties to fasten the crates together. There you go—more space in a snap!

Friday On My Mind

To make sharing the school week with parents part of your students' regular routine, try preparing Friday Files for your students. Purchase a class supply of 10" x 13" manila envelopes. Decorate the envelopes and label each one with a different student's name. Send the envelopes through the laminator with the flaps open. Use an X-acto® knife to carefully slit through the plastic laminate at the envelope opening. Apply Velcro® closures to the envelopes for easy opening and closing. On Thursday evenings, fill the envelopes with students' work as well as with important notes and information for parents. On Friday students can take home their packets for weekend reviews. Make youngsters responsible for returning their envelopes on Monday with any appropriate at-home activities or notes from parents.

WEEK IN A WINK

You can easily keep track of those daily details with this handy system. Purchase five stackable letter trays at a variety or office-supply store. Label each one with a day of the school week. Stack your daily trays on or near your desk. As you plan activities for the week, put all of the activity notes, lesson plans, and reproducibles you need in the letter tray for the corresponding day. By planning ahead, all of your materials will be within easy reach when you need them.

Soda-Bottle Supply Storage

If you prefer that students maintain their own individual supplies, try this idea for handy storage. For each child, cut off the top of a two-liter soda bottle. Cover the bottle bottom with solid-colored Con-Tact® paper, paying particular attention to the cut edge. Use a wide, permanent marker to clearly label each soda-bottle bin with a child's name. When students arrive with their supplies, have them fill their bins with their crayons, scissors, pencils, glue, or any other items they'll need on a daily basis.

Teacher's Space

Create your own special place in your classroom. Decorate your desk (or a bookshelf nook or rolling cart) with favorite items that will cheer you on challenging days: photographs of loved ones, your coffee mug, silk flowers, a plant, a framed inspirational message, etc. Explain to students that just as their bookbags and cubby areas are their own, your desk items are yours. Change the items on your desk to reflect special times of the year, or add new photos and memories as the year goes on.

HELPING CHOOSE HELPING HANDS

Try this simple idea for choosing student helpers with complete fairness. Collect craft sticks, one for each student in the class. Label one end of each stick with a different student's name and place a mini reward sticker on the other end. Gather the sticks in a cup with the sticker side up. When you need a helper, randomly pull out a stick and call on that child. Return the stick to the cup name-side-up. When all the names are pointing upward and every child has been chosen, turn the sticks upside down and begin again.

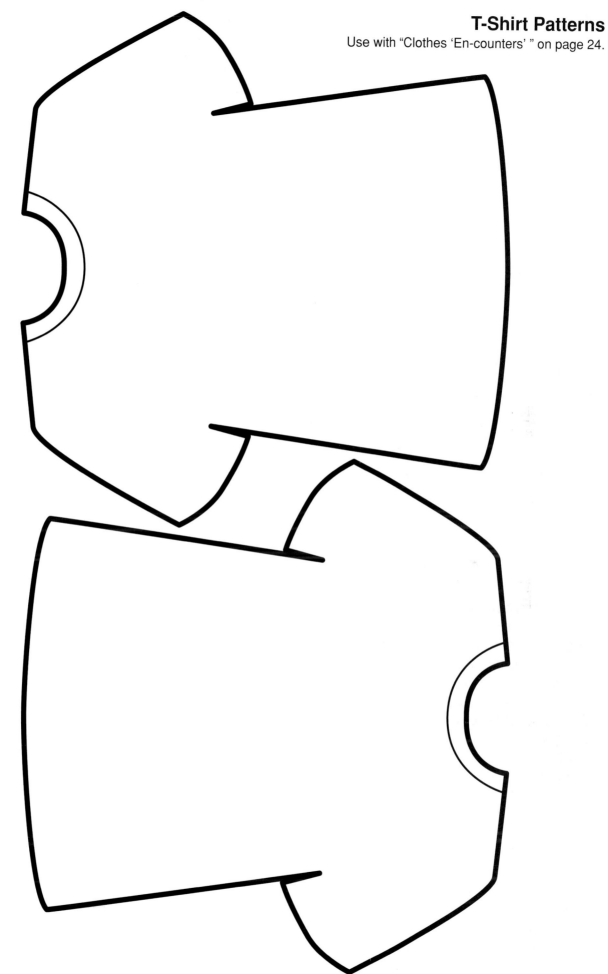

GETTING A GREAT START...
Ahead Of Time!

What better way to start off a school year than with a head start! That's what these practical ideas are all about—preparing yourself, parents, and students for a great school year before it actually begins. So...on your mark, get set, GO! Before the first school bell rings!

ideas contributed by Virginia Zeletzki

HANDLE WITH CARE

Use these special care packages to handle your kindergarten families' first-of-school anxieties. For each student's family, prepare a package to include a parent handbook, a school calendar, transportation details, important school phone numbers, child safety information, PTA information, a class schedule, a list of suggested children's books and books on parenting, and a personal welcome letter from yourself and the principal. Enclose all the materials in a large envelope; then address and mail a care package to each of your families before the first day of school. When they receive their packages, families will be reassured that their youngsters have already been prepared for and cared for.

Charlene McNeil
Parkview School
1234 Parkview Plaza
Charlotte, NC 55555

Wallace Family
330 Flagg St.
Charlotte, NC 55555

CARE

MAP MAGIC

A simple map may provide the mystical magic needed to make your kindergarten families' jitters disappear. Before the first day of school, duplicate a school map for each of your families. Use stickers and a highlighter to indicate important locations around the school, such as your classroom, the cafeteria, the school office, the media center, and rest rooms. Include a note to parents suggesting that they review the map with their kindergartners; then invite them to bring the map to the school's meet-your-teacher event. Mail a copy of the map and an invitation to each family. Then watch the jitters flitter away as each family walks into familiar territory, magical map in hand. Abracadabra!

Parklawn School Map

Art Room
Our classroom
Music Room
Cafeteria
hall restrooms
Library
Office
entry
Tchr Lounge
Nurse
PE Office
Work Room
to playground

COMMON CONCERNS

Kindergarten parents have many common concerns. Address them quickly and efficiently with this idea. Before school begins, send a welcome letter to each family. In the letter, invite parents to anonymously express any concerns or ask questions regarding the class, school, schedule, or any other school-related matter. Then, with each letter, enclose a self-addressed, stamped postcard for parents to use for their responses. After you receive the postcards, list each question with an appropriate response on chart paper. Display the list during your meet-the-teacher event. Parents will appreciate the attention you've shown to their concerns.

What happens if my child gets sick?

You or your designee will be called.

How should I dress my child for class?

Have your child wear seasonally appropriate play clothes.

Does my child need to bring any supplies?

You'll receive a supply list today.

Icebreakers, Smile-Makers

Here's an idea that's sure to break the ice with parents *and* bring smiles to their kindergartners' faces. Prepare a simple questionnaire asking parents to describe particular events from their own kindergarten experience, such as their first day of school or special times with a kindergarten friend. Send a copy of the questionnaire to each parent before school begins, or have copies available for parents to complete during your parent-orientation activities. Display the completed pages with the title "When I Was A Kindergartner…" for everyone to enjoy. Then, during the first week of school, read each parent's memories during a group time. Invite students to try to identify to which classmate each parent belongs.

AUDIO HELLO

Greet your kindergarten families with this special informative cassette. Record a special class greeting to all your new students and families. On the cassette, also include a special song that students will sing in your class at the first of the year, such as "The More We Get Together." Duplicate the cassette for each family; then mail a tape to each family with a letter suggesting that the entire family learn the song together. During kindergarten orientation, invite both parents and students to sing along as you lead a lively rendition of the greeting song to kick off the getting-acquainted events.

My Teacher And Me

Create that first kindergarten keepsake before school even begins. Visit each of your new students to introduce yourself and to take important paperwork or information to parents. Before leaving, ask the parents to snap a photo of you and your future student. Develop the film and mount each photo on a larger rectangle of construction paper. Write "My Teacher And Me" above each photo; then present the photos to your little ones on their first day of school. Seeing the picture of the two of you together will help them remember your visit and ease first-day anxieties.

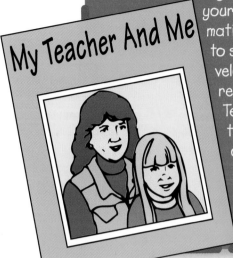

Countdown Chains

Here's a way families can link some important skills to preparing their youngsters for the first day of school. Duplicate the parent note and sentence strips (page 31) on construction paper for each child. Cut the note and strips apart; then mail a set to each of your kindergarten families. On the first day of school, review the links on each child's chain, inviting youngsters to tell about some things that they did to prepare for their first day of school.

Label and pack yo
Recite your first
Recite your addres
Recite your phone
Read a story about
Sing one of your

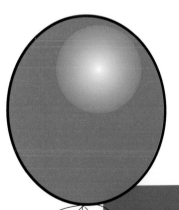

I'm popping with pride to have you in my class!

POPPING WITH PRIDE

If you conduct home visits, consider taking some special treats to each of your students-to-be. For each child, purchase a helium balloon and a pack of bubble gum. On a small notecard, write "I'm popping with pride to have you in my class!" Tape the pack of gum to the back of the notecard. Then present the card, gum, and balloon to each child as you arrive at her house. Youngsters are sure to be bursting with enthusiasm for kindergarten after your visit!

Dear_____,

   Most likely, your kindergartner is really eager for the first day of school to finally arrive! Here's a chain-making activity to help _____ prepare for and count

(child's name)

down the days in the last week before school begins. Select a different sentence strip each day; then help your child follow the directions stated on the strip. After your child completes all the activities, loop and connect the strips to create a chain. Send the chain with your child on the first day of school. Have fun!

Sincerely,

_____

(teacher)

Label and pack your schoolbag.

Recite your first name and last name.

Recite your address.

Recite your phone number.

"Read" a story about the first day of school.

Sing one of your favorite songs.

Pick out your clothes for the first day of school.

Next time you have to miss a day of school, help your substitute keep things running smoothly by providing her with a substitute's survival kit. Use the following suggestions for creating a kit that will make your substitute feel prepared and pampered, too!

ideas contributed by Vicki Mockaitis Pacchetti and Jayne Gammons

THE ART OF BEING PREPARED

Use your creative touch to transform a portable file box into a substitute teacher's treasure chest. Use paint pens, stencils and acrylic paint, stickers, or permanent markers to label and decorate a box. Fill the box with your choice of the items needed for the ideas in this section. Keep the box near your desk so that it will be easy to find and ready to use upon your replacement's arrival.

THE ESSENTIALS

You'll want to begin filling your box with the *essential* information your substitute will need to complete the day. Here's a list of the bare necessities!

- a schedule—Outline the basics of your daily schedule and procedures, leaving spaces to insert details of lesson plans. Laminate the schedule; then when the need arises, use a wipe–off marker to add additional information specific to the day that you'll be absent.

- a class roster—Arrange students' pictures on a sheet of paper; then label each picture with the student's name.

- nametags—Make a class supply of laminated nametags. Provide the teacher with small stickers to attach to the nametags as rewards throughout the day.

- dismissal information—On a bus–shaped cutout, list the bus numbers and riders. Similarly list car riders on a car–shaped cutout and walkers on a sneaker–shaped cutout.

- a list of students' special needs—such as medication, physical limitations, or custody restrictions.

- emergency procedures and a map of your school

- discipline policy

- parents' phone numbers

AWARDS WHEEL

This award-winning wheel will keep your youngsters spinning with good behavior. Divide a tagboard circle into sections; then laminate it. Cut out a paper spinner and attach it to the center of the circle. Use a wipe-off marker to program each section with a simple activity or class privilege—such as singing a favorite song or performing a quick movement activity. (Or leave the wheel blank so that your substitute teacher and your students can decide together how to program the wheel.) To use the wheel, the teacher or a child spins the wheel to determine the privilege. The students then earn the privilege with good behavior. With this management help, goals for good behavior are just a spin away!

Sing a favorite song.

Bubbles at center time.

Have popcorn for snack.

Extra ten minutes on the playground.

BIG-HITS LIST

Reading aloud a class favorite is always a great way for your substitute and class to spend time together. In your survival kit, include a list of favorite read-aloud titles. If desired, include the books as well. Along with the titles, list story extensions that are appropriate for any of the stories. Here are some suggestions!

* STORY EXTENSIONS *

* As a group, list the characters; then describe them.
* Ask each child to draw a favorite scene from the story.
* Dramatize the story.
* Together make a timeline of the story's events.
* Ask each child to draw a poster recommending the book.
* Read two books; then make a graph showing favorites.

The Farmer In The Dell

SAVED BY A SONG

Round up the words to your students' favorite songs so your substitute teacher can lead youngsters in songs during transition times, or conduct a sing-along. Write or photocopy favorite fingerplays and songs onto index cards. Punch a hole in the upper-left corner of each card; then bind the cards with a metal ring. Now, that's a handy resource to have around!

MINIMOTIVATORS

Prepare a class set of this award, and your substitute will have a tasty way to reward your well-behaved class at the end of the day. Prior to your absence, duplicate a class supply of the award on page 35 onto colorful paper; then cut them out. Program the awards with your students' names. Cut each award on the dotted lines; then insert a sucker as shown. At the end of the day, your replacement can sign the awards and give them to your students. Hooray! We had a great day!

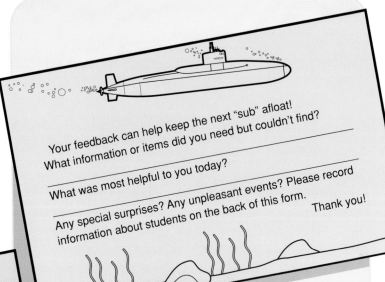

Your feedback can help keep the next "sub" afloat! What information or items did you need but couldn't find?

What was most helpful to you today?

Any special surprises? Any unpleasant events? Please record information about students on the back of this form. Thank you!

HOORAY!

Darren
child's name

helped us have a great day.

Ms. Jones
substitute teacher

Getting Feedback

Along with the other materials that you leave for your replacement, include a copy of the feedback form on page 35. Be sure to take this feedback into consideration as you plan for your next substitute teacher.

Thanks For Coming!

Make your substitute's day by leaving her a brief thank-you note for her efforts and a treat. Consider filling a colorful bag with an assortment of mints, tea bags, or instant coffees. Or tape onto your note enough coins for a soft drink. As a humorous touch, leave her a packet of pain reliever, tissues, cough drops, or a packet of bubble bath. Little things really do mean a lot!

child's name

helped us have a great day.

substitute teacher

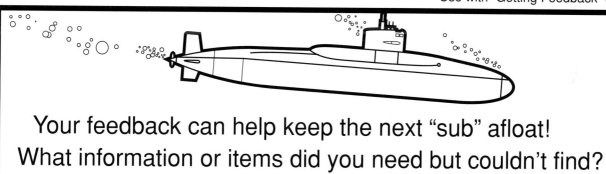

Your feedback can help keep the next "sub" afloat!
What information or items did you need but couldn't find?

What was most helpful to you today?

Any special surprises? Any unpleasant events? Please
record information about students on the back of this form.

Thank you!

Start-Up School Supplies

Keep this wish list on hand when it's time to request supplies from your school or from youngsters' parents, or when you go on your own back-to-school shopping spree!

Helpful Hints:
- Be specific about the number, type, or brand of items you request.
- Give suggestions for stores where parents can find the items on your list.
- Specify a date by which you'd like all supplies brought in.
- Inform parents as to which items will be shared and which will be marked for each child's individual use.
- Consider setting up a snack schedule for parent donations.

Supplies For Each Student	Classroom Supplies	Teacher Supplies
bookbag	crayons	personal planner
resting mat or towel	pencils	hand lotion
spare clothing	markers	stickers
pencil/storage box	glue	rubber stamps
long-sleeve shirt/art smock	safety scissors	thank-you cards
	facial tissues	generic notecards
	baby wipes	carbonless parent notes
	liquid soap	desk calendar
	napkins/paper towels	dictionary
	paper plates	tote bag
	paper cups	headache medication
	plastic spoons	umbrella
	lunch bags	sweater/jacket
	resealable plastic bags	sticky notes/notepads
	adhesive bandages	assorted treats/rewards
	cotton balls/swabs	safety pins
	air freshener	apron
	Con-Tact® covering	rubber gloves
	play dough	first-aid kit
	miscellaneous craft items:	
	wiggle eyes, pom-poms,	
	beads, feathers, buttons,	
	craft sticks, sequins, pipe	
	cleaners, pasta pieces,	
	glitter	

There's more! See page 78 for a reproducible request form for cooking supplies.

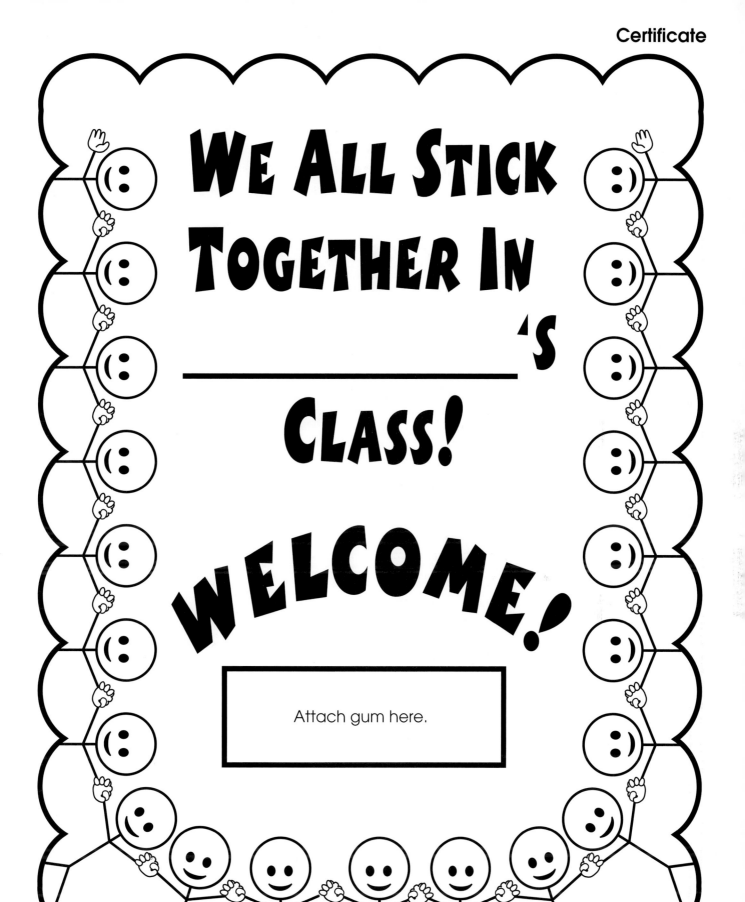

WE ALL STICK TOGETHER IN

_____'S

CLASS!

WELCOME!

Attach gum here.

Note To The Teacher: Duplicate a certificate for each child. Color, cut out, and personalize each one; then tape a piece of gum to the designated area. Distribute the certificates on the first day of school.

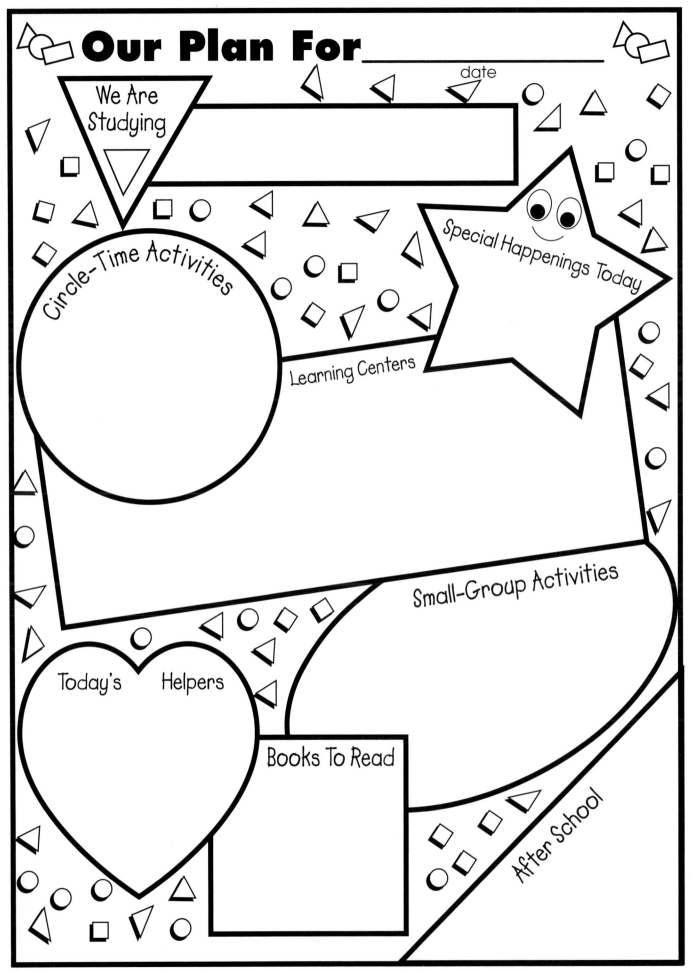

Our Plan For _____
date

We Are Studying

Circle-Time Activities

Special Happenings Today

Learning Centers

Small-Group Activities

Today's Helpers

Books To Read

After School

CENTERS

LET'S BUILD!
GREAT IDEAS FOR THE BLOCK CENTER

Help your little ones construct new understandings in the block center as they build on their basic foundations. Use the following list to assist you in providing a variety of building materials. Then try out these sky-scraping ideas. Slow down and observe what goes on in *this* work zone!

ideas contributed by Linda Gordetsky

TOOLS OF THE TRADE

- unit blocks
- empty detergent boxes wrapped in Con-Tact® covering
- empty gift boxes stuffed with newspaper, then taped closed
- Tinkertoys®
- Bristle Blocks®
- miniature traffic signs
- dollhouse furniture
- Lincoln Logs®
- animal/people figures
- clean, empty food boxes/containers
- toy vehicles
- theme-related books
- DUPLO® blocks
- road playmats
- train sets
- cardboard tubes
- egg-carton cups (pretend rocks)
- fabric scraps (for window, door, or bed coverings)
- hard hats
- an assortment of paper
- tape
- markers, pencils, and crayons

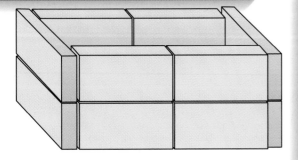

Tick-Tock Tower

Here's a building race that your little construction workers won't want to miss. Designate one child as the timekeeper and provide him with a timer. On his signal, instruct each of the other children in the center to build a block tower. When time is called, encourage the group to compare to see whose tower is tallest. Have the winner be the timekeeper for the next round. Get set…BUILD!

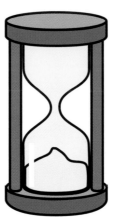

SHAPELY STRUCTURES

Work on shape-recognition skills with this building plan. Assign each builder in a small group a different shape. Have her construct a building using her designated shape as its foundation. Once all buildings are complete, invite other students to visit the block center and name each building's shape.

ON THE ROAD AGAIN!

Begin a patterned road using building materials from your block center. Make sure there are enough blocks to extend the road for some distance. During center time, ask students in the center to observe your patterned road and continue it until there are no more blocks that fit that pattern. Then have each child push a toy vehicle along the road and "read" the pattern aloud. Are we there yet?

Blocks And Blueprints

Encourage your youngsters to use these blueprints to practice visual and spatial relationship skills. To make a blueprint, lay blocks of a variety of shapes and sizes on pieces of 12" x 18" construction paper to create building designs. Laminate the papers for durability. Store the blueprints in the block center. As a child visits the center, challenge him to build using the blueprint of his choice. For a variation to this activity, invite each student to create his own block structure; then provide block-shaped cutouts for him to make his own blueprint for other students to follow. Who knows? You just might inspire a future architect!

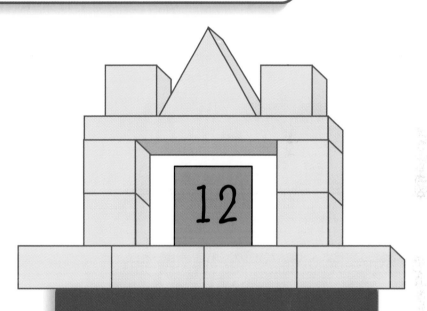

STICK TO THE BUDGET

This construction budget will lead to lots of creativity and critical thinking. Explain to your little contractors what a budget is; then give each of them a budget of blocks to use in constructing a house. For example, if the budget is 12, each child can use only 12 blocks to build her structure. Write the budget numeral on a sheet of construction paper, and post it in the center as a reminder. At the end of center time, have a student inspector check the houses to see if each child stuck to her budget. Then bring in the demolition and cleanup crew!

Ease On Over To The Easel:
Great Ideas For The Art Center

Use these ideas to make your art center more inviting, more organized, and more FUN!

ideas contributed by Tricia Daughtry and Holly Dunham

A "Hole" Lot Of Creativity

Encourage children to think creatively about shapes and spaces with this idea. Before hanging a sheet of art paper on the easel, cut a hole in it. The hole can be any shape—try circles, squares, stars, or diamonds for starters. If desired, hang a solid piece of paper behind the one with the hole. Then observe how your youngsters react: do they paint inside the cutout shape or around it?

Crayons-On-A-String

If your art center routine is "Crayons at the table, paints at the easel," then think again! Attach one end of a long length of yarn to the top of your easel, and tie the opposite end around a crayon. (You might add a dab of hot glue for security.) Youngsters will love drawing with this crayon-on-a-string. Tie two or three crayons together for a multicolored effect.

Sticky Stuff

Want youngsters to stick with their artistic endeavors? Stock your art center with some of these peel-and-stick materials. Youngsters will be creating with new media *and* building fine-motor skills as they peel and place these materials.

stickers
adhesive bandages
colored masking tape
magnetic tape
scraps of Con-Tact® paper
adhesive Velcro®

Provide variety in painting activities by encouraging children to use paintbrushes of different sizes. You probably have very small watercolor brushes and fatter children's paintbrushes on hand. Visit a home-improvement store and purchase a few inexpensive brushes with greater widths (the type used for painting walls and trim). Of course, you'll need to provide large sheets of paper or lengths of bulletin-board paper for this BIG brush exploration.

Paint Prints—Neat!

If you've ever invited children to dip a printing item—such as a cookie cutter or a cut vegetable—into a container of paint, you know how messy the results can be. Try this tip for neater printing: place a wet sponge in a disposable pie plate, sprinkle dry tempera paint on it, and then have children press the printing object onto the sponge to take on the color. Add water as necessary to keep the sponge wet.

FINGERPAINTING FEVER!

Your youngsters will catch fingerpainting fever when you provide some unusual surfaces on which to paint. Try any or all of the following:

aluminum foil
plastic picture or poster frames
waxed paper
a shower curtain
large mirrors
cafeteria trays
vinyl tile samples
cookie sheets
grocery bags

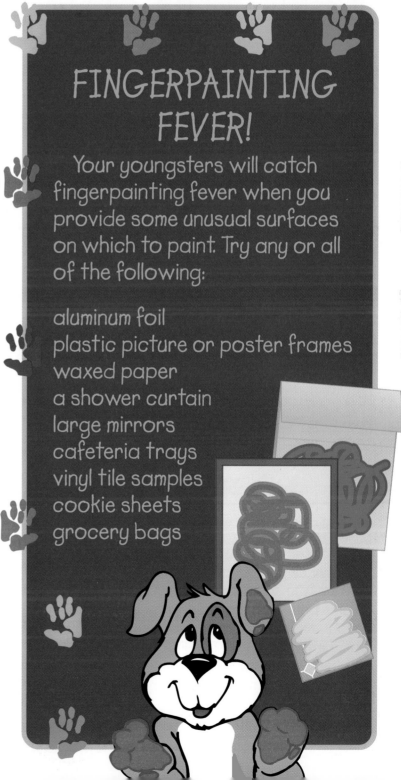

WRITE AWAY!
Great Ideas For The Writing Center

Make writing fun for little scribblers. Pencil these exciting ideas into your planner, and make your writing center a popular place to doodle, draw, dream, and learn about writing.

ideas contributed by Vicki Mockaitis Pachetti

SPELLING SQUARES

Nurture beginning spelling skills with letter tiles. Bring in squares from a Scrabble® game, or visit a home improvement store to find small tiles and make your own low-cost letter tiles. Use a permanent marker to label one tile for each letter of the alphabet. Make multiples of often-used letters. Place the letter tiles in your writing center along with a list of seasonal or sight words. Then invite your youngsters to let their fingers do the writing as they use the tiles to copy the words on the list. Extend the hands-on learning by asking youngsters visiting your writing center to alphabetize the letter tiles.

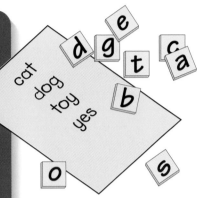

Pretty Printing

Motivate your youngsters to write with some interesting implements. Join together two to four different colors of crayons, pens, pencils, or fine-line markers with a rubber band. Place these multicolored writing utensils where little ones can use them to add a fanciful touch to their writing.

CARD STOCK

Coax creative writing from your youngsters with festive writing prompts. Ask parents to cut off the fronts of holiday cards they've received and donate them to your class. Place the card fronts in a basket and include them in your writing center. Encourage each student to select a card. On the back, have him write imaginative words or sentences inspired by the card. For a larger project, have him choose several card fronts, write on the back of each, and staple them together along the left edge to make a picture book. Continue collecting cards throughout the year to keep your writing center stocked and students' interest piqued.

PERSONALIZED STATIONERY

Introduce letter writing with a personal touch by encouraging youngsters to design their own stationery. On sheets of white paper, mark off a one-inch border. Instruct each youngster to use crayons or rubber stamps to create a design within the border. Duplicate a small supply of each student's design so she can have a personal pack of her own paper. Follow this activity by asking each student to write or dictate a letter home to her mom or dad. Provide a variety of envelopes to decorate. Your students will be bursting with pride when they present their personalized letters to their parents.

BUDDY BOOKMARKS

Turn reading buddies into writing buddies by inviting youngsters to create buddy bookmarks. Give each child a tagboard sentence strip. Encourage each youngster to use his best handwriting to write his name on the strip. Have him flip over and illustrate the strip, then trade strips with his buddy. What a great way to always have a buddy with you when reading!

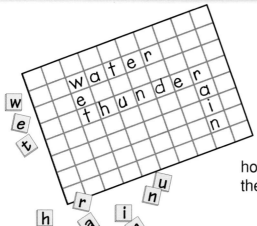

Creative Crosswords

Simplified crossword puzzles will provide writing-center fun. Create grids on sheets of white copy paper. Laminate the grids; then program each one with seasonal or sight words. Show youngsters how to use the tiles from a game of Scrabble® to cover the letters, making words on the puzzle paper.

CLASSROOM CLIP ART

Jazz up your weekly parent notes with a collection of clip art created by your young artists. Supply your writing table with 3" x 5" plain index cards and black, fine-tip markers. On an index card, have each child draw a picture that illustrates an upcoming theme or season. Direct him to write his name beneath his drawing. After your little ones complete their pictures, place several of their index cards at a time on a copy machine, and reduce the pictures to approximately 1" x 2". Cut out pictures as needed to enhance newsletters or parent communications. Youngsters will be eager to pass along your notes to parents when they see their own clip art decorating the page.

COLORFUL CRAYON GRAPHS

Combine math and letter discrimination for a colorful addition to your writing center. In advance purchase a box of 64 crayons. Choose six letters that begin one or more crayon names. Design a graph with 6 columns and 16 rows. Label each column with one of the six letters chosen. Duplicate a class supply of these grids. Remove one of the cardboard sleeves from the crayon box and fill it with crayons whose color names begin with the letters on your graph. Invite visitors to your writing center to complete a graph by coloring in a square in the corresponding beginning-letter column for each of the 16 crayons in the sleeve. Now, that's a colorful way to practice beginning letters!

Beyond Housekeeping
Great Ideas For The Dramatic-Play Center

Take the housekeeping ho-hum out of your dramatic-play center
with this collection of ideas designed to let students' imaginations soar.

ideas contributed by Lucia Kemp Henry

A-Camping We Will Go

Your little ones will be making tracks to your dramatic-play center when you transform it into this cool campsite. Roll out a piece of green or brown outdoor carpet in an open area of your classroom to resemble the forest floor. Set up a simple pop-up tent on the carpet. Arrange several rocks into a circle nearby. Place a few blocks in the center of the rock circle; then add some crumpled red tissue paper to represent a fire. To give this area the feel of a real campsite, stock it with plenty of camping gear, such as backpacks, flashlights, toy lanterns, mess kits, and forest maps. Add some camping hats and hiking boots, and your little campers will be ready to sing around the campfire.

Working In The Garden

Your youngsters will rake up bushels of dramatic-play opportunities in this center. Fill a child-sized wheelbarrow or small garden cart with a variety of plastic garden tools, a rake, a watering can, plastic flowerpots, a short length of garden hose, a spray nozzle, a lawn sprinkler, and a variety of artificial flowers and leaves. Place the wheelbarrow in a center along with a sensory table filled with potting soil. Add some garden garb, such as overalls, tall garden boots, gardening gloves, and a variety of gardening hats. As youngsters plant flowers and rake up leaves, you'll see sprouts of creative imagination begin to take root!

Under Construction

Merge dramatic play with your block area to create a construction site. Stock the area with a variety of toy dump trucks, bulldozers, and loaders. Then break ground for some big block building by adding a collection of measuring tapes, tool belts, masking tape, flagging tape, tagboard construction-site signs, and orange safety cones. Make some orange safety vests by cutting a hole in the center of each of several orange fabric rectangles. Place the vests and some hard hats in the center. Encourage equal opportunity use of the center by inviting both girls and boys to don hard hats and get to work. Now, that's a blueprint for success!

Spring Cleaning

Add a touch of springtime freshness to your housekeeping center! Stock the area with some spring-cleaning essentials, such as small buckets; a feather duster; a child-sized broom, dustpan, and mop; sponges; and a few spray bottles filled with water (add a few drops of lemon extract to give the water a lemony scent, if desired). Place all the cleaning props in a large laundry basket in your housekeeping center.

Encourage youngsters to use the cleaning supplies to spruce up the furniture and accessories in the area. Then, when the area is sparkling clean and lemony fresh, prepare for a few home improvements. Mount a sheet of bulletin-board paper on a wall in the area. Place a bucket of paintbrushes, paint rollers, paint samples, glue, and wallpaper scraps in the area. Invite students to redecorate the area by painting the paper, then gluing wallpaper and paint samples onto the paper. Now, that's a housekeeping area that's springtime fresh and pretty as a picture!

Puppy Love

Create a classroom version of a veterinary clinic. Begin by stacking some boxes along one wall; then place a stuffed animal in each box to resemble a kennel. Cover an "examining" table with a white sheet; then place some medical supplies—such as a stethoscope, toy thermometer, fabric bandage strips, masking-tape Band-Aids®, empty prescription containers, and some cotton balls—near the table. Your little veterinarians will need to write some prescriptions, so include some notepaper, pencils, and clipboards. Finally, provide some oversized white shirts for each pet doctor to wear. The doctor will see you now!

Masquerade Ball

For a variation on traditional dress-up activities, invite your youngsters to attend a masquerade ball. Pack a suitcase with a variety of interesting clothes, shoes, gloves, and hats. (Thrift shops are a wonderful source for funky fashions.) Also include fun eyeglass frames (with the lenses removed), jewelry, wigs, false noses, and mustaches. Invite students to dress up in their choice of items. Then, when everyone has donned a disguise, play some lively instrumental music and let the dancing begin!

BANK ON BOOKS
Great Ideas For The Reading Center

Has your reading-center account made too many withdrawals on your creativity while earning poor student interest? Then read on to find some deposits you can give to your center that will make it more print-rich and gain substantial student literacy returns. You can bank on it!

ideas contributed by Angie Kutzer and Bonnie Elizabeth Vontz

Reading Deposits

Expose your bookworms to the power of print by including lots of reading materials. Use the following list to get you started. Incorporating these materials into your reading center will show youngsters that reading has many purposes and is essential to living in our world.

- posters
- fiction and nonfiction books
- pictures
- magazines
- newspapers
- brochures and pamphlets
- menus
- store circulars and advertisements
- receipts
- coupons
- telephone books
- food-box front panels
- maps
- junk mail
- catalogs
- wordless books
- recipes
- greeting cards
- old grocery lists
- calendars
- class photo album/scrapbook
- picture dictionaries

Transferring Accounts

Change your reading center periodically to keep it fresh and exciting in order to entice new readers and welcome back frequent visitors. Consider organizing it by theme to correlate with your current unit of study, or seasonally to associate it with upcoming holidays and celebrations. Fill the center with stories related to your topic. Then, for added interest, include a space (table, shelf, or corner of the floor) for manipulatives and props related to the theme. For example, if your current unit is "The Farm," you might want to include plastic farm animals, a seed collection, miniature garden tools, a barn replica, and a toy tractor. Invite students to contribute to the collection and to take turns choosing a book from the center for storytime. Your planning and providing, along with students' learning and participation, will balance out to the penny!

Literacy Mutual Fund

Provide this funny-money incentive for youngsters who invest their time in your reading center. Prepare a supply of construction-paper book bucks, or use play money. Each time a student visits the center, pay him one buck; then periodically have book sales where students can buy books you acquire from yard sales, book clubs, or parent donations. This investment really pays off!

High-Yield I.R.A. (Individual Reading Area)

Not enough space in your classroom for a permanent reading center? Then make it portable with a pool! Fill a small plastic or inflatable pool with pillows, and store books in baskets around the pool's edge for an inviting reading environment. If desired, make the pool seasonal by filling it with straw in the fall; polyester fiberfill in the winter; plastic grass or raffia and craft feathers in the spring; and blue packing chips in the summer. This high-yielding I.R.A. may need to be adjusted to a P.R.A. (Partner Reading Area) to accommodate more growth!

Family Trusts

Encourage families to contribute to your reading center with this take-home project. In advance, place a book, a plain standard-sized pillowcase, a letter explaining the project, and various craft materials—such as craft glue, scissors, fabric paints, fabric pens, buttons, felt, sequins, and wiggle eyes—into a large resealable plastic bag. Give the bag to one student to take home. Have her family decorate the pillowcase together after reading the enclosed book. When the bag is returned, replenish the supplies, insert a different book, and send it home with another child. Ask parents to donate inexpensive pillows to use with the literacy pillowcases. An idea worth saving!

Ready For 'Rithmetic?

Great Ideas For The Math Center

Add these hands-on activities to your math center, and watch students' interest and skills multiply!

ideas contributed by Diane Gilliam

LEAFY LADYBUG MATH

Your little ones will go buggy over matching numerals to sets with these fun props! In advance create a leaf pattern and duplicate 21 copies. Program each leaf with a different numeral from 0 to 20; then color each leaf and laminate it for extended use, if desired. Next spread dried lima beans on sheets of newspaper. Spray-paint one side of the beans red. When the paint dries, use a permanent black marker to decorate each bean to resemble a ladybug. Place the leaves and a jar of ladybug beans in your math center. Have students place ladybugs on the leaves to form numerals. Or have them count and place the corresponding number of bugs on each numbered leaf. Expand youngsters' counting skills by teaching them this ladybug song:

Ten Little Ladybugs
(sung to the tune of "Ten Little Indians")
One little, two little, three little ladybugs,
Four little, five little, six little ladybugs,
Seven little, eight little, nine little ladybugs,
Ten ladybugs on a leaf.

Hooked On Numerals

Link counting and cooperation with this center idea. First use cardboard and dimensional fabric paints to create numeral cards (1–10). Add the appropriate number of dots at the bottom of each card for self-checking. For each numeral card, connect an equal number of learning links together to form a chain. Hang the chains on a simple clothesline, and place the numeral cards nearby. Instruct your little ones to remove each chain and lay it next to the corresponding numeral card. Invite the center participants to check each other's work. They'll be hooked on this activity!

Walking The Dog

This patterning activity will be a walk in the park for your bright learners! Gather a pile of multicolored learning links. Draw various chain-link patterns of varying difficulty on sentence strips, making sure that they match the colors of your learning links. Place them in a tub with three or four small stuffed dogs. Encourage youngsters to pretend the stuffed animals are their pets. Invite each child to select a pattern strip and use the learning links to create a matching pattern collar and leash for her dog. After the proud owner takes her furry friend for a walk around the room, invite her to choose another pattern strip and begin again.

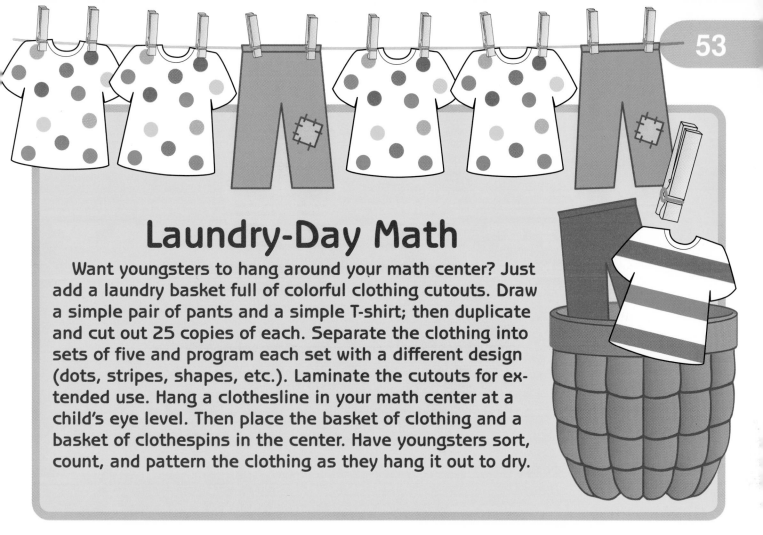

Laundry-Day Math

Want youngsters to hang around your math center? Just add a laundry basket full of colorful clothing cutouts. Draw a simple pair of pants and a simple T-shirt; then duplicate and cut out 25 copies of each. Separate the clothing into sets of five and program each set with a different design (dots, stripes, shapes, etc.). Laminate the cutouts for extended use. Hang a clothesline in your math center at a child's eye level. Then place the basket of clothing and a basket of clothespins in the center. Have youngsters sort, count, and pattern the clothing as they hang it out to dry.

Clothing That Measures Up

Challenge students to measure various classroom objects using the T-shirt and pants cutouts created for "Laundry-Day Math." Before children begin, review measurement tips, such as measuring in a straight line and evenly spacing the cutouts. Have each student measure an object using the T-shirt cutouts, then using the pants cutouts. Afterward have them discuss which items are the longest, the same size, and the shortest. If students get different measurement results for the same object, have them discuss possible reasons why. Provide additional practice with other nonstandard units of measurement, such as Legos®, tennis shoes, or seasonal cut-out shapes.

Estimation Station

Your little ones will be counting the days until they can visit the estimation station! Gather several baby-food jars and fill each one with a different treasure, such as postmarked stamps, pom-poms, bottle caps, and jingle bells. Provide paper and pencils. Invite each student, in turn, to select a jar and estimate the number of objects inside the jar. Have him record his estimation on a slip of paper. Then have him count the objects and record the correct number. After he compares his estimation to the actual count, have him select another estimation jar and repeat the process. Add a little jingle to this center by teaching your students this song to sing as they work:

(sung to the tune of "Jingle Bells")

Estimate, estimate, estimate today.
Guess how many in the jar,
Then count them right away. Hey!

Inquiring Minds Want To Know!

Great Ideas For The Science Center

These ideas will encourage students to get their "hands on" science!

ideas contributed by Ann Flagg

PET FOR A DAY

Teach your little scientists about observation when you bring out their animal instincts. If your classroom doesn't have a permanent class pet, ask colleagues or students if anyone owns a small animal that lives in a cage. Make arrangements for the animal to spend a day or two in your classroom.

Ask students what a scientist does. Emphasize the importance of observation to the scientific process. Then give youngsters some time to observe their new pet. Their observations can be general—or ask them to notice specific behaviors such as eating, sleeping, and exercising. Provide paper and crayons at the center so students can record their observations in drawings.

Window On The World

Create a simple weather station by placing your science center in front of a window. Cut streamers from a plastic garbage bag to make a wind gauge, and use duct tape to hang it outside the window. Mount a thermometer with suction cups on the outside of the window. Make weather watching a regular activity by asking one student or a small group of students to report on the weather each day. They may describe the strength of the wind and keep track of the temperature on a monthly graph, or they may try to draw the cloud formations they see each day on a blank calendar. Encourage students to discuss the patterns they see: what do the clouds look like before it rains? What time of year is the weather the warmest or the wettest? Your young meteorologists will put on sunny smiles when they give their daily weather reports!

The Magic Paper Clip

Young minds will find themselves attracted to this fun puzzle. Fill a glass jar with water. Drop a large paper clip into the jar, and screw the lid on tight. Provide a strong magnet. Challenge students to make the paper clip move without touching the jar with their hands. Let the children discover they can move the paper clip with the magnet.

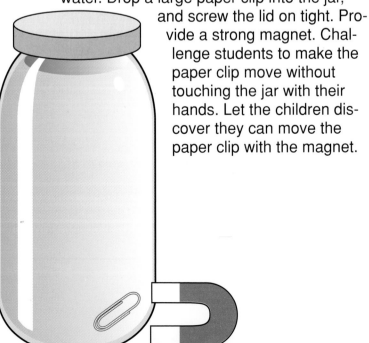

Give students a feel for their sense of touch with a touching box. Cut a circle in the side of a box. Glue the top edge of a square of material over the circle so students cannot see inside. Place common items inside the box, such as a paper clip, a glue bottle, an unsharpened pencil, and a block. Tape the top of the box shut. Invite youngsters to visit the center in pairs and take turns reaching inside. Ask them to identify the items they feel inside the box. Once they've made their guesses, open the box and show them what is inside.

A Penny For Your (Scientific) Thoughts

Students will be quick to add their two cents to the discussion on this water activity. Ask children to estimate how many drops of water will fit on the top of a penny. Use an eyedropper with blue-tinted water, and count the number of drops that fill up the tiny tub before it spills over the sides. Invite children to repeat the experiment using nickels, quarters, water with a bit of soap added, warm water, or ice water. Encourage the youngsters to design their own experiments with these materials and demonstrate the procedures to others.

"A-maze-ing" Water

This water experiment will make a big splash with students. Draw a simple maze on a piece of tagboard. Laminate the tagboard or cover it with Con-Tact® paper. Provide blue-tinted water, paper towels, eyedroppers, and toothpicks. Challenge students to place one drop of water at the start of the maze and move it with a toothpick to the end of the maze. Invite youngsters to experiment with different-sized drops or more than one drop at a time on the maze. As they work, encourage them to discuss their observations about the drops of water.

AIRTIGHT AROMAS

This sensory investigation is right on the nose. Sprinkle one strong-smelling item inside each of several deflated balloons. Substances that work well are coffee grounds, minced onions, perfume, vanilla flavoring, and vinegar. Blow up the balloons and hang them from the ceiling so they dangle in front of your science center. Challenge children to smell the balloons and identify the mystery smells. When all students have made their guesses, reveal the secret scents.

TEXTURE TEMPTATIONS

Great Ideas For The Sand And Water Table

Slippery, gritty, ooey, gooey sand and water…oh, what fun! Invite your youngsters to dig into these innovative activities and splash around in the kindergarten curriculum. The discovery table isn't just for sand and water anymore!

ideas contributed by Suzanne Moore

BUBBLES, BUBBLES

Your little ones will be bursting with excitement when your water table turns into Bubble-Blowing Central! Replace the water in your table with the mixture listed below. Use your imagination to stock the center with a variety of bubble-making tools. Some objects that work well are berry baskets, cookie cutters, scissor handles, and cardboard tubes. Invite your students to experiment with bubble making; then turn exploration into problem solving by challenging them to find other objects to use in the solution that will make bubbles. Have baby wipes or paper towels nearby for easy cleanup so that the bubbles cause no troubles!

BUBBLE SOLUTION
1 gallon water
1/2 cup Dawn® dishwashing detergent
1 tablespoon glycerin

Combine these liquids and allow the solution to cure for one week (or longer, if possible).

Wacky, Wonderful Water

With just a sprinkle of this and a dash of that, you can turn your water table into a wonderful phenomenon. Simply add a few capfuls of flavoring extract to the water and just listen to the sniffs! Try lemon extract during a fruit unit or peppermint extract during the holiday season. For more visual appeal, add glitter, plastic confetti, or crayon shavings to the water. A word of caution: Avoid adding the visual stimuli to the water if you've already scented it. Little ones may be tempted to taste!

Dig This!

Bury objects related to your current theme or unit of study in the discovery table, and watch as your little ones uncover their sorting, classifying, and problem-solving skills. For example, during a dinosaur unit, bury the pieces to a wooden dinosaur puzzle in a gravel-filled table, and encourage your little paleontologists to put together the mystery. Or for a more skill-oriented center, bury an assortment of seashells during a beach unit, and invite the children to find them and sort them by shape, kind, color, and size. The possibilities are endless; just dig it!

Other things to bury:

- **vegetables**
- **nuts**
- **manipulatives**
- **dog bones**
- **plastic worms and bugs**
- **rocks**
- **plastic eggs**

A Work Of Art

Turn your sand table into a canvas fit for a "sand-sational" nature portrait. Moisten the sand with water and pack it down evenly and firmly. Encourage a small group of students to draw a picture using sticks as drawing tools. Then encourage them to use other outdoor objects—such as leaves, nuts, grass, rocks, and twigs—for embellishing the picture.

Pour The Water Out!

Here are some super substitutions for the water or sand in your discovery table. Are *you* brave enough to pour the water out?

- **gelatin blocks**
  (Make sure you have extras for snacking!)
- **shaving cream or whipped topping**
- **crushed ice**
- **cotton balls**
- **aquarium gravel**
- **beans**
- **assorted pasta**
- **cereal**
- **pudding**
- **potting soil**
- **leaves**

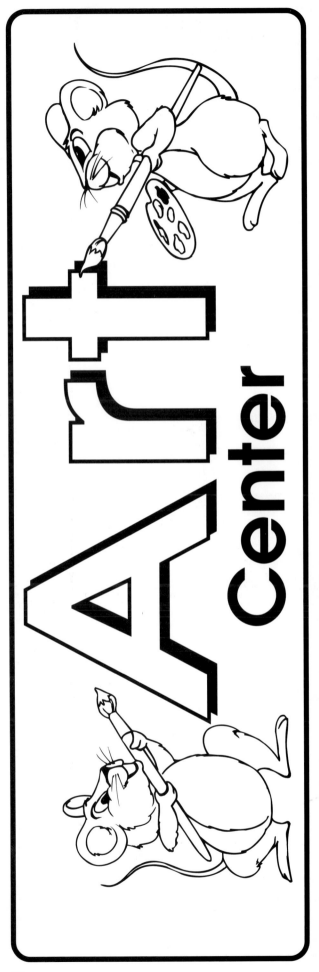

Art center

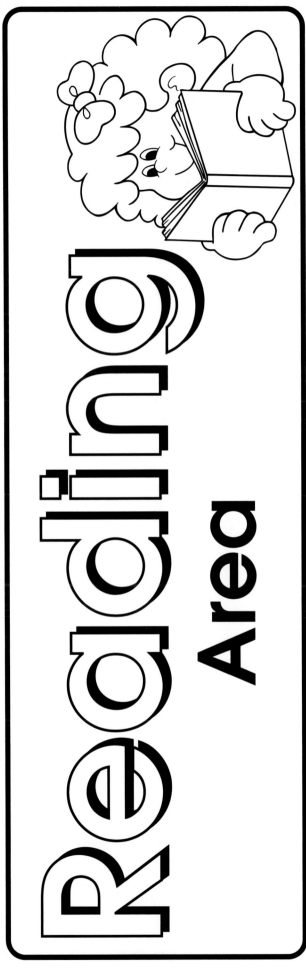

Reading Area

Note To The Teacher: Duplicate, color, and cut out the labels on this page to use for work charts or other center-scheduling methods. If desired, enlarge the labels, color them, and then hang or post them in the designated spaces of your classroom.

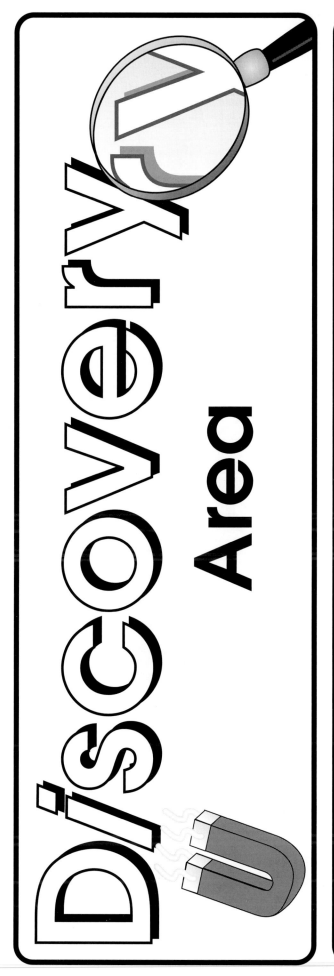

Discovery Area

Manipulatives

Note To The Teacher: Duplicate, color, and cut out the labels on this page to use for work charts or other center-scheduling methods. If desired, enlarge the labels, color them, and then hang or post them in the designated spaces of your classroom.

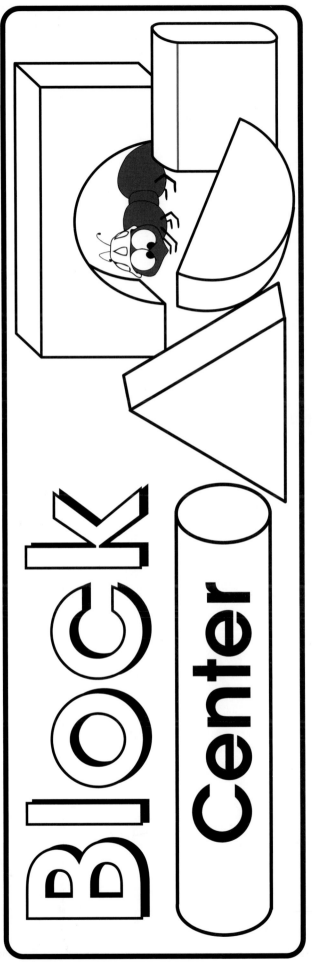

Note To The Teacher: Duplicate, color, and cut out the labels on this page to use for work charts or other center-scheduling methods. If desired, enlarge the labels, color them, and then hang or post them in the designated spaces of your classroom.

Writing Center

Dramatic-Play Area

Note To The Teacher: Duplicate, color, and cut out the labels on this page to use for work charts or other center-scheduling methods. If desired, enlarge the labels, color them, and then hang or post them in the designated spaces of your classroom.

It's CENTER Time!

CLASSROOM MANAGEMENT

CLASSROOM MANAGEMENT

Relax and enjoy your little ones when you use these tips to help manage and organize your kindergarten classroom.

ideas contributed by Jean Feldman and Marie Iannetti

CIRCLE-TIME SEATING

Make seating your little ones for circle time a snap with this helpful hint. In advance collect a classroom supply of margarine-tub lids. Attach a different sticker or shape cutout to each lid. Place the lids in a decorative basket. Mount matching stickers or cutouts on small sheets of tagboard; then laminate the tagboard if desired. Each day before circle time, place each sheet of tagboard in a designated spot on the floor in your circle-time location. Then have each child choose a margarine lid from the basket and find the spot with the matching sheet of tagboard. Everyone will soon be seated and ready for circle time!

A Postcard Of Praise

Your little ones will anxiously await the mail carrier if they know they'll be receiving postcards of praise. Periodically record positive behavior you've observed on a postcard, and mail it to the child's home to inform parents of his good deed. Now, that's first-class mail!

Jim did a great job at the library!
Ms. Anderson

To:
The Parents of
Jim Turner
123 Park Drive
Springton, MA 10012

Note Tote

This organizational tip will help you keep up with notes from parents. Use fabric paint to label a tote bag "Note Tote"; then mount the tote bag within an arm's reach of your desk. When a student hands you a note from his parent(s), read the note and immediately place it in the Note Tote. Later, you'll know right where to find it and be able to respond if necessary. Empty the tote at the end of the day, and file the notes as necessary.

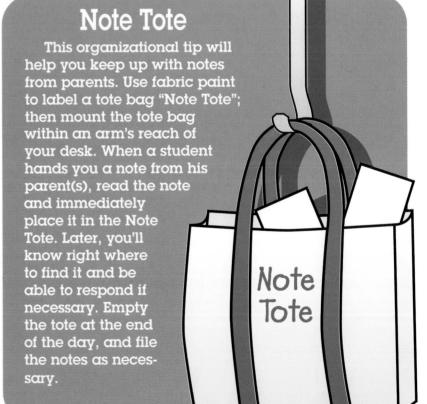

Note Tote

Helping-Hand Necklace

Do you get interrupted when working with individuals and small groups of children? If so, try this handy suggestion. In advance cut out a hand shape from tagboard. Write "I need a helping hand!" on the cutout. Laminate the cutout if desired. Punch a hole in one finger of the hand shape; then thread a length of yarn thorough the hole to create a necklace. When a child needs your help, have him get your attention by wearing the necklace and waiting near you until you have finished what you are doing.

I need a helping hand!

Get-Well Greetings

Send this get-well greeting to a youngster who has been sick and absent from school for several days. Program the outside of a grocery bag with a get-well greeting. Then have each child in your class sign the outside of the bag. Place any projects the child has missed while sick, stickers, and perhaps a few sweet treats in the bag, and take it to the child. What a nice way to show him that he's missed!

TOY STORAGE

This idea will end your search for a place to store large toys and manipulatives. Purchase a few standard-sized outdoor trash cans. Use craft items, such as paint or Con-Tact® paper, to decorate each container; then label the outside. Store items such as large toy trucks, blocks, jump ropes, and playground balls in the corresponding containers. These trash cans are a treasure!

Beth Aaron John

Get well, Suzie!

Ashley Marcia Freddy

Show-And-Tell Tote

To help schedule show-and-tell, use a tote bag or a small suitcase to help remind students on which day they are scheduled to share. In advance, label a tote bag or small suitcase "Show-And-Tell" and decorate the bag. Inside the bag, place a note telling parents about the bag and how it will be used during the year. The day before a designated child is scheduled for show-and-tell, give her the bag to take home. Encourage her to place her show-and-tell item in the bag to bring to school with her the next day.

SPECIAL FRIENDS

Children enjoy sitting next to the teacher and being special helpers. Make sure everyone has that opportunity with this idea. Write each child's name on a craft stick, then place all the sticks in a decorated can or cup. As you begin circle time each day, pull two sticks from the container. Ask the two children whose names are chosen to sit on either side of you and be your special helpers for the day. Place the two sticks chosen into a string-tie envelope and set it aside, assuring that different children will be chosen on subsequent days. After everyone has had a turn, return all the sticks to the container and begin again.

Workspace Dividers

Help students stay within their own workspaces when doing an assignment. Attach strips of thin, colored tape to your tables to create individual sections. These visual lines will remind your youngsters of their boundaries during work time.

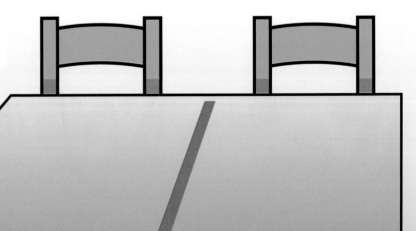

No More Messy Tables

If you need a quick-and-easy solution to messy tables, then give this neat idea a try. Purchase a plastic sand pail for each table in your classroom. Place a pail on each table. Throughout the day, have your youngsters discard paper scraps and trash in the pails. At the end of the day, designate one child from each table to empty the pail. Tabletops will be spotless!

Good-Morning Boxes

Get your youngsters off to a positive start *and* take attendance with good-morning boxes. In advance paint or cover the outside of a shoebox for each child. Have each child personalize her box. Before students arrive each morning, place a puzzle, manipulative, game, or book in each child's box; then place each box on a table or shelf within students' reach. When each child arrives in the morning, have her find her box and take it to her table to use the materials inside. You'll be able to tell at a glance who's absent while your little ones are actively working.

Pop Goes The Bubble!

Your little ones will float through transitional times when you use this attention-getting idea. Each time you want your youngsters to move from one area of your room to another, use bubbles to help keep things moving smoothly. First tell your youngsters which area of the room you'd like them to move to. Then use a wand and bubble solution to blow bubbles. Tell youngsters that you'd like them to walk quietly to the designated area and be ready to work before all of the bubbles pop. They'll pop right into place!

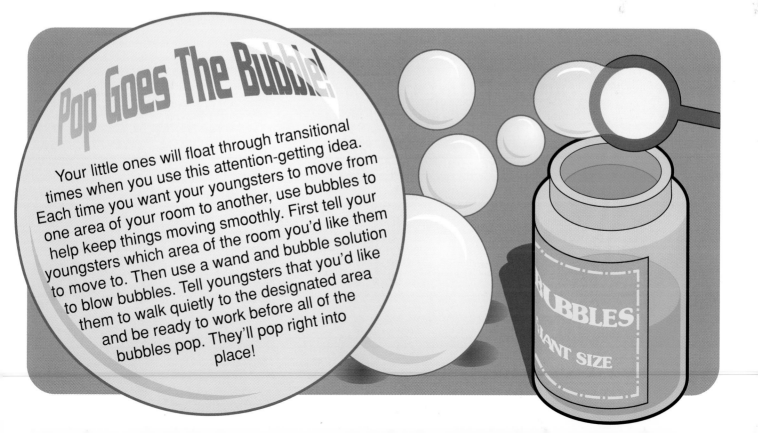

MUSICAL MANAGEMENT

Use these tunes and chants as transitions to move your youngsters through the day.

ideas contributed by Lisa Cowman, Mackie Rhodes, and Betty Silkunas

MORNING RAP

Start the day in a cool sort of way with this lively rap.

Say, "Hi! Hi! Hi!
Hello! Hello!
What a great day
For school, you know!"

Say, "Hi! Hi! Hi!
Hello! Hello!
Time to get started.
Let's go, go, go!"

LINE UP, CHILDREN

Here's a snappy tune that will prepare youngsters for a transitional trek down the hall.

(sung to the tune of "Head And Shoulders, Knees And Toes")

Line up, children.
Line up one. Line up all.
Quiet children.
Quiet one. Quiet all.
Let's walk softly down the hall.
Line up, children.
Line up one. Line up all.

A-CLEANING WE WILL GO

Everyone will want to join in the cleanup fun when you sing this song.

(sung to the tune of "A-Hunting We Will Go")

A-cleaning we will go!
A-cleaning we will go!
We'll pick up toys and blocks and books
And put them where they go!

IT'S TIME TO PICK UP

Make cleanup time quick and breezy with this bouncy tune.

(sung to the tune of "She'll Be Coming 'Round The Mountain")

Oh, it's time to pick up all our toys right now.
Yes, it's time to pick up all our toys right now.
When we work together, it's easy—
Cleanup time is quick and breezy.
Oh, it's time to pick up all our toys right now!

LISTEN CLOSELY

Sing this song with youngsters to call the attention of all ears and eyes to the teacher.

(sung to the tune of "I've Been Working On The Railroad")

Listen closely to the teacher.
Listen as (s)he speaks.
Listen closely to the teacher.
No grunts, no growls, no squeaks.
Everyone is oh, so quiet
And looking the teacher's way.
Everyone is still and ready
To hear what (s)he has to say.

LET'S GET SHAKIN'!

Round up your youngsters to shake, stamp, snap, and clap their way into group time.

(sung to the tune of "The Wheels On The Bus")

It's time to shake
And shake and shake.
Stamp and stamp.
Snap and clap.

It's time to shake
And shake and shake.
Now everyone sit down!

WIGGLE-TIME RHYME

Get those wiggles out with some
movement music.

*(sung to the tune of
"Twinkle, Twinkle, Little Star")*

Wiggle your toes and bend your legs;
Sway your hips and nod your head.
Shake your shoulders, blink your eyes;
Stretch your arms up to the sky!
Cross your legs; sit on the floor.
Wiggles are gone—we have no more!

GOOD-BYE FRIENDS

Softly sing this sweet end-of-the-day
send-off to your little friends.

*(sung to the tune of "Make New Friends,
But Keep The Old")*

Good-bye, friends,
I'll miss you so.
We've had fun,
But now it's time to go.

Moving Right Along

Fill **a** few spare moments, or help your little ones get ready for the next activity, with these fun transitions and time-fillers.

ideas contributed by Jean Feldman and Betty Silkunas

BOOK-BUDDY BASKET

Here's a cozy way to settle students down for a rest or quiet time. Fill a large basket with small stuffed animals, puppets, books, and magazines. Encourage each child to select a buddy (a stuffed animal or puppet) and a book or magazine to read with that buddy. Shhh...we're reading!

ALL ABOARD

Students will chug right along to the next destination on the Classroom Express. Use a train engineer's hat from your dramatic-play area, or a child's baseball cap. Choose one child to be the engineer and wear the hat. When he calls, "All aboard!" have the other children get in line behind him. Direct each child to put his hands on the shoulders of the person in front of him to make a train. Then it's chug, chug, chug—on to the next stop in your school day!

On another day, invite your class to move like a caterpillar by putting their hands on one another's waists. Encourage students to think of other creative ways they can move together.

PICK A FRIEND

Friendship is in the cards with this student-pairing idea! To prepare friendship cards, collect a different set of two identical stickers or pictures for each pair of students in your class. Attach each sticker or picture to a separate notecard; then shuffle the cards. Before assigning students to paired activities, invite each child to draw a card from the deck. After each child has a card, ask him to find the classmate with the matching card; that child will be his partner for the activity. It's that simple—pick a card, pick a friend.

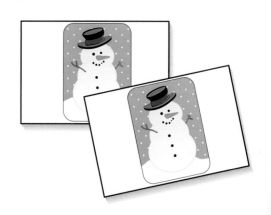

Double Simon

Here's a variation on a favorite time-filler game. Have children sit at a table or on the floor. Offer children instructions with two variables. For example:

— Simon says, "People with sneakers and turtlenecks, stand up."

— Simon says, "People with sneakers and turtlenecks, sit down."

— Simon says, "People wearing white socks and zippers, jog in place."

— Simon says, "People wearing white socks and zippers, sit down."

Once the rules are familiar, invite a student to be the leader of this fun, new game.

TICKET TO RIDE (OR READ, OR PLAY)

Try this transition tip after a messy art session, and your classroom will be clean in a snap. Tell students that to join you for the next activity, they'll each need a ticket. The ticket consists of one scrap of paper off the floor. (On really messy days, request two or more tickets.) Have them bring the scraps to the next activity where you or your assistant collect them in a wastebasket. What a tidy transition!

ROLL 'EM

This quick and easy counting game will help little ones get the wiggles out. Make a pair of jumbo foam dice by cutting a giant car-wash sponge in half. Place the appropriate number of dot stickers on each side of each die. To play, have students take turns rolling one die or both dice. When the dice have been rolled, have the child announce the number of dots showing on top of the dice. Ask the child to pick an activity for the whole class to repeat that number of times. For example, if four is rolled, students might do four jumping jacks, toe-touches, sit-ups, or hand claps.

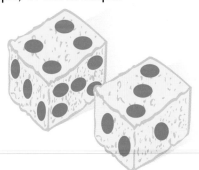

STEP-BY-STEP

It's easy to sneak in a little estimation practice each day. Ask a small group of students to estimate and then figure out the distance between two objects or places. Try guessing the number of footsteps from your classroom door to the bathroom door, from the water fountain to the swings, from the windows to the easel, or from your classroom to the gym. Invite student volunteers to do the measuring; then compare the results with students' predictions.

COLORFUL CHAIRS

Color practice becomes a variation on Musical Chairs in this fun game. Ask each student to sit in a chair. Scan the room to determine the most popular colors of clothing. Tell children you are going to clap your hands and say a color. If they are wearing that color, they should get up and find a new seat. Clap and call colors as time permits. Every so often clap and call, "All colors." Your little ones will love this game of chair-changing fun.

Silly Human Alphabet Tricks

How many children would need to lie on the floor to make a W? The letter A? The letter X? Choose students to predict and test body-letter solutions. For added fun, use a larger number of children to spell out simple words. F-U-N!

KID IN A BLANKET

How well do your little ones know their classmates? Have students sit in a circle on the floor. While students close their eyes, tap one child to tiptoe to the center of the circle. Cover that student with a large blanket. When the class opens their eyes, challenge them to guess who is under the blanket. After two or three guesses, ask the student under the blanket to poke out one hand to give the guessers a clue. Next ask the blanket person to poke out a foot. Continue until students guess correctly or until you run out of time.

SOMETHING'S DIFFERENT

Youngsters will get the giggles when they play this nifty memory game. Ask one student to stand in front of the class where everyone can see her. Tell the class to carefully study the student's appearance and remember as many details as possible. Then, while your little ones cover their eyes, quickly change one aspect of the student's appearance, such as taking off a sock, cuffing one pant leg, or untucking her shirt. Challenge the class to guess what's different about their classmate.

ONE-MINUTE CHALLENGE

Have some fun with the classroom clock or a stopwatch. Ask students to see how many times they can write their names in one minute. Start and stop the challenge with the help of students, who will take turns being the timekeeper. Other one-minute challenges could include counting how many times students can jump up and down, how many blocks they can stack, or how many times they can clap their hands.

COOKING UP SOME FUN

Put on your apron, find your spoon, and mix up some fun! Cooking involves all of the senses and provides a meaningful way for children to use math and reading skills. Cooking also enhances social skills, cooperation, language, motor skills, and independence. Here are some helpful hints for providing cooking experiences that are "tasteful"!

ideas contributed by Jean Feldman

A RECIPE FOR SUCCESS

- Illustrate recipes with pictures, either on step-by-step recipe cards or on charts.
- Keep it simple! Choose cooking activities that are developmentally appropriate so youngsters can experience success and feel independent.
- Explain cooking terms and demonstrate what each child should do.
- When possible, give children choices and select recipes that allow them to make their food and eat it right away!

ESSENTIAL INGREDIENTS

- measuring cups and spoons
- nonbreakable mixing bowls
- kitchen gadgets (such as eggbeaters and potato mashers)
- sharp knives (securely placed out of little hands' reach!)
- cookie sheet, pots and pans, muffin tins
- electric frying pan, toaster oven, blender
- oven mitt and dish towels
- disposable plates, bowls, cups, and utensils
- aluminum foil, waxed paper, plastic wrap, zippered plastic bags
- food coloring
- parent request forms for recipe items and supplies (see page 78)

AN OUNCE OF PREVENTION

- Be aware of food allergies.
- Stress good health habits: washing hands, cleaning up, and making healthy food choices.
- Know what to do if a child chokes on his food.
- Provide adequate adult supervision when using electrical appliances.

STIR UP A LESSON

- Discuss science concepts, such as where foods come from, how they are grown, and to what food group they belong.
- Make a graph to compare which foods students like best.
- Serve ethnic foods to children and tie in multicultural education with foods you eat.
- Relate cooking experiences to classroom themes and skills. Cook something that relates to a sound you are working on, a field trip, or a story.
- Ask parents to take turns being "Chef Of The Week." They can come in and cook with the children or simply provide the ingredients for a cooking activity.

SHARE YOUR TREAT!

- Send copies of recipes home with the children so they can prepare them again with their parents. (You might want to put them all together and make a book for the end of the year.)

- Let the children dictate their own recipes for the best thing their mother cooks. Compile these into a book for Mother's Day.

- Make a video of the children cooking, or take photographs of them so you can share the experience with their parents during an Open House or conference time.

LOOK WHAT'S COOKING!

Dear Family,

With your help, we'll be cooking up something special in our classroom!

What's cooking? _____
(name of recipe)

What the cooks need:

_____

_____

Please help our budding chefs by supplying the item(s) listed above. We'll need all our ingredients by _____ .
(date)

Let me know if you'll be unable to send in the items requested.
Thank you for helping us cook up some learning fun!

Sincerely,

_____
(teacher)

KINDERGARTEN
BASICS

YEARLONG DISPLAYS

Birthdays are sweet with this display. Cut one edge on each of 12 half-sheets of construction paper to resemble a paper bag. Decorate the bags as desired. Label each bag with a different month; then glue each bag onto a separate sheet of construction paper, leaving the top edge free. Personalize a separate candy shape (patterns on page 84) with each child's name and birthdate. Mount the bags and title onto a wall or bulletin board; then tuck the candies into the appropriate bags.

Your little ones will shine with pride over this display. Brush glue on top of a large star shape; then sprinkle it with iridescent glitter. Glue construction-paper features to the star; then laminate it. Mount the star on a bulletin board with the title "Shining Star." Use a dry-erase marker to personalize the star with a different child's name each week. Encourage your little shining star to bring in pictures of himself and his family, and a few of his favorite things. Display the items on the board.

To keep track of helpers, duplicate a desired number of honey pots (page 85) onto construction paper. Color as shown; then label each one with a classroom job. Personalize a bear for each child (pattern on page 85). Stack and pin the bears inside a brown paper cave. Staple the honey pots on the board, and assign classroom helpers by pinning a child's bear next to the appropriate honey pot.

This display will have students grinning from ear to ear! Enlarge and color the character on page 86. Mount it on one side of a background. Add a rope lasso border and a title as shown. Duplicate and cut out a supply of the same character. Each time a child loses a tooth, write his name and the date on the hat of a cutout. Have the child color the cutout, then blacken in the missing tooth before adding it to the display.

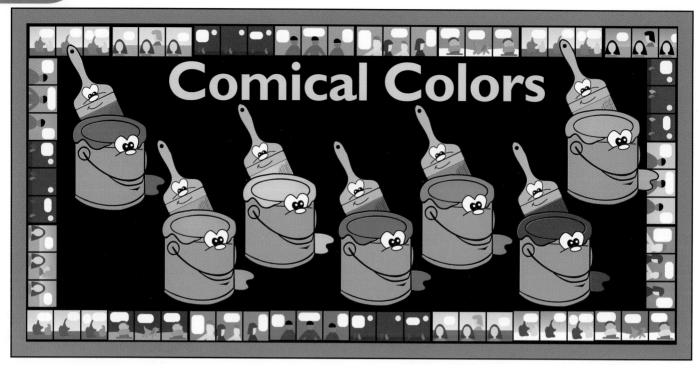

Comical Colors

To create this colorful display, duplicate a paint can and paintbrush (patterns on page 87) for each color you wish to display. Color the paint in each can a different color; then color a brush to match each can. Staple the bottom and sides of each can to the bulletin board, creating a pocket at the top. Slip the matching paintbrush into each can. Add the title "Comical Colors" and strips of colored newspaper comics for a border. If desired, invite youngsters to match the brushes and cans.

Cookie Counters

Help your children take a bite out of counting! Duplicate ten cookie jars (pattern on page 88). Label each jar with a different numeral from one to ten. Mount the jars and title on a wall or bulletin board. Duplicate a large supply of cookies (on page 84) onto construction paper. Staple the corresponding numbers of cookies on each jar. For a variation, store the cookie cutouts and a supply of Sticky-Tac near your display; then invite a student to place the correct number of cookies on each jar.

Keep alphabet skills on the right track with this display. Enlarge the engine pattern on page 89 and color it as desired. Mount the engine on a wall. Add the title in a bulletin-board-paper puff of smoke. Add a labeled construction-paper car for each letter of the alphabet. As each letter is being studied, have children cut out magazine pictures of items that begin with that letter, then glue them onto the corresponding car.

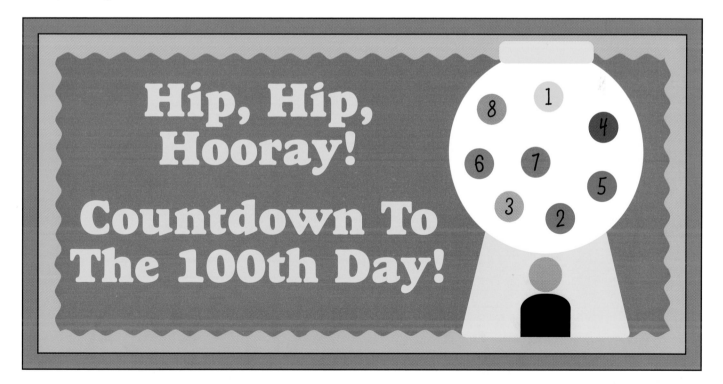

Use this display to count down to the 100th day of school. Mount a large gumball machine cut-out—or make one using large construction-paper shapes—on a wall or bulletin board. Cut out a large supply of colored circles or use large colored sticky dots to represent gumballs. Each day, write the day's number on a gumball; then place it "inside" the machine. When the 100th gumball is posted, celebrate with a Hundredth-Day-Of-School Party.

Candy Patterns

Use with "Sweet Celebrations" on page 80.

Cookie Patterns

Use with "Cookie Counters" on page 82.

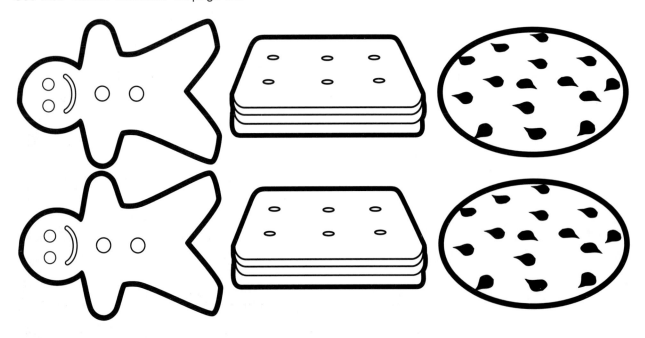

Tooth Character Pattern
Use with "The Gappy Grin Gang" on page 81.

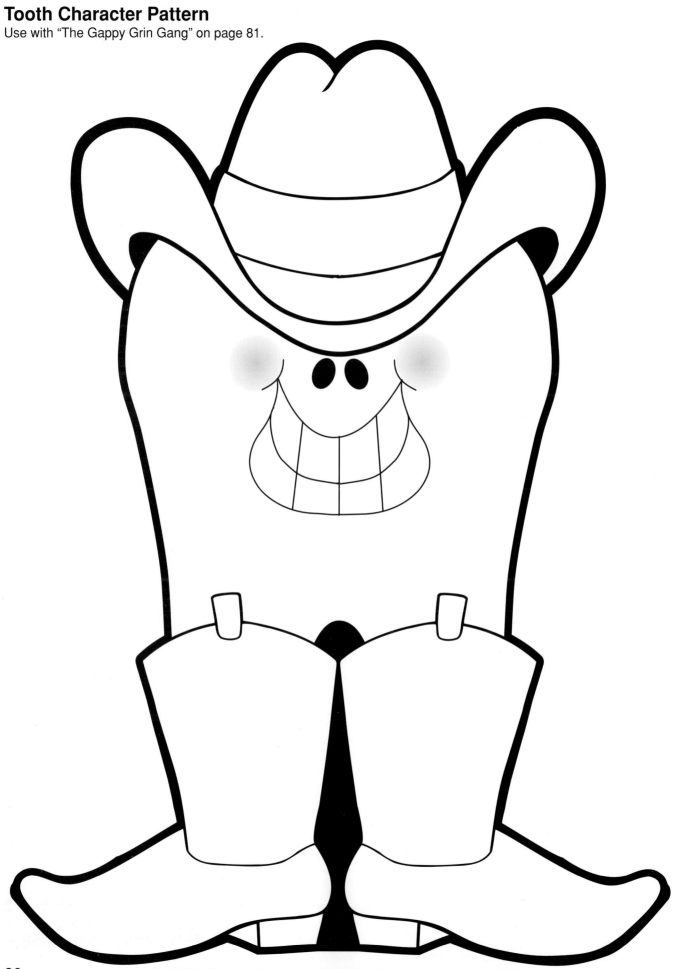

Cookie Jar Pattern

Use with "Cookie Counters" on page 82.

ABC Express

A IS FOR ALPHABET

Make every day a red-letter day with this collection of alphabet activities that offers visual and tactile explorations of letter shapes. We are certain that they will suit your little learners to a "T"!

ideas contributed by Lucia Kemp Henry

Letter Boards

Your little ones will be eager to get their hands on this letter activity. Create a letter "feely" board by tracing a desired letter onto several materials of different textures. Cut them out; then glue the letters in a row onto a strip of tagboard. Next cut out an additional letter, plus several different letters, from tagboard. Place the letter cutouts into a bag; then store the bag with the letter board. To use the board, encourage a child to use her finger to touch and trace each textured letter several times. Then challenge her to close her eyes and find the matching letter in the bag.

On The Road Again

Get students on the road to letter learning with this activity that will shift them into high gear! Cut large letters from 9" x 12" sheets of black construction paper. Glue each letter cutout onto a sheet of tagboard. Paint yellow road stripes on each letter; then cut away the excess tagboard to create a sturdy letter road. Place the letter roads and a supply of tiny cars and trucks in a center. Encourage students to work together to create an alphabet highway by laying the letter roads on the floor. Have a child name each letter as she "drives" a car along the letter-learning highway. Vroooo-oommmmmmm!

Stamp-A-Letter

Recycle Styrofoam® trays into supersized letter stamps; then watch your little ones stamp their way to letter recognition! To make a stamp, use an X-acto® knife to cut a 2" x 2 1/2" block letter from a Styrofoam® tray. Make a backing piece for the stamp by cutting out a Styrofoam® square that is slightly longer and wider than the letter. Glue the foam letter to the backing piece with craft glue. Place a set of letters, several large stamp pads, and paper in a center. Invite students to stamp their choice of letters onto sheets of paper. For added challenge, have students stamp their names or simple words onto paper. Use the decorated papers for book covers, folders, or wrapping paper.

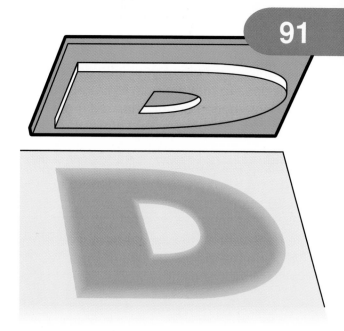

Letter Collections

Send your youngsters out on a scavenger hunt to collect letters for this collaborative alphabet mural. Prepare by mounting a large sheet of bulletin-board paper on a wall or bulletin board. Cut out a class supply of the letter you wish to focus on; then hide them around your classroom. During a group time, discuss with your students the letter being learned, and show them a cutout. Invite them to search the room to find the matching letter cutouts. When each child has found a letter, have him embellish it with stickers, stamps, or other collage materials; then have him glue his letter onto a section of the bulletin-board paper. Each time a new letter is learned, add it to the mural. At the end of the alphabet, you'll have a cool collection of collaged letters.

PUT IT ON A POSTER

Have your little ones chart their alphabet know-how with these letter posters. Use a wide marker to program squares of tagboard, each with a different letter of the alphabet. Provide each youngster with a letter and a bottle of Elmer's® GluColors™. Direct him to trace his letter shape with the glue. When the glue is dry, have him glue his letter to the top of a large sheet of construction paper to make a poster. As you are studying a particular letter of the alphabet, display the corresponding poster. Encourage students to decorate the poster with magazine pictures or drawings of things that begin with that letter.

It's A Puzzler!

Enlist the help of your little detectives in solving these mystery letter puzzles. To make a puzzle, trace a letter onto a large sheet of construction paper; then cut it out. Cut the letter into a few simple pieces, and place them into a resealable plastic bag. Trace an identical letter onto a piece of cardboard using a wide-tipped black marker. Color it; then place the cardboard in the bag along with the construction-paper pieces. Challenge a youngster to solve the mystery puzzle by correctly placing the pieces within the cardboard outline. For a variation, include the pieces for two or three puzzles in one bag. Now, that's a mystery worth piecing together!

Soup's On!

Students will cook up letter-recognition skills when playing this tasty game of Alphabet Soup Concentration. Duplicate a double set of the alphabet cards on page 95. Cut the cards apart; then laminate them for durability. Cut a very large soup-pot shape from poster board and program it with 52 squares equal in size to an alphabet card. Place the gameboard on a tabletop or floor. Place one card facedown in each square of the playing board.

To play, a child turns over two cards. If the cards match, she may keep them. If they do not match, she returns them, facedown, to the gameboard. Play then passes to the next child. Continue the game until all the letters have been removed from the pot.

Letter Laundry

Looking to air a little laundry? Then try this clothesline of letters. String a clothesline in your classroom. Into a basket, place pictures and real items that begin with a desired letter. Add a couple of items that do not begin with the designated letter. Program a set of clothespins with the corresponding letter. Place the clothespins and the basket near the clothesline. Have each youngster search the basket for the items that begin with the selected letter, then clip them to the clothesline. When he has finished, have him tell you the names of the clipped items and the name of the letter being studied. Vary the center by changing the letter or adding two or three different letter items to the basket.

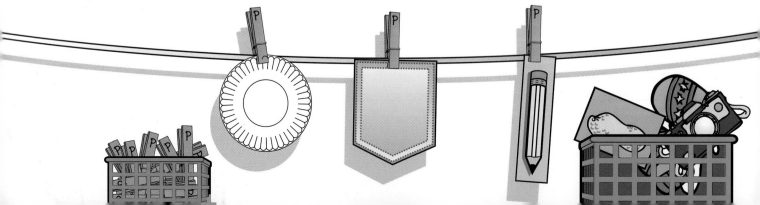

I Spy Collages

Creating these collages will help your students work out the riddle of learning letters. Prepare by stocking your art center with large Styrofoam® trays, glue, scissors, and alphabet collage materials, such as letter stickers, letters cut from newspapers, Alpha-Bits® cereal pieces, and letter pasta. Also include additional collage materials, such as pom-poms, feathers, buttons, etc.

Invite each student to create his own letter collage by randomly gluing his choice of letters to a foam tray. Direct him to arrange additional collage materials around the letters, then glue them to his tray. When each child has completed a collage, have pairs exchange collages and try to spy specific letters. Then display the collages on a wall or bulletin board with the heading "I Spy Letters."

What's That Letter?

Try this delightful ditty to accompany your favorite alphabet book. Randomly turn to a page in the book; then quietly sing the first verse of the song below, being sure to allow each child time to visually identify the letter illustrated. Have each child silently indicate that she has identified the letter; then have students name the letter as you sing the second verse of the song together. Continue in the same manner until everyone is singing to the letter-recognition beat!

(sung to the tune of "Bingo")

> Oh, what's this letter?
> Do you know?
> What letter can this be-O?

> [B], [B], it's a [B],
> [B], [B], it's a [B],
> [B], [B], it's a [B].
> This letter is a [B]!

Hop, Skip, And Jump A Letter

This gross-motor alternative to alphabet recognition will have your youngsters moving in letter formation. Each time you introduce a new letter, use colorful masking tape to create a supersized version of that letter on the floor of your classroom. Invite your little ones to hop, skip, creep, or crawl along the lines of the letter. What a letter-perfect movement activity!

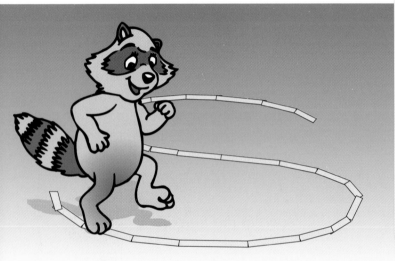

Dig Those Letters!

Here's the scoop on a fun way to practice letter-identification skills that your youngsters will really dig! Program a sheet of tagboard with each letter of the alphabet. Bury a set of magnetic letters in your sand table; then place the prepared gameboard nearby.

To play, encourage each child in a small group to dig up a letter in the table. Have him identify the letter, then place it on the corresponding letter on the gameboard. When each letter has been discovered, have the children bury the letters in preparation for the next group.

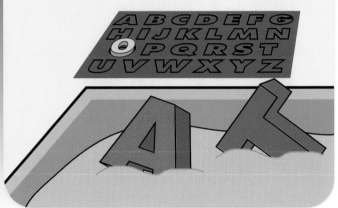

Alphabet Antics

It's always a beautiful day in this alphabet neighborhood! Prepare a display by stapling cutouts of houses, hills, and trees to a bulletin board. Place a polka-dot border around the edges of the display. Finally, enlarge, duplicate, and then cut out the alphabet cards on page 95.

Read aloud the classic book *Chicka Chicka Boom Boom* by Bill Martin, Jr., and John Archambault (Simon & Schuster Children's Books). Then tell youngsters they are going to help you make up a new adventure for the letters. Give each child one alphabet card; then invite her to place it somewhere on the neighborhood display. Encourage her to tell you something she imagines her letter could do, such as run, sit, jump, go in a house, or climb a tree. Write her dictated sentence on a strip of paper; then display it next to her letter. When each child has had an opportunity to place a letter on the board, "read" the story. Your youngsters will delight in collaborating to bring this neighborhood to life!

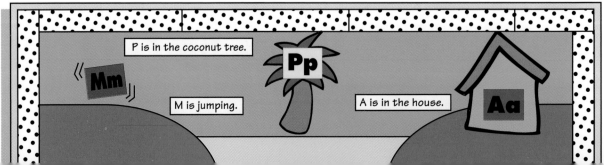

Aa	Bb	Cc	Dd
Ee	Ff	Gg	Hh
Ii	Jj	Kk	Ll
Mm	Nn	Oo	Pp
Qq	Rr	Ss	Tt
Uu	Vv	Ww	Xx
	Yy	Zz	

NUMBERS!

Use this unique unit to fill your classroom with lots of opportunities for children to identify and manipulate numerals. The following activities provide you with ideas to incorporate numerals during circle time, in centers, and with whole-group and individual projects. So buckle up and hold on tight for a number unit that's out of this world. 5, 4, 3, 2, 1…blast off!

ideas contributed by Diane Gilliam

TEN LITTLE FROGGIES

Ribbet, ribbet! Your little ones will hop with delight when you teach them this counting rhyme. As they say each verse, encourage them to use their fingers to count the number of times they hop. On the last verse, have students fall to the floor on "Drop!" Here we go!

One little froggie goes hop.   *(Hop once and hold up one finger.)*
Along comes another and they just can't stop, so…

Two little froggies go hop, hop.   *(Hop twice and count on fingers.)*
Along comes another and they just can't stop, so…

Three little froggies go hop, hop, hop.   *(Hop three times and count on fingers.)*
Along comes another and they just can't stop, so…

Continue in this manner and end as follows:

Ten little froggies go hop, hop, hop, hop, hop….   *(Hop ten times and count on fingers.)*
Drop! Time to stop!   *(Fall gently to floor.)*

High Five, Numbers Alive!

This adaptation of the traditional Hot Potato game will have your youngsters jumping up to recognize numerals. Prepare for the game by making identical numeral necklaces for each pair of children. To make two necklaces, draw the same numeral on two separate tagboard cards, punch a hole in the top of each card, and thread each card onto a different piece of yarn. Tie the yarn ends together to complete each necklace. Give a necklace to each child; then direct the group to sit in a circle. Have your students pass a ball around the circle while you play music (or if you have an odd number of students, have the extra child play the music). When the music stops, instruct the child holding the ball to jump up and announce his numeral. Then ask the child who is wearing the matching numeral to jump up, meet his partner in the middle of the circle, give a high five, and switch places in the circle. Continue playing until each pair has had a chance to jump up and come alive with numbers!

Number Chant

Keep little ones' numeral-recognition skills improving with this rhythmic chant. Create large numeral cards or use the ones made in "Handy Numerals" on page 100. Hold up one card and ask your youngsters to identify the numeral; then invite them to clap and chant the verse below. Repeat the verse with the rest of the numeral cards.

I went to school,   *(Clap on the offbeats: "went," "school,"*
And what did I see?   *"what," "see," "num-," "four," "front," "me.")*
The number [four],
In front of me.
[One, two, three, four]!   *(Clap and count to each number.)*

Numbers In The News

Where can you find lots of numerals to identify and sets to count? Look no further than your local newspaper! Post a section of the newspaper in front of your group. Have each child find a numeral in the news, identify it, and circle it with a marker. Use a different-colored marker to have each student volunteer circle a set of objects, count it, and write the corresponding numeral. Extra! Extra! We know our numbers!

"Exer-dice"

Use this number warm-up for gross-motor development and rote counting practice. Have a student roll a large die in front of the group. Ask the student to identify the number showing on the die, and then designate an exercise for the group to perform that number of times. Have everyone count aloud as they exercise. For more advanced children or later in the school year, add another die. Now drop and give me six!

CENTERS

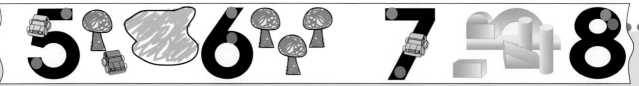

Cruisin' Through Numberville

Invite youngsters to practice numeral formation in the block center by driving through Numberville. To create Numberville, use black paint to make the numerals 0–9 on a length of white bulletin-board paper. Use green and red sticky dots to show where each numeral starts and stops. If desired, provide markers and crayons for children to draw more scenery. Lay the paper town in the block center and encourage children to "drive" toy vehicles over each numeral. For added fun, challenge each child to use the corresponding number of blocks to build a structure beside each numeral.

Classroom Counting

Turn your classroom into Counting Central with sets of numeral cards. For each set, number each of ten tagboard cards with a different numeral from 1 to 10. Have a child spread a set of the cards out on the floor or on a table. Then let the counting begin! Encourage the child to collect small objects from the room to match the quantity shown on each of the numeral cards. For example, she might put three blocks on the 3 card and five crayons on the 5 card. Use this activity as an individual assessment tool, or allow partners to work together.

"Number-roni"

Say cheese! Macaroni and cheese, that is. Obtain several boxes of Kraft® Macaroni & Cheese Dinner 1•2•3 (with numeral-shaped pasta). If desired, color the pasta before using it. Then set out a few tubs of the noodle numerals for the following activities. Be sure to buy an extra box or two, and prepare it as a special treat for your little number munchers!

Sorting
Encourage each child to sort a bowl of numerals by color, numeral, broken/not broken, etc.

Numeral Soup
Put numeral pasta in a pot and provide bowls, spoons, and a dipper. Have each child dip out a serving of pasta, then use his spoon to scoop up numerals and identify them.

Numeral Strip
Give each child a tagboard strip, a bowl of pasta, and glue. Have her find the numerals 0 through 9 and glue them in sequential order on her strip.

Hidden Numerals
Use the numeral pasta pieces to complete the activity "How Many?" on page 100.

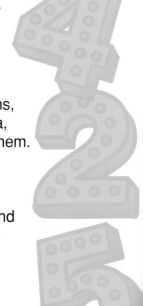

COUNT!

Counting Cash

Use youngsters' curiosity about money to cash in on counting and one-to-one correspondence practice. To prepare for this activity, draw a simple wallet on each of ten envelopes similar to the one shown. Seal the envelopes and laminate them. Then slit the top of each envelope front. Use a permanent marker to program the front of each envelope with a different numeral from 1 to 10. Provide a supply of play money, or make your own from green construction paper. To complete the center activity, have a student place the appropriate number of bills in each wallet. Sorry, no credit!

DIG IN!

Invite your little ones to a treasure hunt in your sand table. Ahead of time, bury several sets of wooden, plastic, or magnetic numerals. Then provide shovels and buckets. Encourage each child in a small group to find the numerals 0 through 9. Once a child has found a set, reward him with a piece of "gold" (candy) and have him bury his set of numerals for the next participant. Methinks me spies some numerals!

Twist And Count

Get to the nuts and bolts of counting with this center. Collect a supply of nuts and bolts in assorted sizes. Have each child at the center choose a bolt, cover it with nuts, and then count the nuts. Encourage him to repeat the activity with several different bolts. Then for an added challenge, have the student order the bolts from the one with the fewest nuts to the one with the most. As a variation, include a set of numeral cards in the center, and have the child cover a bolt with the number of nuts indicated by each card. So come on baby now, twist and count!

How Many?

Just lift the flaps to find out in this activity. Duplicate the scene on page 101 onto white construction paper for each child. Have each child color his page. When he is finished coloring, use an X-acto® knife to open the flaps. Then glue the scene to another piece of construction paper, making sure the flaps remain open. Have each child search the numeral-shaped macaroni from the activities on page 98 to find the numerals 1 through 6. Then instruct him to count each set on his scene and glue the corresponding pasta numeral under the correct flap. Peekaboo, it's number 2!

Handy Numerals

Brighten your room with this handy numeral display. Draw the outline of a different numeral from 1 to 10 on each of ten large sheets of white construction paper. Place one of the sheets of paper on a table. Paint a student volunteer's hand with a vivid color of washable paint. Guide her in pressing her hand along the outline several times in order to form the numeral. Stop and repaint her hand if necessary. Repeat this process for the rest of the numerals, using a different child and a different color of paint each time. After the paint dries, cut around the numerals, mount them onto colored pieces of construction paper, and display them in sequential order at students' eye level or use them as large numeral cards. What a handy reference!

Numeral Cakes

Finish this number unit by tempting taste buds with numeral cakes. To make them, simply prepare pancake batter, pour it into a squeeze bottle, and squirt it onto a hot griddle to form a numeral of each child's choice. As you squirt, be sure to verbalize and model the correct numeral formations. When the numeral cakes are done, provide syrup, whipped topping, fruit, sprinkles, or other edibles for each child to decorate his cake. Ask the child to tell you his number and clap that many times before he gobbles up the numeral!

The "Tree-mendous" Five Senses

Trees in autumn provide a feast for the senses—vivid colors, crunchy sounds, distinctive smells, and a tasty harvest of nuts and fruits. If you introduce the topic of the five senses to your students in autumn, why not use trees as the focus of your exploration? As you involve students in each of the activities in this unit, remind them that they are using the sense or senses noted in each heading.

ideas contributed by Suzanne Moore

Before And After

(Sight)

Encourage your little ones to see trees more clearly with this activity. Have each student draw a tree on a 12" x 18" sheet of construction paper. Set the drawings aside. Next take an observation walk to a tree-filled area. Encourage youngsters to use their sense of sight as you ask questions, such as:

- What size and shape are the leaves on this tree?
- What color are they?
- Do all trees have leaves?
- Where do the branches start?
- Does the tree have any buds, flowers, fruit, or seeds?

Return to your classroom and encourage students to discuss their discoveries. Next have each child draw a second picture of a tree, adding details discovered during the walk. Display each student's "before" and "after" drawings side by side. Ask students to decide if there were more details in the second drawing. Their answers will be "tree-mendously" informative!

A Look At Leaves

(Sight)

Open your youngsters' eyes to the differences in leaves with a leaf-gathering expedition. Pair students and give each pair a plastic bag to fill. Remind youngsters to gather only those leaves that have fallen to the ground. After the bags are full, return to your classroom and have students examine their findings. Are the leaves different colors? Shapes? Who found the largest leaf? Set aside some of the leaves for " 'Leaf' The Printing To Us!" (page 103) and preserve the rest by ironing them between sheets of waxed paper. (Or laminate the leaves if they are not too brittle.) Place the preserved leaves in a center, and challenge students to exercise their sense of sight as they sort them by size, shape, color, edging, and vein pattern.

"Leaf" The Printing To Us!

(Sight, Touch)

Gather a small group of students and give each of them a leaf set aside from "A Look At Leaves" (page 102). Have your little ones trace the veins on the leaf with their fingers. Explain to your youngsters that leaves make food for trees and the veins carry food to the rest of the tree. Place the leaf on a paper plate or a thickness of newspaper. Have each student lightly daub the back of the leaf

with liquid shoe polish (the type with a sponge applicator). Turn the leaf polish-side-down on a sheet of construction paper. Cover the leaf with another thickness of newspaper. Firmly rub the newspaper with the palm; then slowly lift the paper and leaf to reveal the print. To extend this activity, place the leaf prints and real leaves in a center. Challenge your students to look closely and match each leaf to its leaf print.

There's The Rub!

(Touch)

Since bark is the protective covering of the tree—the tree's skin—it provides a perfect introduction to the sense of touch. In advance duplicate a class set of page 106. Scout out a location with several kinds of trees. Provide crayons in various shades of gray and brown. Give each child a copy of page 106; then head outside to touch trees. As each student feels a tree, ask her to make a bark rubbing on her handout. Then have her write or dictate the color of the bark, and decide whether the bark is smooth, rough, or shaggy. After returning to the classroom, have students fill in the final blank on their papers by writing or dictating a description of what the bark felt like. Bind all your students' rubbings between two sheets of construction paper to make a class book about bark.

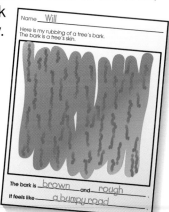

Name Will
Here is my rubbing of a tree's bark.
The bark is a tree's skin.

The bark is brown and rough
It feels like a bumpy road

Feely Sacks

(Touch)

Prepare this center for tactile matching fun. Gather two of each of the following items. (They all come from trees!)

acorns	walnuts
lemons	cinnamon sticks
almonds	pistachios
pinecones	pecans

Then make eight simple feely sacks. To make a feely sack, fold a brown paper lunch bag lengthwise. Draw a half-circle the size of a child's fist on the fold. Divide the half-circle into four equal slices. Beginning at the fold, cut each slice to the edge of the circle. Then open the bag, place one item from a pair inside, fold the top down, and staple the bag closed. Place all the bags and the matching items in a center. Can your students find the match for each item by touch alone?

My Nose Knows!

(Smell)

Allspice, cinnamon, cloves, mace, nutmeg—many of the spices we love are products of trees. Duplicate a class supply of page 107; then bring in a jar of each spice. Invite one small group of students at a time to join you in smelling these spices. Give each student a copy of page 107 and provide glue. Pass one spice container at a time to let each student smell the spice's aroma. Then have him spread a small amount of glue over the corresponding square on his handout and sprinkle on a bit of the spice. If he likes the smell, have him color in the happy face. If he does not, have him color in the sad face. Encourage each student to copy the name of the spice he likes best in the blank space provided.

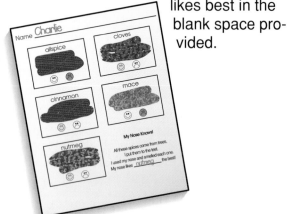

Follow Your Nose

(Smell)

Do trees have a scent? A good whiff of a sprig from a pine or cedar tree will remind students that trees have an odor. Since many products from trees also have distinctive aromas, challenge your students to a scent-matching activity. Collect 12 empty, plastic film canisters; then prepare a smelling center focusing on tree products. Place a cotton ball inside each film canister. Choose one of the spices or extracts listed below. Sprinkle a bit of the spice or a few drops of the extract into a pair of canisters. Program the bottoms of the paired canisters with matching color dots for self-checking. Repeat for each of six spices or extracts.

allspice

banana extract

chocolate syrup or extract

cloves

lemon extract or peel

orange extract or peel

nutmeg

almond extract

cinnamon

coconut extract

mace

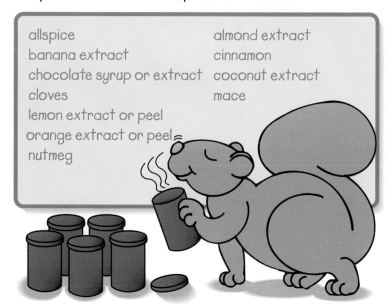

Sweet Or Not Sweet?

(Taste)

Tempt your youngsters' tongues with a tasty selection of fruits that grow on trees. In advance prepare a large graph as shown. Set up a taste test with sliced oranges, pink grapefruits, apples, and bananas. Place corresponding colored stickers in front of each fruit. Instruct each student to taste each fruit, then decide whether it tastes sweet or not. Then have him take a corresponding sticker and place it on the graph in the column he feels is appropriate. Which fruits did *your* class think were sweet?

	Sweet	Not Sweet
Grapefruit	○○	○○○○○ ○○○○○
Orange	○○○○○	○○○○
Apple	●●●●● ●●●●●	●●●
Banana	○○○○○ ○○○	

The Wind In The Trees

(Sound)

Rustle up a lesson on tree sounds with this lively movement exercise. For dramatic sound effects, have each child fill a plastic grocery sack with dry leaves and knot the top of the bag closed.

The Wind In The Trees

The leaves up in the top of trees,
(Hold hands above head; stand on toes.)
Sway from left to right.
(Sway from left to right.)
Rustling softly in the breeze
(Slowly rub bag with hands.)
They swish throughout the night.
(Swish bag to left then right.)

A strong wind comes and shakes the tree,
(Shake arms above head.)
It rattles in the wind.
(Shake bag vigorously.)
Swaying wildly to and fro,
(Sway arms above head.)
The branches bend and bend!
(Bend from side to side.)

The strong wind blows the leaves all off!
(Drop bag.)
They flitter to the ground.
(Wiggle fingers from over head to floor.)
Swirling, twirling, silently
(Twirl.)
They fall without a sound.
(Touch floor.)

The leaves now crunch beneath my feet,
(Step on bag.)
I listen with a grin.
(Smile broadly.)
I rake them in a great big pile.
(Pretend to rake.)
And then I jump right in!
(Sit on the bag.)

It's A Nutty Thing!

(Sight, Smell, Touch, Sound, Taste)

It may seem nutty, but tree products, such as nuts, are a great source for hands-on activities. In advance purchase an assortment of nuts in their shells; then provide several magnifying glasses, nutcrackers, and pictures of the kinds of trees the nuts grow on. Invite a small group of students at a time to join you in investigating nuts. Show students each nut in turn, and ask them to match the nuts to the trees they grow on. Then give each student a handful of nuts to explore, using all five senses.

Sight
- Look closely at each nut using the magnifying glass.
- Sort the nuts according to shape, color, and size.

Smell
- Describe the odor of each shell.
- Show students how to safely crack the nutshell. Smell the nut meat after it has been removed from the shell.

Touch
- Sort the nuts according to smooth, rough, or bumpy.
- Feel the nut after it has been removed from the shell.

Sound
- Roll the nuts on the table.
- Listen to the sounds made when cracking the nutshell.

Taste
- Taste each nut after removing it from the shell.

Afterward ask students what senses they used to investigate the nuts.

Name _____

Here is my rubbing of a tree's bark.
The bark is a tree's skin.

The bark is _____ and _____.
                   (color)   (smooth, rough, or shaggy)

It feels like _____.

Note To The Teacher: Use with "There's The Rub!" on page 103.

Name _____

allspice	cloves
🙂 ☹️	🙂 ☹️

cinnamon	mace
🙂 ☹️	🙂 ☹️

nutmeg	**My nose knows!**
🙂 ☹️	All these spices come from trees. I put them to the test. I used my nose and smelled each one. My nose likes _____ the best!

Note To The Teacher: Use with "My Nose Knows!" on page 104.

IT'S TIME FOR RHYMES!

Keep rhyming skills alive in your classroom with these fun-filled activities.
Your youngsters will be rhyming in no time.

ideas contributed by Marie Iannetti

Sticker Buddies

Your little ones will be stuck on this fun rhyming activity. In advance collect pairs of picture stickers that show rhyming words. Match the total number of stickers to children in your class. After reviewing rhyming pictures with your students, place a picture sticker on each child's hand. Have each child name the picture on his hand. While arranging your class in a circle, play a recording of upbeat music. When you stop the music, ask each child to find his rhyming partner. In turn, have each set of sticker buddies say their rhymes aloud. Afterward have each child exchange his sticker with a child other than his rhyming buddy; then restart the music.

Transition Rhyme Time

Move youngsters from one destination to another with this rhyme time idea. In advance photocopy the rhyming pictures on page 112; then cut out each picture. Glue each cutout onto a separate notecard. Color the pictures if desired, and laminate them for durability. To use, give each child a card. Ask him to say a word that rhymes with his card before he goes to his assigned destination (such as to a center, to the library, or to line up for dismissal).

RHYMING WITH SHAPE PADS

Use this versatile seasonal center throughout the year. To prepare, photocopy the rhyming pictures on page 112. Glue each of the pictures onto a separate sheet from a seasonal-shaped notepad. Place the notepad sheets and spring-type clothespins in a center. To use this center, a child matches each picture to a corresponding rhyming picture and uses a clothespin to clip each pair together.

A-DIGGING WE WILL GO

Your little ones will really dig those rhymes when they use this fun center. In advance collect a clean, half-pint milk carton for each rhyming word family that you plan to study. Cut off the top of each carton; then glue a picture representing each different word family onto each carton. (You may find the picturers on pages 112 and 113 useful.) Place the cartons near your sand table. Bury in the sand a variety of small objects that rhyme with the pictures on the cartons. To use the center, a child digs an object out of the sand, then places it in the corresponding carton. It's true—kids dig rhymes!

Outdoor Rhyme Time

Head outdoors for some fun with chalk to reinforce rhyming skills. On a nice day, take your youngsters and a box of colored chalk to a paved section of your playground. Have each child use a stick of chalk to draw boundaries for her own workspace; then assign a different word for each child to illustrate in her space. Challenge the child to then draw different pictures to represent words that rhyme with her word. After each student completes her drawings, have your class members visit each workspace to "read" the rhyming pictures.

A Heap Of Sheep In A Jeep

This heap of sheep will help youngsters make that rhyming leap! Read aloud *Sheep In A Jeep* by Nancy Shaw (Houghton Mifflin Company). After the story, list student-generated words that rhyme with *sheep* on a sheet of chart paper. Then encourage students to each write or dictate a sentence about sheep using words from the list. Have each child illustrate his sentence; then invite each child to share his picture with the class. Display the illustrations with the title "Take A Peep At Our Sheep!"

My sheep needs some sleep.

Jump 'N' Rhyme

Youngsters will be jumping at the chance to chant rhymes with this idea. To prepare, collect several jump ropes. Divide your class into groups of three students, providing each group with a rope. Ask the groups to each make up a jump-rope rhyme or to recite a rhyming chant, such as "Miss Mary Mac" or "Teddy Bear, Teddy Bear." As each group recites its rhyme, have two students turn the rope while one student jumps. Then, in turn, have each group perform its rhyme or chant for the rest of the class. After each performance, ask the class to identify the rhyming words.

Poets In Progress

Use this activity to help little ones identify rhyming and spelling patterns. In advance select poems or nursery rhymes that contain rhyming words with similar spelling patterns. Write each poem and/or nursery rhyme on a separate sheet of chart paper. Read one of the selections aloud; then ask students to identify the rhyming words. Invite a student volunteer to use a highlighting marker to accent the rhyming words in the selection. Continue in this manner using the other poems or nursery rhymes. Then encourage each student to write (or dictate) and illustrate his own simple rhyming verse. After each child shares his poem with the class, display it on a wall or bulletin board entitled "Our Little Poets."

RHYMING SHOW-AND-SHARE BOOK

This book of rhymes is sure to become a class favorite. To begin, ask each child to bring in two rhyming items from home. During circle time, have each child, in turn, show and name her rhyming objects. Then photograph the child holding both objects. Mount each developed photo onto a sheet of construction paper programmed with "[Child's name]'s rhyming objects." Write the label for the two objects under the picture; then bind the pages together to create a classroom rhyming book.

Rhyming Show-And-Share Book

Ms. Kenneth's Class

Angela's rhyming objects

hat   cat

I Spy

Stretch your students' listening and observation skills with this rhyming version of I Spy. Have your students sit in a circle. Ask a student volunteer to be the Caller. Have him whisper to you the name of an object in the room; then help him think of a rhyming word for the object. Have the Caller then announce, "I spy something that rhymes with [the rhyming word]." Instruct the students to raise their hands when they think they have visually located the object. After a brief period of time, ask the Caller to select a child to share his guess. If that child's guess is correct, he becomes the Caller for the next round of play.

This version of the ever-popular lotto game can be used as a center activity or as a take-home game. Duplicate the caller cards and several copies of the gameboards (page 113) on construction paper; then cut them out. Laminate all the game pieces for durability. To use, place the gameboards and stacked caller cards in a center with a bowl of markers such as beans or pennies. Each player in a small group chooses a gameboard and eight markers. In turn, a Caller draws the top caller card and announces the rhyming picture to be covered with a marker. When a player covers all of the rhyming pictures on his gameboard, he calls out, "Lotto!" Then that player becomes the Caller for the next game.

If desired, put the game pieces in a large, resealable plastic bag. Include a note explaining how to play the game and encouraging a child's family to play it together; then send the game home with a different child each day.

Rhyming Pictures

Use with "Transition Rhyme Time" and "Rhyming With Shape Pads" on page 108.

PATTERNING POSSIBILITIES

Here's a potpourri of possibilities to help you provide your children with lots of practice in picking out, prolonging, and planning patterns. Practice makes perfect!

ideas contributed by Vicki Mockaitis Pacchetti

Paper-Clip Patterns

No need to buy expensive patterning manipulatives. A box of color-coated paper clips will do just fine! Give each child a handful of clips and encourage her to link them together to create a colorful pattern. Then have her join the ends of her paper-clip chain to create a necklace or bracelet. Now, that's a jewel of an idea!

Follow Me!

Patterns and movement go hand in hand in this activity. Gather your little ones around you; then pat your legs as you say the rhyme below. Create a simple pattern using claps, snaps, and pats. Invite each child to join in as soon as he discovers the pattern. Then repeat the rhyme with a new pattern. Clap, clap, snap, snap!

Patterns, patterns all around.
See them, feel them, hear their sound.
Watch to see just what I do,
Then everybody do it, too!

Stick To Your Theme

Use stickers to incorporate patterning into any of your teaching units. Simply cut a supply of construction paper to make bookmarks, wristbands, notecards, or long strips; then have each child use stickers to create a pattern on one of the pieces of paper. As a variation, start a sticker pattern on a paper strip; then have a student extend the pattern the length of the strip. With the variety of stickers available, patterning can be a part of every theme!

Palatable Patterning

Patterns you can eat? You bet! What better way to get children into patterning? Give each child a licorice string knotted at one end and a cup of colored cereal rings. Encourage him to thread the cereal onto the licorice in a pattern. Then have him read the pattern to you before munching. Patterns will appear *and* disappear right in front of your very eyes!

MONKEYING AROUND

Youngsters will go ape over this patterning activity. Duplicate several copies of the monkey patterns on page 118 onto red, yellow, green, and blue construction paper. Cut out the monkeys and laminate them for durability. Attach self-adhesive Velcro®, felt tape, or magnetic tape to the back of each monkey so that it can stick to a flannelboard or magnetic board. Then store the monkeys in a basket near the board. During group time, teach your little ones the first verse of the rhyme at the right, inserting a student's name as indicated. Once the child creates a monkey pattern, chant the second verse of the rhyme together, and select a volunteer to extend the pattern. Continue until all of your students have had a chance to monkey around.

MONKEY MADNESS

Verse One:

Down, down in Jungle Town,
There's monkey madness all around.
Silly monkeys can be seen,
In blue and red, yellow and green.
No other monkeys are quite like these.
[Student's name], make a pattern,
please.

Verse Two:

Down, down in Jungle Town,
A monkey pattern can be found.
They're in a row, looking fine.
Each with a special place in line.
Let's add more. Here we go!
Who can make this pattern grow?

Patterning With Puppets

Making paper-bag puppets is always a favorite activity, so why not use them with patterning? Divide your class into small groups; then assign each group a different animal. Provide a supply of paper bags, yarn, glue, wiggle eyes, crayons, fabric scraps, and other decorative materials for each child to use in creating her assigned animal. When the puppets are completed, ask a few students to hold their puppets up in a particular order. Encourage the rest of the class to figure out the pattern, then join the puppet line, if appropriate, in order to extend the pattern. Once there are no more puppets that can be used in the pattern, have everyone be seated and start again with a new pattern.

Petal Patterns

Patterns will be in full bloom when youngsters complete this activity. Make several workmats by coloring and mounting copies of page 119 onto tagboard. Store the mats in your math center along with a supply of different-colored plastic spoons. Encourage children in the center to arrange the spoons in circular patterns on the mats to create unique flowers. The mats also work well with pattern blocks, colored pasta pieces, and two-sided counters. For added fun, teach children the traditional "He Loves Me" chant as they pick apart their patterned petals.

Pattern Power

Excite your students by teaching them to play this power-packed patterning card game with a partner. Prepare for the game by cutting 12 cards from each of four different colors of tagboard or poster board. Have one child in the duo shuffle the cards, deal seven cards to each player, and then place the extras in a pile. To play the game, each player looks at his cards and tries to make one or more patterns with them. The first player lays his pattern(s) in the playing area. The other player can then lay down cards to extend the first player's patterns and/or lay down his own pattern(s). The game continues with making and extending patterns until both players run out of cards. If a player can't lay down one of his cards, he must draw a card from the pile. He may lay down that card if it is playable; otherwise he keeps it in his hand until his next turn.

Creative Quilts

Expand children's knowledge of patterning with quilts. Explain that patterns are not necessarily always linear; then show students some examples of quilts. After discussing the patterns found on each quilt, have a quilting bee! Give each child a sheet of tagboard, glue, and a supply of one-inch fabric scraps. Have the child fill the tagboard with patterned fabric rows to resemble a quilt. Challenge more advanced children to create a patterned design that's more complex. Hang the quilted creations on a bulletin board titled "Patchwork Patterns."

They're Everywhere!

Patterns, that is. Encourage each child to be on the lookout for patterns in his environment. When one is spotted, take a picture of it, and reward the spotter with a pattern point toward a class incentive—such as patterned pizza (pepperoni, mushroom, pepperoni, mushroom) or fruit kabobs (pineapple, grape, apple, pineapple, grape, apple). Compile the pattern photos in a class book. Under each photo, write the child's dictation as he explains the pattern and tells where it was found. Encourage children to bring photos of patterns found during family outings as well. When the book is complete, enjoy your class pattern treat!

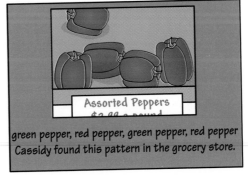

Assorted Peppers
$2.99 a pound

green pepper, red pepper, green pepper, red pepper
Cassidy found this pattern in the grocery store.

People Patterns

Giggle, wiggle, giggle, wiggle will be the pattern during this activity! During circle time, arrange a small group of student volunteers into a pattern, such as *stand/sit/stand/sit* or *front/front/back/back.* Encourage the other students to examine the arrangement and reveal the pattern. Then ask a few students to place themselves in the line and extend the pattern. Continue until each child has had a chance to participate in a pattern.

Monkey Patterns
Use with "Monkeying Around" on page 115.

Playing With OPPOSITES

This collection of activities and games to help teach opposites is sure to be a **big** hit with your **little** learners!

ideas contributed by Linda Gordetsky

Opposites Day

Begin your study of opposites by sending home the parent note on page 124. When your youngsters arrive wearing opposites, have a video camera on hand to catch them entering the room. Roll the film again as you have students walk backward to circle time. Encourage students to discuss one another's clothing. Remind them that their clothes are being worn the *opposite* of the way they should be. Use terms such as *inside out* and *right-side out, upside down* and *right-side up,* and *backward* and *forward.* Then watch your video in reverse as it rewinds. Ask students if this is the opposite of the way it should be viewed. Then watch the movie going forward. Soon your little ones will get the picture!

Crickets And Snails

Your students will quickly begin to recognize opposites with a bit of book-related dramatic play. Read aloud the wonderful descriptions of animal opposites in *Quick As A Cricket* by Audrey Wood (Scholastic Inc.). Read the text a second time, but pause after each introductory descriptive phrase. Ask your students to recall the phrase's opposite; then continue reading. Read the text a third time. Pause after each introductory descriptive phrase and ask students to act out the phrase. Have them act out its opposite, too; then read the opposite phrase.

Your active learners will love being as loud as lions and as slow as snails!

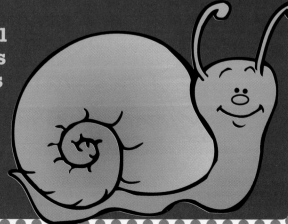

We will be having
OPPOSITES DAY
at school on

Tuesday, April 13th
(date)

Please help your child dress wearing opposites.

Games To Play

Teach youngsters the games on these pages to help them learn the concept of opposites. For most of the games, you'll need one or more sets of the opposites cards on pages 124–125. Simply duplicate the cards on sturdy tagboard and cut them apart. Color them if desired.

Simon Does Not Say

Add a new twist to an old game by challenging little ones to do the *opposite* of each thing Simon says to do. Demonstrate first with a few examples, such as "Simon says frown." *(Smile instead of frown.)* Or "Simon says stand up." *(Sit down.)* This may take practice, but your students will beg to play this game again and again. Simon says this is the only time students will be encouraged to do the opposite of what you say!

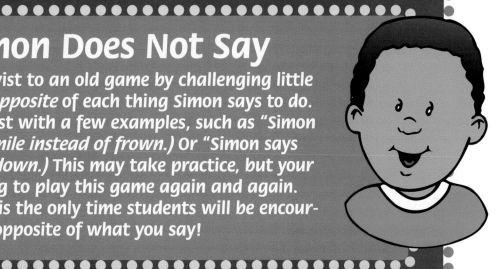

Concentrate On Opposites

Your students will pay close attention to opposites when they play Opposites Concentration. Arrange a few rows of opposites cards in your pocket chart picture-side-in. To begin the game, ask a child to turn over two cards. Using the picture clues, have him guess the words. If the two cards chosen depict opposites, instruct him to leave them picture-side-out. If not, have him turn them both back over and have another child choose two cards. Continue play until all the opposite pairs have been revealed. Opposites Concentration can be played in teams, if desired.

Fishing For Opposites

Invite children to go fishing for opposites with this small-group game. To prepare, make a fishing pole by tying a string around a magnet, then tying the string to one end of a dowel. Create a pond by cutting a length of blue bulletin-board paper into an abstract shape. Attach a large paper clip to one card from each opposite pair. Lay all the paper-clipped cards facedown on the pond. Stack the remaining opposite cards nearby.

To play, give the pole to one child. Have her choose a card from the stack and name the opposite of the picture shown on the card. Then invite her to "fish" for that corresponding opposite card. Once she "catches" a paper-clipped card with her magnetic fishing pole, have her look at it and determine if it is indeed the opposite of the card she chose from the stack. If it is, she may keep the pair of cards. If it is not the opposite, have her replace the paper-clipped card in its original position on the pond and put the other card on the bottom of the stack. Continue with the other players in the group until all the opposite pairs have been "caught."

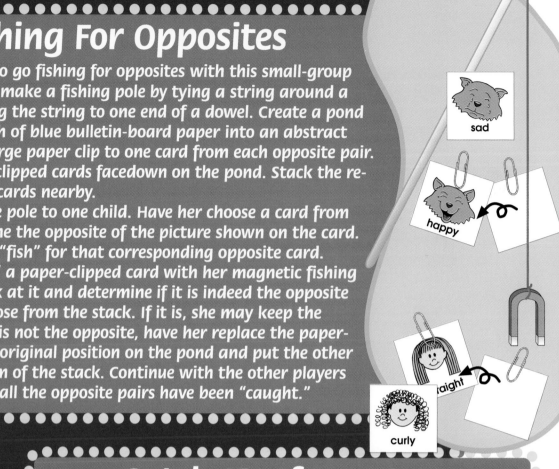

Catch Me If You Can

Transform Duck, Duck, Goose into a game that reinforces opposites. Prepare two sets of opposites cards. Staple each card from one set to a separate construction-paper headband. (Set aside the second set of cards.) Review each opposite pair represented as you distribute the headbands to pairs of children. Instruct children to sit in a circle and wear the headbands so that the pictures face the outside of the circle. Designate one child to be It. Give It a card from the extra set that represents the opposite of one of the seated children's headbands (not his own). Invite It to walk around the outside of the circle, naming the word represented on each child's headband as he goes. When It reaches the child wearing the headband that shows the opposite of the picture in his hand, have him shout, "Opposite!" The seated child should jump up and chase It as It tries to run around the circle and claim the chaser's spot. Whether It gets tagged or not, review the opposite pair; then begin the game again with the chaser taking on the role of It for the new round.

Lost My Opposite

Do-si-do and around you go with opposite partners. Stick a piece of double-sided tape or rolled masking tape to the back of each opposite card in a set. Separate the opposites so that you have two groups of cards. Then separate students into two equal groups. Have each student in the first group choose a card from one group of opposites; then have each student in the second group choose a card from the other group of opposites. Instruct each student to stick his card to the front of his shirt. Line the groups up facing one another. Call out a word represented by one of the picture cards. Direct the student wearing that picture to skip along the opposite line, looking for his opposite, as the rest of the class sings "Lost My Opposite" to the tune of "Skip To My Lou."

Lost my opposite, what'll I do? *(Repeat three times.)*
Skip to my Lou, my darling.

When the student finds the child wearing the opposite picture card, have the pair join hands, swing around in the middle, and then go back to their original places as everyone sings:

Opposite, opposite, I found you. *(Repeat three times.)*
Skip to my Lou, my darling.

Musical Pairs

Reinforce the concept of opposites with a musical matchup. Set up two rows of chairs back-to-back, as in a game of Musical Chairs. Hand each player a card and attach the card showing its opposite to a chair back. Play some lively music and have the children march around the chairs holding their pictures. When the music stops, instruct each child to sit in the chair displaying the opposite of the picture he holds. After the first round, direct each youngster to pass his picture to the child on his right. Then play the music and invite each child to once again find the chair that makes a pair!

Parent Note

Use with "Opposites Day" on page 120.

We will be having
OPPOSITES DAY
at school on

_____.
(date)

Please help your child
dress wearing opposites.

Opposite Concept Cards

Use with the activities on pages 121–123.

curly	straight	up
down	happy	sad

sun

moon

empty

full

plain

fancy

big

little

open

closed

front

back

Student Awards
Duplicate, personalize, and distribute these awards as appropriate.

Now I Know My ABCs!

Great Job,

_____
Name

_____
Date

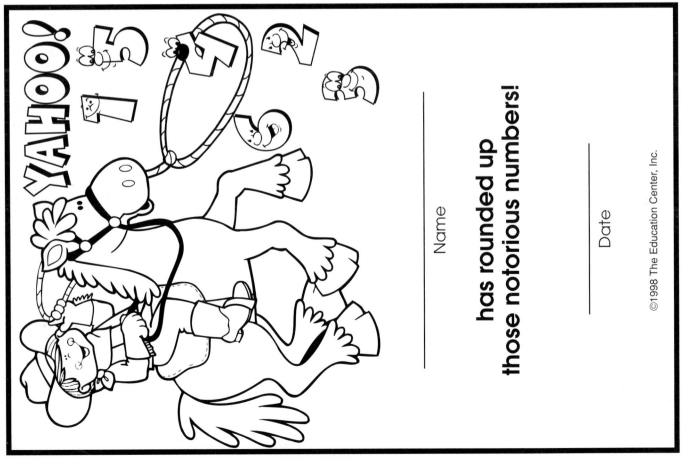

YAHOO!

_____
Name

has rounded up those notorious numbers!

_____
Date

Student Awards
Duplicate, personalize, and distribute these
awards as appropriate.

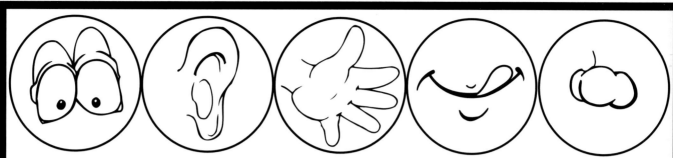

See, Hear, Feel, Taste, and Smell

_____
Name

knows the senses very well!

_____
Date

©1998 The Education Center, Inc.

_____
Name

can make a rhyme
anytime!

_____
Date

©1998 The Education Center, Inc.

Student Awards

Duplicate, personalize, and distribute these awards as appropriate. For the patterning award, have the child color the pawprints to make a pattern of his choice.

Name

Is "Purr-fect" With Patterns!

Date

Name

knows the **in**s and **out**s of Opposites!

Date

SPECIAL EVENTS

BIRTHDAY BONANZA!

You'll strike gold when you dig into this collection of birthday ideas that will help your birthday children feel like a million!
ideas contributed by Betty Silkunas and Lori Kent

Greg
1–27

Paul
1–16

Emily
1–6

January

BIRTHDAY SUNDAES

Here's the scoop on a mouthwatering birthday display that's really dishy! On a wall or bulletin board, display a construction-paper cutout of an ice-cream dish for each month of the year. Personalize construction-paper scoops of ice cream with each child's birthdate; then attach each scoop to the appropriate dish. Top off each dish with a cherry cutout.

At the end of each month, bring in some ice cream and assorted toppings. Invite the "scoops" in that month's dish to join you after school for an ice-cream sundae party. (Don't forget to plan a special day for children with summer birthdays.) Youngsters won't soon forget this sweet birthday treat.

Today is Zach's birthday!

Birthday Banner

Your birthday honoree will have a banner day when you welcome him with this birthday banner. To make one, cut balloon and birthday gift shapes from different colors of felt. Glue the cutouts onto a 36" x 48" piece of burlap. Use fabric pens and dimensional paints to add festive details to the banner. Hot-glue the top of the banner onto a wooden dowel; then tie a length of string to either end of the dowel for hanging.

When it is time to celebrate a child's birthday, write "Today is [child's name]'s birthday!" on a sentence strip. Use clothespins or paper clips to attach the strip to the bottom of the banner. Hang the banner on your classroom door. Happy birthday!

A BIRTHDAY SHIRT

Celebrate birthdays in style with this festive shirt. Use dimensional paints and fabric markers to decorate a brightly colored T-shirt with a birthday cake or balloon shapes. For added delight, sprinkle iridescent glitter over the design. Your birthday child is sure to love the birthday greetings she will receive when wearing this birthday shirt!

A DAY TO REMEMBER

This birthday keepsake is sure to draw a cheer from your birthday student. First, program each of four giant flash cards with a part of the sentence "Today Is [Child's name]'s Birthday." Gather the class around the birthday child, and ask volunteers to hold the flash cards above their heads. Use an instant camera to snap a photo; then mount the photo onto a pennant-shaped piece of poster board. Invite the birthday child to decorate the pennant with markers and stickers. Have each child in the class write his name on the pennant. Tape the pennant to a paint-stirring stick or dowel; then add some lengths of colorful curling ribbon. Hip, hip, hooray—today's your special day!

Put On A Happy Face

Celebrate each child's birthday in a special way by inviting the birthday child to have her face painted. Use face paints to paint a simple design on the child's cheek. Then hand her a mirror and watch her smile with birthday pride!

A Throne Of Honor

Make your birthday child feel like a king—or queen—with this chair topper. To make one, use pinking shears to cut the bottom off of a pillowcase so that it fits over the back of a child-sized chair. Decorate the topper with brightly colored dimensional paints, sequins, and fake jewels. Attach a large bow to the back panel of the topper. On a child's birthday, slip the topper over the back of the student's chair. Now, that's some royal treatment!

A Zippy Birthday Song!

Here's a birthday ditty with a little zip! Introduce this song at circle time for a birthday greeting that is sure to make your birthday child feel special. For each new verse, substitute a different movement. In no time at all, your students will be moving to the birthday beat!

(sung to the chorus of "Zip-A-Dee-Doo-Dah")

Zip-a-dee-doo-dah!
Zip-a-dee-ay!
Let's [clap our hands]—
'cause it's [Child's name]'s
birthday!
Lots of good wishes
headed [his/her] way!
Zip-a-dee-doo-dah!
Zip-a-dee-ay!

Balloon Pop

You'll hear squeals of laughter when your youngsters play this party game similar to Hot Potato. In advance, add a spoonful of confetti to each balloon in a class supply. Blow up each balloon; then knot the end. Have your students form a group circle in an open area of your classroom. Direct the group to pass a balloon around the circle as you play some party music. Stop the music; then invite the child holding the balloon to sit on the balloon to pop it. (If a child is fearful, give him a handful of confetti to toss into the air as an alternative.) That child then leaves the circle. Continue in the same manner—adding one or more balloons each time one is popped—until each child has had an opportunity to pop a balloon.

Safety Note: Remove all popped pieces immediately to eliminate any choking hazard.

DON'T FORGET THE PRESENTS

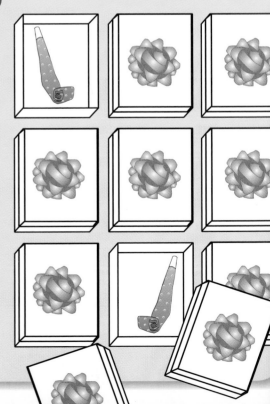

Visual memory skills are the gifts your students will receive when playing this Concentration-style game. In advance, collect enough identical pairs of small party favors so that each child may have one. Obtain small gift boxes equal to the number of items you have. Place each item in a box; then stick a bow to the top of each box. Arrange the boxes on a tabletop or floor.

To play, have a player open two boxes. If the items match, have the child place them in a basket. If the items do not match, the child replaces the lid on each box. Play then passes to the next child. Continue in the same manner until all the matches have been found. Then distribute the favors to the children to take home.

Birthday celebrations will take center stage when you add some festive touches with these classroom centers.

Birthday Bakery

Your little ones will whip up the best birthday cakes in town in this classroom bakery. Collect a variety of muffin cups and small tart tins. Place the pans in a center along with some play dough, plastic knives, decorative birthday plates, doilies, bits of rickrack, and birthday candles. Make a wish!

Kindergarten Cakes

Decorating birthday cupcakes will be the focus of fun in this center celebration. Invite the birthday child's parent to donate a class supply of unfrosted cupcakes. Place the cupcakes in a center along with frosting, candy sprinkles, colored sugars, and plastic knives. Invite each child to frost a cupcake, then sprinkle on his choice of toppings. When it is time to eat, place a candle on the birthday child's cupcake. Happy birthday to you!

CARDS BY DESIGN

Birthday greetings will abound in this writing center. Brainstorm with your students a list of birthday-related words. Write each word on a separate birthday-cake cutout. Display the cutouts in a center along with birthday gift wrap, construction paper, stickers, construction-paper shapes, discarded birthday cards, curling ribbon, birthday confetti, envelopes, scissors, glue, and markers. Encourage a student in this center to create a birthday card using his choice of materials. Have him place his completed card in an envelope, then deliver it to the birthday child. What a special delivery!

A Birthday Backpack

This birthday backpack is a sure way to make your birthday child's day! Stock a backpack with a birthday journal (blank paper bound between laminated birthday gift-wrap covers), scented markers or sparkle crayons, and some of the items from the suggested list. On a child's birthday, send the backpack home, along with a parent note requesting that the child draw a picture in the birthday journal. Ask parents to write their child's descriptions of his drawing at the bottom of his page, then return the backpack and journal to school. Invite the birthday child to keep the prizes and party favors; then restock the backpack for the next birthday child.

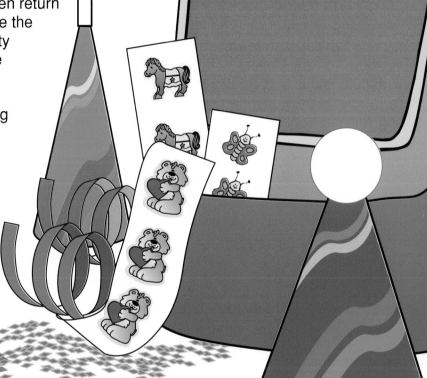

- a birthday bear (a stuffed bear wearing a birthday hat and bandana)
- birthday favors such as noisemakers, party blowers, and a birthday hat
- a specially decorated birthday plate
- a small bag of birthday prizes
- a birthday-related book (see the suggested list)
- a birthday game, such as Pin The Tail On The Donkey

BIRTHDAY-BOOK BONANZA

Arthur's Birthday
Written by Marc Brown
Published by Little, Brown and Company

Jimmy's Boa And The Big Splash Birthday Bash
Written by Trinka Hakes Noble
Published by Puffin Books

Angelina's Birthday Surprise
Written by Katharine Holabird
Published by Crown Books For Young Readers

Don't Wake Up Mama! Another Five Little Monkeys Story
Written by Eileen Christelow
Published by Houghton Mifflin Company

Will It Ever Be My Birthday?
Written by Dorothy Corey
Published by Albert Whitman & Company

HAPPY BIRTHDAY

©1998 The Education Center, Inc. • The Mailbox® Superbook • Grade K • TEC459

IT'S YOUR BIRTHDAY,

GO WILD!

©1998 The Education Center, Inc. • The Mailbox® Superbook • Grade K • TEC459

Note To The Teacher: Duplicate cards on white construction paper. Color, cut out, and personalize each card. Distribute a card to each child on his birthday.

TIPS For Good Trips

Permission slips, admission money, bag lunches, bus reservations… aren't field trips fun? Ease the stress and worry of putting a trip together by using these organizational tips for hassle-free trips. Then sit back and enjoy the ride!

ideas contributed by Vicki Mockaitis Pacchetti

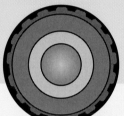

Where Are We Going?

The realm of field trips for little learners is unlimited. Just traveling as a group is a learning experience in itself for youngsters—maybe for you, too! Even if a child has been to the grocery store countless times with a parent, there is still value in experiencing a tour with a group of peers. Here are a few possibilities for places to visit and people to see.

post office	bakery	fire station	police station
bank	pet store	grocery store	museum
park	theater	circus	fair
newspaper office	local TV station	library	farm
zoo	fast-food restaurant	shopping mall	manufacturing facility
hospital	doctor/veterinarian	dentist	planetarium
airport	your house	walk around the neighborhood	

Personal Preview

Start planning for your classroom excursion by taking a solo trip to your destination for a preview. Drive the same route you plan to take so that you are aware of any road construction, heavy traffic, or other transportation happenings. Time your trip so that you can let parents know approximate departure and arrival times. As you walk through and visit, make note of any potential problems that may occur as well as any "must-sees." Talk with a guide, if one is available, and find out any background information that will be beneficial in preparing little ones for the trip. With luck, a preliminary run-through will eliminate any surprises that will cause your trip to be less than enjoyable. So be a good scout, and be prepared!

Setting The Stage

Even though you may not want to be extremely detailed (because surprise can be fun), preparing youngsters for a field trip can add value to what they actually take away from the trip. Make a simple semantic map with your students, listing what might be seen at the location. If available, show brochures so that youngsters can get a visual idea of what the trip is going to be like. Finally write down a list of students' questions that can be answered during the trip. Once students have a purpose for the outing, you'll see lots of excitement and anticipation!

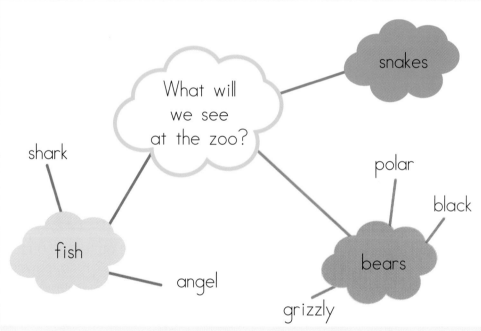

Plastic And/Or Paper!

If you're planning an all-day trip that will require youngsters to bring their own lunches, request that parents use disposable containers. Paper bags, zippered sandwich baggies, and juice boxes will take up less room, cleanup will be a breeze, *and* you'll be returning to school with a lighter load!

Color-Coded Crew

Put safety and security at the top of your priority list with these colorful tips. On the day of the trip, have everyone wear coordinated clothing. Choose a very common article of clothing—such as a red T-shirt or a school sweatshirt—for youngsters and their parents to wear so that your group sticks out and is easily recognizable.

Once you've divided your class into chaperoned groups, assign each group a different color. Then make each group's nametags in its designated color with colored paper, markers, or colored sticky dots. The adults will be able to see in a flash who belongs in their groups. Be sure to make a master list of the colored groupings so that you can sort out any stragglers.

Parent Packs

There's no greater asset on a field trip than a prepared parent. Help your chaperones by assembling these handy travel packs. Collect several fanny packs and stock each one with baby wipes, bandages, an instant cold pack, spare change, a pen, safety pins, emergency first-aid information, and the phone number of the school. If desired, include an inexpensive watch so that each group is synchronized with the others. Now you'll have first-aid supplies that are readily accessible and convenient. After the trip, collect the packs and restock them as necessary.

Classroom Caravan

Playing Follow The Leader is fun, but it's not always reliable when you're traveling. If parents are driving, make sure each one has a detailed map showing the route you'd like him to take. You may want to use a marker to highlight the route so that the map is easier to follow. Include the name and phone number of the destination on the map just in case someone gets separated. See you there!

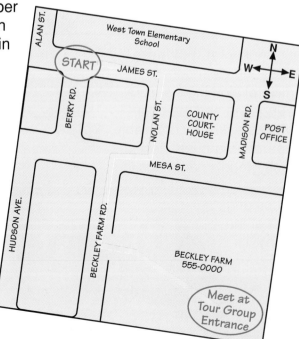

Can't Travel?

Are field trips out of the question for your group? If so, consider bringing the trip to school! Ask community helpers to visit your class and bring some tools of their trades. Often firefighters can drive a truck over for children to investigate. Parents can be great resources, too, giving you lots of suggestions and using their connections. For example, host a petting zoo on school grounds with animals owned by your students' acquaintances. Susie's aunt's friend can bring a goat; Jamar's third cousin has a miniature horse; Cassie's grandpa raises rabbits; etc. You may also research the wide variety of videos available to find some video field trips for your children's level. It's the next best thing to being there!

"I'm Tired!"

If you've planned an all-day trip, you can bet little bodies will be dragging upon returning to school. Ease the hectic pace of getting ready to go home by having children pack up their belongings *before* leaving for the trip. When they return, they can just grab their bookbags and be ready to go home. You may even have a little time left over for sharing or a story to end the day on a pleasant note instead of rushing students out the door.

Field-Trip *Tribune*

Turn field trips into lasting memories with this post-trip report. After the excursion, give each child a copy of pages 140 and 141. (Program the empty boxes on page 140 for your outing if it is not already represented.) Read aloud the *Tribune's* basic framework, then have a student volunteer reveal which picture from page 140 should go in each box on page 141. Direct each student to color, cut out, and glue the designated pictures to the corresponding boxes on her *Tribune.* Then help her complete her page by writing her dictation to fill in the blanks. Have each child record every trip with a *Tribune,* then compile the pages at the the end of the year to create a travel log for the year. Oh, the places we've gone!

Thanks A Bunch!

Extend a hearty thanks to your host or visitor with this gigantic thank-you note. Gather your little ones around you and create a letter by writing their comments about the trip on a sheet of chart paper. Add a short greeting; then have each child sign his name. Have volunteers decorate the letter with small drawings. (Use two sheets of paper if necessary.) Fold the paper, insert it in a large brown envelope, and model how to address the envelope and add the postage. For added fun, invite your youngsters to walk with you to a nearby mailbox. What a trip!

Dear Mr. Beckley,

We enjoyed our visit to your farm. Thanks for having us!

"I like the pigs the best."

"Those cows sure can moo!"

"I wanted to ride that horse!"

"The lamb was so soft and cuddly."

"I want my mom to take me back!"

Newsletter Pieces

Use with "Field-Trip *Tribune*" on page 139.

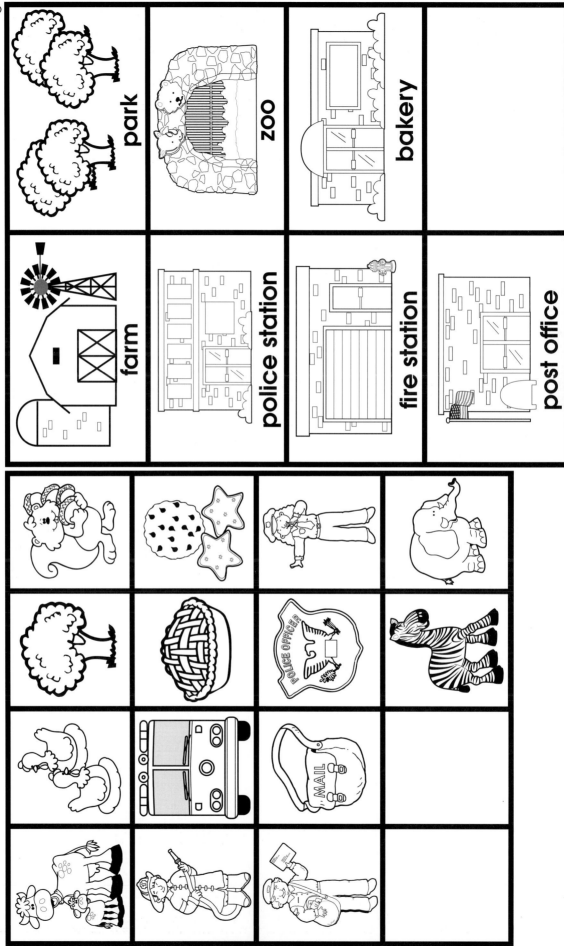

park

zoo

bakery

farm

police station

fire station

post office

MAIL

POLICE OFFICER

Field-Trip Tribune

Read All About It!

On _____ we went
(date)

to the ⬜ .

We saw ⬜ and ⬜ .

I liked _____ the best!

My favorite part of the trip.

Name _____

MAKE YOURSELF AT HOME

Welcome parents into their children's home-away-from-home with these ideas and activities for a successful Open House.

ideas contributed by Patricia A. Staino and Virginia Zeletzki

MAKE IT AND TAKE IT...HOME!

Encourage students to create Open House invitations to present to their families. Make one copy of the invitation on page 146; then fill in the date and time of your Open House in the blank spaces on the copy. For each student, duplicate the schoolhouse pattern on red construction paper and the programmed text box on white copy paper. Have each child cut out the schoolhouse and the text box, then cut along the dotted lines. Help her glue the text box to the back of her schoolhouse so the information shows through the doors when they are folded back. Complete the invitations by hot-gluing a jingle bell to the box at the top of each schoolhouse.

Come On In!

We're getting ready—
There's so much to do!
We're eager for guests;
We're waiting for you!
Please come
to our Open House

on _____

at _____

We Are Family

A busy-hands center will keep younger siblings occupied while parents participate in the evening's activities. Stock an area of your classroom with toys, books, and activities that will hold the interest of younger children. Arrange for an older child or adult helper to supervise the area while you visit with parents.

Warm Welcome

Place a welcoming message outside your front door. Print the message on a large sheet of poster board, and clip it to your art easel. Prop a friendly stuffed animal (perhaps your school's mascot) on top of the easel for a finishing touch. Or, if your classroom entryway is outside, use chalk to write a welcoming message, and draw your school mascot on the sidewalk.

Welcome
To Ms. Caudle's
Room
GO TIGERS

PRIZE PINS

Boost attendance at your Open House by awarding a door prize. Ask a local business (such as a bookstore) to donate a gift certificate as a prize. Before the Open House, write each child's name on a clothespin. Place the clothespins on a clothesline mounted in your classroom. Use each child's clothespin to hold his parents' nametags and the evening's schedule.

When parents enter the classroom, ask them to find their child's clothespin, remove it from the line, and place it into a box or basket nearby. When all the parents have arrived or at a predetermined time, draw one clothespin from the container, and award the winner's parents the gift certificate.

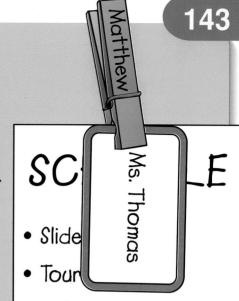

SC_____LE
- Slide
- Tour
- Refreshments
- Meet The Principal

Matthew

Ms. Thomas

SCHOOL SCAVENGERS

Families will have fun with this game, which will familiarize them with their children's school. Make up a list of destinations and items to find at each location, similar to the example.

- school office—a school calendar
- nurse's office—an adhesive bandage
- art room—a crayon
- music room—a sticker or stamp of a musical note
- playground—a rock or wood chip
- cafeteria—a cookie
- hall bathroom—a paper towel
- guidance office—a "Free Hug" pass

Inform the staff at each location that parents will be coming by, and place a supply of the items in each location ahead of time.

At Open House, give each family a copy of the list and a large zippered plastic bag. When parents return with all the items, present them with a small prize, such as an edible treat.

Slide-Show Schedule

Parents will enjoy seeing their children in action! In the weeks prior to Open House, use slide film to take photos of each part of your school day, such as arrival, circle time, centers, recess, etc. Then prepare a slide show that illustrates your class's daily schedule. With the lights out and their focus on the slides, parents will be giving their full attention to your explanation of a typical school day.

Rock Around The Room

During your Open House, play recordings of some of the songs you use each day in class. Parents will probably recognize the songs from hearing their children sing them. List the names of the recordings, and display the list where parents can see it, in case they would like to purchase their own copies for their children. Even if parents don't recognize the songs, a little upbeat music will add to the Open House atmosphere!

Graffiti Board

Find out what's on parents' minds with this handy idea. Cover a bulletin board or tabletop with bulletin-board paper. Provide markers, and invite parents to jot down any advice, good wishes, comments, or questions they have. Be sure to answer any questions either during Open House or in a future issue of your class newsletter.

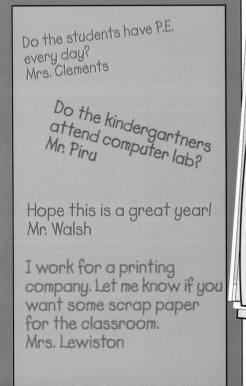

Do the students have P.E. every day?
Mrs. Clements

Do the kindergartners attend computer lab?
Mr. Piru

Hope this is a great year!
Mr. Walsh

I work for a printing company. Let me know if you want some scrap paper for the classroom.
Mrs. Lewiston

HANDLE WITH CARE

Many kindergartners' parents need reassurance, information, and a little TLC (Teacher's Loving Care) at the beginning of the school year. Before the Open House, prepare a care package for each family. Duplicate a class supply of the cover sheet on page 147 on tan construction paper. For each child, glue a cover sheet to the front of a file folder. Fill each folder with artwork and other creations made by the student, as well as important papers—such as your school handbook, a school lunch menu, a volunteer form, and a class newsletter. Add an herbal tea bag or a candy treat. "Address" each care package and tie red ribbon into a big bow around the folder.

FROM:
Your Child's Teacher,
Ms. Eakers

CARE PACKAGE

HANDLE WITH CARE

TO:
The Family Of
Seth Noel

"WHAT ARE THEY LEARNING?"

Parents like to know what their children are learning. Show them what you teach and *how* you teach it with this simple idea. Post a sheet of chart paper in each of your classroom centers—as well as your group area—explaining briefly to parents what children learn in that area of the classroom. If there isn't any wall space near a center, fold a sheet of poster board into thirds (as shown) to make a tabletop sign.

ART CENTER

- creativity
- fine-motor skills
- sensory exploration

Build-A-Snack

Looking for a refreshing way to serve refreshments? Why not invite parents to experience snacktime the way your students do? Choose a simple, no-cook recipe, and illustrate it on a chart or on step-by-step picture cards similar to those your kindergartners would use. Set out the ingredients and utensils needed, along with the instructions, and have parents make their own snacks.

Our First Photo Gallery

Invite little ones to help you decide what to show their parents at Open House. At least two weeks before your Open House, purchase a few disposable cameras (with film for indoor use). Demonstrate how to use the cameras. Keep them handy in the classroom, and encourage students to take pictures of each other during various activities. A few days before Open House, have the pictures developed; then display them on a bulletin board or around a doorway. Ask students to help you compose captions for the pictures that will tell their parents about their school experiences.

Open House Invitation

Use with "Make It And Take It...Home!" on page 142.

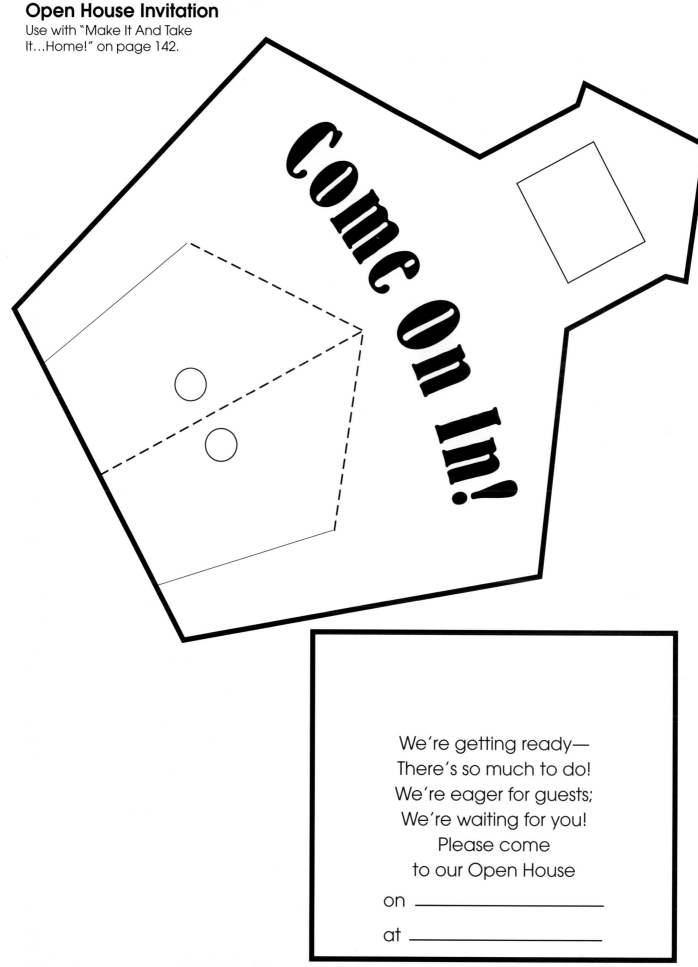

Come On In!

We're getting ready—
There's so much to do!
We're eager for guests;
We're waiting for you!
Please come
to our Open House

on _____

at _____

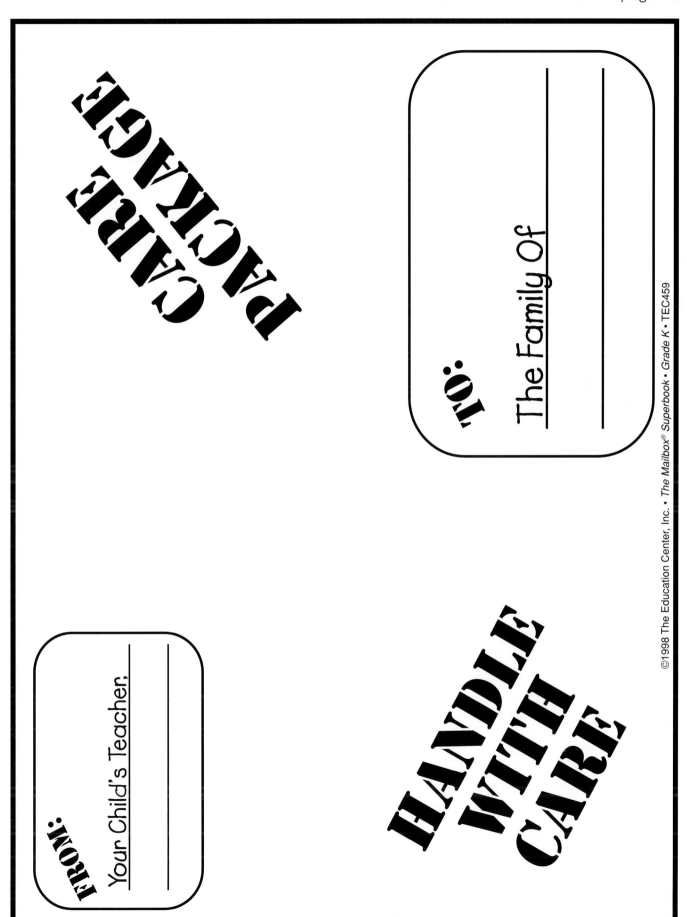

TO:

The Family Of _____

_____

FROM:

Your Child's Teacher, _____

_____

CARE PACKAGE

HANDLE WITH CARE

CLASS PARTIES That Are Always In Season

Turn ho-hum class parties into inviting celebrations
with these seasonally themed ideas.

ideas contributed by Lucia Kemp Henry

COME FOR SOME FALL FUN!

DECOR: LOVELY LEAF TABLE SETTINGS

You'll fall for these pretty party decorations! Invite each child to sponge-paint leaf shapes in fall colors onto a personalized 12" x 18" sheet of white construction paper and a plain white party napkin. Set the placemats and napkins aside to dry. Just before the party, roll out lengths of bulletin-board paper to serve as table runners. Scatter real leaves or fingerpainted leaf shapes down the table runners. Arrange the placemats and napkins. Beautiful!

DRESS: Festive Fall Headbands

For each headband, you'll need:
- a black construction-paper headband
- 3 copies of the leaf patterns (page 152)
- three 3" x 3/4" strips of paper, accordion-folded to make paper "springs"

Have each youngster color and cut out his leaves, then glue three of them to his headband. Have him glue each of the other three leaves to one end of a separate paper spring, then glue the opposite end of the spring to his head-band. These leaves will wiggle and dance—just like fall leaves blowing in the wind!

ACTIVITY: Beanbag Leaf Toss

Use the leaf patterns on page 152 to make red, orange, and yellow felt leaf shapes. Hot-glue the felt leaves to plain beanbags. Cut out three large leaf shapes from red, orange, and yellow construction paper. Glue each paper leaf to a large brown paper grocery sack. Scatter the beanbags around the floor of the classroom, and challenge students to gather up all the "fallen leaves." Then have them toss each colorful beanbag into its matching leaf sack.

To make this into a game, divide your class into three teams and assign each team a color of leaf beanbag to collect. The first team to toss all its beanbags into the matching grocery bag wins!

Food: Cinnamon-Apple Stackers

Ingredients (per child):
- 1 Tbsp. spreadable cream cheese
- 1 dried apple ring
- 1 tsp. applesauce
- 1 cinnamon graham cracker square

"Stack" the cream cheese, applesauce, and apple ring on top of a cinnamon graham cracker square. Now, bite into fall!

IT'S A SNOWY CELEBRATION

DECOR: STYROFOAM® SNOWFOLKS

Your room will be a winter wonderland when you set these supercute snowfolk on the tables. Give each child a small white foam cup and a three-inch foam ball along with a variety of colorful buttons, wiggle eyes, tiny pom-poms, real twigs, pipe-cleaner pieces, and strips of felt. To make a snowperson, glue a foam ball to the bottom of a cup to create the head and body. Insert two twigs into the sides of the cup for arms, securing the twigs with glue. Add details by gluing on the materials of your choice.

DRESS: SNOWFLAKE NECKLACES

For each necklace, you'll need:
- a square of waxed paper
- white school glue
- silver or iridescent glitter
- an 18-inch length of yarn

Use a pencil to sketch a simple snowflake shape on each child's waxed paper. Have him trace over the pencil lines with thick streams of glue. Have him shake a small amount of glitter over the glue; then leave the shape to dry overnight. When the shape is firm, peel it off the waxed paper, punch a hole near one tip, and thread the yarn length through the hole. Tie the ends of the yarn to create a necklace.

ACTIVITY: Snowball Throw

A flurry of fun will follow this safe and dry indoor snowball toss! Gather a supply of large Styrofoam® balls. Pile these faux snowballs onto a small plastic snow saucer or sled. Hang several large tagboard snowflake shapes (from the patterns on page 152) from a classroom clothesline. Challenge several students to throw foam snowballs at the snowflake targets. When their snowball supply is gone, ask the players to gather up the foam balls for the next group.

Food: Blizzard Bites

Ingredients (per child):
- vanilla wafer
- spreadable cream cheese
- flaked coconut

Spread the cream cheese on top of the vanilla wafer. Press the cookie, cream-cheese-side-down, onto a dish of flaked coconut. Mmmm…perfect with a cup of hot cocoa!

SPRING FLING

DECOR: A GREAT BIG BOUQUET

Giant flower decorations will have little ones blooming with party spirit! Paint empty cardboard gift-wrap tubes with green tempera paint to make oversized flower stems. Enlarge the flower patterns on page 153, and use them as templates to cut out large flower shapes from students' colorful finger-paintings; then cut smaller duplicate shapes from colored construction paper. Glue a fingerpainted flower to one end of a cardboard tube; then glue a construction-paper flower on top. Glue half of a painted foam ball to the middle of each flower, as shown. Arrange these blossoms in a large plastic flowerpot filled with sand, and set the bouquet on your party table.

ACTIVITY: Planting Packets

Youngsters will enjoy this hand-eye coordination activity filled with flower-planting paraphernalia. Gather plastic flowerpots in three or four graduated sizes, five flower-seed packets, and a pair of garden gloves. Set the flowerpots on the floor in a row from largest to smallest. Ask a child to put on the gloves and stand next to the largest flowerpot while she holds a seed packet. Have her hold the packet at chin level and drop it straight down into the flowerpot, then repeat the action with the remaining four packets. After she successfully drops the five packets into the largest pot, have her continue with the remaining pots, ending with the smallest.

DRESS: Buggy Bands

For each headband, you'll need:
• an inexpensive plastic headband
• 2 pipe cleaners
• 2 jingle bells
  Thread one end of each pipe cleaner through the loop on a jingle bell. Bend the pipe cleaners to hold the bells on the ends. Wrap the opposite end of each pipe cleaner around the headband (near its center).

Food: Springtime Snacks

Ingredients (per child):
• 1 cheese sandwich, cut in half diagonally
• 1 tiny sweet pickle

Set the sweet pickle in the center of a paper plate. Arrange the sandwich wings on the plate on either side of the pickle to make a butterfly. Watch your appetite bloom!

A SUMMER SPREE

DECOR: SUNSHINE CENTERPIECE

Sand, shells, and the sun are the perfect summer party decorations. To make a sunshine centerpiece, paint a large foam ball yellow. Push a one-foot wooden dowel into the painted ball and secure it with glue. Push yellow poster-board sun rays into the ball around its circumference to create a sun shape. Place this sun-on-a-stick into a child's beach bucket filled with sand, and then scatter shells on the sand. Set the sun centerpiece on your party table.

DRESS: Seashell Shirts

You will need:
- a solid-colored T-shirt per child
- newspaper
- sponges cut into shell shapes (patterns on page 153)
- fabric paint (dark and light shades)

Slide a section of newspaper inside each shirt before painting. Have each child sponge-paint several shell shapes on the front of his T-shirt and add lines by "drawing" with the paint bottles. Let the shirts dry overnight. Follow directions on the fabric-paint bottle for setting the paint.

ACTIVITY: Seaside Sand Table

Turn your sand table into a game space, and your youngsters will feel like they're playing at the beach. Gather several large seashells or make shell-shaped beanbags from the patterns on page 153. Place the shells in a child's sand pail. Then lay three targets out on the sand: bury a wide cup so that its rim is *level* with the sand's surface, lay an embroidery hoop *on* the sand, and set a round sand sieve or pie pan on top of the sand so that its rim is *above* the sand's surface. Ask youngsters to take turns tossing the shells onto the sand table, attempting to hit the targets.

Food: Sunny Snacks

Ingredients (per child):
- 1 English muffin half
- 1 slice American cheese (cut into eight triangles as shown)
- 2 pineapple chunks
- yellow-tinted cream cheese
- 1 half of a pineapple ring

Spread the cream cheese atop the muffin half. Set the muffin half on a paper plate, and arrange the cheese triangles around it to resemble sun rays. Use the pineapple chunks and half-ring to create a face. What a sizzling good snack!

Leaf Patterns

Use with "Festive Fall Headbands" and "Beanbag Leaf Toss" on page 148.

Snowflake Patterns

Use with "Snowball Throw" on page 149.

Flower Patterns
Use with "A Great Big Bouquet" on page 150.

Seashell Patterns
Use with "Seashell Shirts" and "Seaside Sand Table" on page 151.

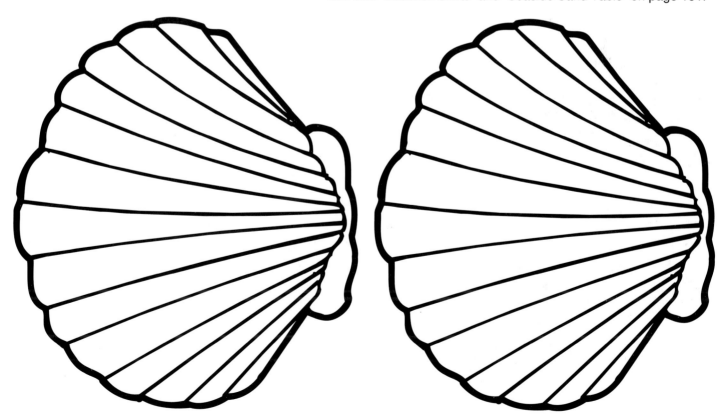

Calendar Of SPECIAL

AUGUST

- Children's Vision And Learning Month

- Friendship Day—First Sunday in August

- National Smile Week—First full week in August

- Book Lovers Day—August 9

- National I Love Cowboys and Cowgirls Day—August 15

- National Aviation Week—Week of August 19

SEPTEMBER

- Children's Good Manners Month
- Library Card Sign-Up Month
- National Better Breakfast Month
- National Honey Month
- Labor Day—First Monday in September
- National Grandparents Day—First Sunday after Labor Day
- National Farm Animals Awareness Week—Third full week in September
- Johnny Appleseed's Birthday (John Chapman)—September 26

OCTOBER

- National Dental Hygiene Month

- National Pasta Month

- National Pizza Month

- National Popcorn Poppin' Month

- Fire Prevention Week—First or second week of October

- Columbus Day—Second Monday in October

- National School Bus Safety Week—Third full week of October

- Halloween—October 31

NOVEMBER

- Peanut Butter Lovers' Month
- International Drum Month
- National Author's Day—November 1
- Sandwich Day (birthday of John Montague, sandwich inventor)—November 3
- National Children's Book Week—Week prior to Thanksgiving
- American Education Week—Week prior to week of Thanksgiving
- Thanksgiving Day—Fourth Thursday in November
- National Game And Puzzle Week—Last week in November

EVENTS

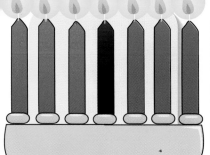

DECEMBER

- International Calendar Awareness Month

- National Poinsettia Day— December 12

- Christmas— December 25

- Hanukkah— Date based on Jewish calendar (usually in December)

- Kwanzaa— December 26– January 1

JANUARY

- National Soup Month
- Oatmeal Month
- Eye Care Month
- New Year's Day—January 1
- International Thank-You Day— January 11
- Pooh Day (A. A. Milne's Birthday)— January 18
- National Hugging Day™— January 21
- Martin Luther King, Jr. Federal Holiday—Third Monday in January
- National School Nurse Day— Fourth Wednesday in January

FEBRUARY

- American Heart Month
- Black History Month
- National Children's Dental Health Month
- Groundhog Day— February 2
- Random Acts Of Kindness Week— Week including February 14
- Read To Your Child Day— February 14
- Valentine's Day— February 14
- Presidents' Day—Third Monday in February
- International Friendship Week—Last full week of February

MARCH

- National Nutrition Month®

- National Peanut Month

- Music In Our Schools Month

- Youth Art Month

- Share A Smile Day—March 1

- Newspapers In Education Week—First full week of March

- St. Patrick's Day—March 17

APRIL

- Keep America Beautiful Month

- National Library Month

- Month Of The Young Child

- Easter—Date based on lunar calendar (between March 22 and April 25)

- April Fools' Day—April 1

- International Children's Book Day—April 2

- Kindergarten Day—April 21

- Earth Day—April 22

- National Arbor Day—Last Friday in April

MAY

- National Physical Fitness And Sports Month
- National Strawberry Month
- National Family Week—First full week in May
- May Day—May 1
- Mother Goose Day—May 1
- National Weather Observer's Day—May 4
- Mother's Day—Second Sunday in May
- National Transportation Week—Week including third Friday in May
- Memorial Day—Last Monday in May

JUNE

- Dairy Month

- National Fresh Fruit And Vegetable Month

- Pet Appreciation Week—June 6–12

- National Hug Holiday Week—Second week in June

- Flag Day—June 14

- Father's Day—Third Sunday in June

- Celebration Of The Senses Day—June 24

JULY

- National Hot Dog Month

- National Ice Cream Month

- National Picnic Month

- Independence Day—July 4

- Space Week—Week including July 20

CIRCLE TIME

Round Up For Circle Time

Gather youngsters together for some rootin'-tootin' circle-time fun with these ideas—and rope in a herd of language, math, and social skills along the way.

by Mackie Rhodes

Turn-Taking Magic

Go head-to-head with the circle-time turn-taking challenge with this charming idea. In advance, create a magic wand by covering a ruler, dowel, or sturdy plastic tube with sparkly stickers or glitter fabric paint. To one end of the wand, attach a small item or construction-paper cutout that represents your unit of study or an appropriate special occasion. For example, you might attach a silk leaf to the wand during your fall unit. Or use a plastic frog at the end of the wand during a study of pond life. Introduce the concept of taking turns by explaining that when a student's head is tapped lightly with the wand, it is her turn to talk. Ask the other students to listen quietly and attentively during each child's turn. Abracadabra! Let the magic begin!

MOUSE NIBBLES

For more practice with turn-taking skills, try this sweet idea. Obtain a large cardboard pizza round; then cut out a poster-board circle the same size as the pizza round. Decorate the cutout to resemble a chocolate chip cookie. Laminate the cookie; then puzzle-cut it into the same number of pieces as there are students in your class. Assemble the cookie puzzle onto the pizza round, tracing the outline of each piece. During circle time, explain that students are little mice waiting to take a nibble out of the big cookie. When an occasion calls for taking turns, invite each child to "nibble" a puzzle piece from the cookie as he takes his turn. Then on the next turn-taking sequence, have each student return his cookie nibble after he takes his turn. On a subsequent day when students exhibit good turn-taking skills, reward them with a snack of *real* chocolate chip cookies!

Sitting Pretty

Try this clever game to position youngsters for some attentive circle-time sitting. When youngsters have gathered for circle-time activities, toss a beanbag to a child. Ask that child to sit in any position he chooses; then challenge the rest of the class to imitate his position. Repeat the procedure, tossing the bag to a different child each time. Conclude the game by tossing the beanbag to yourself, and modeling the preferred position—such as cross-legged—for youngsters to imitate. Now that youngsters are sitting pretty, circle time can begin!

Operation: Jingle Bell

Your mission: to promote those all-important listening skills. Your method: jingle-bell signals. Your classroom will resound with joyful ringing when you use this idea to practice students' listening skills. At the beginning of circle time, give each child a set of jingle bells. Announce a special code word for circle time—such as a color, a book character's name, or even a silly nonsense word. Explain that each time students hear the word, they are to ring their bells three times. Then proceed with your planned activities, inserting the code word randomly throughout circle time. Youngsters will enthusiastically signal their sharp listening skills. Mission accomplished.

FITTING THE PIECES TOGETHER

If you're puzzled over how to involve youngsters in making activity choices (or in summarizing their day's activities), try this simple solution. To prepare, obtain a puzzle with the same number of pieces as there are children in your class. At the beginning of your first and/or last circle time, give each child a piece of the puzzle. During your first circle time, explain the day's activity offerings. Invite each child, in turn, to place his puzzle piece in its appropriate space and tell in which activity he would like to participate. Or, during the day's last circle time, have each child summarize his day's activities after placing his puzzle piece. What a neat way to piece the day together!

Initial Sounds In Action

Prick up youngsters' ears and energy levels with this listen-and-move activity. To begin, purchase or prepare a set of alphabet cards. During circle time, instruct each student to look and listen for the card with the letter that begins his name; then show one card at a time. When a child identifies the letter corresponding to his name, have him stand up. Then invite the standing student(s) to perform a named action that also corresponds to the letter. For instance, children with names beginning with *A* might do the alligator crawl. Or students whose names begin with *G* might gallop. When a card does not correspond to any child's name, invite the entire class to perform the named action. Ready? Look… listen…move!

Hungry Puppy Puppet

Youngsters will work up an appetite for counting when you introduce them to your Hungry Puppy puppet. To prepare, create a sock puppet with wiggle eyes, a pom-pom nose, and felt ears. You'll also need a box of bone-shaped dog treats. Each day during circle time, invite a child to place the puppet on her hand and say, "This hungry puppy ate [number] bones." Have her choose a number from one to ten. Then ask her to manipulate the puppet so that it "eats" the corresponding number of bones out of the box. (Have her remove one bone at a time and drop the bones into a box or basket nearby.) As she counts, encourage the other children to make the crunching and munching sound effects for the Hungry Puppy. Afterward, invite the class to chorally count the "eaten" bones to check the child's counting. Return the bones to the box for more counting and crunching the next day!

THE SHAPES ON THE BUS

Roll into shape recognition with a familiar song in a slightly different form. To begin, create a large picture of a school bus on a sheet of bulletin-board paper. Include lots of different shapes to represent the different parts of the bus. For instance, you might use circles for the wheels, squares for the windows, rectangles for the doors, and triangles for the lights. Display your school bus during circle time; then invite youngsters to sing this song, filling in a different bus part and its corresponding shape each time the song is repeated.

(sung to the tune of "The Wheels On The Bus")

The [wheels] on the bus are [round, round, round], [round, round, round], [round, round, round], The [wheels] on the bus are [round, round, round], On our shape-time school bus!

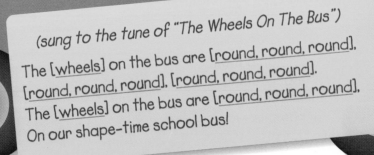

BOXED RHYMES

Add a bit of guesswork and giddiness to liven up student interest in nursery rhymes. Separately cover a large shoebox and lid with decorative wrapping paper. Then select a rhyme to use during circle time, such as "Hey Diddle, Diddle." Place a few items or pictures in the box to represent parts of the rhyme. For example, you might include plastic models of a cat and a cow, a plastic spoon and dish from your house-keeping center, and a picture of a fiddle. Place the lid on the box; then, during circle time, invite a child to slip her hand into the box and remove an item. Ask students to guess which rhyme the item might represent. (If desired, have the class recite rhymes that go with any reasonable guesses.) Have youngsters continue removing the items one at a time until the correct rhyme is guessed or the box is empty. Display all the items together; then invite the class to chorally recite—and act out—the rhyme.

Spy Light

This spirited adaptation of I Spy will keep youngsters on the lookout for mystery objects. At circle time, explain to youngsters that they will play a game called Spy Light. To play, the spy mentally notes a specific object in the room and whispers the name and location of that object to you. Then the class sings the song below, with the spy filling in the blank with a characteristic of his chosen object, such as its shape, color, or size. The other students try to guess the identity of the mystery object. The spy points a flashlight at each guessed object but does not actually turn on the light until it is pointed at the correct object. Turn on the spy light—the guess is right!

(sung to the tune of "This Little Light Of Mine")

This little light of mine,
I'm gonna let it shine.
This little light of mine,
I'm gonna let it shine.
This little light of mine,
I'm gonna let it shine.
Let it shine, let it shine, let it shine....
On something [blue]. *(spoken)*

STORY CHAIN

Link youngsters' thoughts into a story with this special story chain. As a group, select a story topic; then give each child a long construction-paper strip, and keep one strip for yourself. Write the numeral 1 and your dictated story starter on your paper strip. Staple the strip into a loop, printed side out. Then invite a volunteer to dictate the next sentence of the story, labeling her strip with the numeral 2. Write her dictation on her paper strip; then loop her strip through the first paper loop and staple the ends together. Repeat this procedure, labeling each child's paper strip with the next numeral in the sequence and having her add a sentence to the story. If desired, sketch a simple illustration next to each sentence to help children recall the story. After completing the story chain, reread the story. Then place it in your reading center for students to enjoy.

Cooperative Creations

Promote a spirit of creative cooperation with this circle-time illustration. Post a large sheet of bulletin-board paper in your circle-time area. During group time, use a marker to draw a simple design or figure on the paper. Ask youngsters to discuss how different designs or figures might be added to the drawing to create something recognizable, such as a clown or train. Then invite each child, in turn, to add her choice of designs to the illustration. As youngsters build the illustration, continue the group's discussion about what might be created from the new additions. Does the final picture represent the group's original ideas? Label the creation with a student-generated title; then display the class illustration along with a sheet of chart paper listing each child's comment about it. Now, that's creativity with class!

"Hand-y" Rebus Tales

Hand it to this storytelling idea to really hold youngsters' attention. To prepare to tell a hand-sign rebus tale, obtain a hand-sign dictionary or a children's book of hand signs. Select a story, such as "The Three Bears," with repetitive characters, actions, or simple phrases; then teach your students the simple signs for these. Tell the story in your own words, inviting students to fill in the repetitive words and phrases with the corresponding hand sign; for example, students might make the sign for "bear" (shown below), each time the bears are mentioned in "The Three Bears." Youngsters will get so involved that you'll want to expand this idea to include your song selections as well. Hands up for hand-sign rebuses!

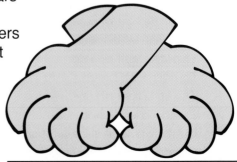

bear: "clawed" hands crossed at wrist

SHARE TIME...LIVE!

Amplify your circle-time sharing experiences with this neat idea. Write each child's name on a separate notecard; then put the cards in a bag. Invite a volunteer to be the announcer. Have the announcer draw a card from the bag and silently read the name on the card (whisper the name to her if she cannot read it). Then ask the announcer to talk into a toy microphone as she describes the person labeled on the card—without using her name, of course! When the described child recognizes her own description, invite her to take the microphone to tell about her share topic for the day. Then have that child assume the announcer role. Continue until sharing time ends. It's share time...live!

The Gift Of Expression

Use this language idea to help youngsters express their imaginations. Wrap several boxes of different sizes in decorative gift-wrapping paper; then tie a ribbon around each box. Have students sit in a circle during group time. Ask a volunteer to select a wrapped box and imagine the gift he would like to find inside. Have him whisper his thought to you; then instruct him to describe his imaginary gift to the child on his right. If this child has difficulty identifying the imaginary gift, invite other class members to help him guess until it is correctly named. Then invite that child to choose a box and repeat the game, describing his imaginary gift to the child on his right. Continue around the circle in this manner so that each child has an opportunity to describe his imaginary gift. Conclude by describing *your* imaginary gift and asking the class to identify it. This special gift of expression will surely last a lifetime.

GATHER AROUND—IT'S STORYTIME!

Invite your youngsters into the magical world of books with tips that add a special touch to storytime.

ideas by Bonnie Elizabeth Vontz and Kim T. Griswell

STORYTIME RITUALS

Signal your little ones that it's time for a story with one of these special read-aloud rituals.

▶ Dim the classroom lights, cozy up in a rocking chair, and turn on a reading lamp to signal that it's time to gather around the reading rug.

▶ Bring out a story bag filled with items that represent stories in your collection. Have a child pick an item from the bag; then read the book that relates to that item.

▶ Play or sing a special song that signals storytime is about to begin.

▶ Decoupage a wooden chair with storybook art cut from worn-out books, or provide a director's chair with a canvas back and seat. Invite visiting authors and illustrators to decorate the chair by signing their names and drawing book characters on the canvas. Sit in the chair only when it's storytime.

▶ Announce storytime with the special cheer at right that will help your little ones get the wiggles out before settling down to listen.

S!	(Stand and raise your hands.)
T!	(Hold your arms out straight from each side.)
O!	(Bend to the left.)
R!	(Bend to the right.)
Y!	(Hold your arms above your head.)
T!	(Bend forward and touch your toes.)
I!	(Stand and fold arms over chest.)
M!	(Walk your students to your storytime spot.)
E!	(Sit down and pick up your book.)

Dress For Successful Reading

Do you need to dress up storytime? Then dress to match the story you'll be reading. Don overalls to read about a farm. Wear a floppy, striped felt hat to read *The Cat In The Hat.* Put on bunny ears before reading a rabbit tale. Before announcing the title of a book you'll be sharing, invite youngsters to predict what it's about, based on what you're wearing.

Story Aprons

Stir up interest in each book by introducing the characters before you read. In advance attach the hook side of a number of large Velcro® dots to the front of an apron. On tagboard draw characters from the book you'll be reading, and cut them out. Attach the loop side of a Velcro® dot to the back of each cutout. Before reading the book, don the apron. Stick each character, in turn, on the story apron; then tell the children something about that character.

Dramatic Read-Alouds

Turn storytime into dramatic playtime by choosing stories that allow audience participation. Pick a story that has defined speakers with short, repetitive dialogue, or spoken sounds. Assign a different child to play the part of each character that speaks. Become the narrator and read the story, stopping to allow each character to speak his dialogue or make the appropriate sound. As they wait for their cues, your little actors will develop better listening skills, and they'll line up to take part in the next storytime play.

Puppet Power

Your little listeners will be all ears when books are read aloud by puppets. Collect a variety of storytelling puppets that relate to a number of your favorite read-alouds. Since so many children's stories feature animals, a small collection of animal puppets—such as a spider, a monkey, a dog, and a bat—will provide hours of read-aloud enjoyment.

Together Time

Want to get families more involved in your classroom? Then host a family storytime. Invite the family of each child to come to school for a morning or an afternoon of reading. Invite each family to bring along a book to read to the class. Videotape the readings and keep copies of the video in your classroom library for families to borrow. Watch clips from the video throughout the year to make families an ongoing part of your classroom fun!

Read-Alouds That Captivate Kindergartners

Encourage young listeners to love language with one or more of these appealing, age-appropriate books. Many feature rollicking, repetitive text that invites kindergartners to chime in. Others lend themselves to drama, encouraging little ones to imitate movements, mimic sounds, or deliver dialogue. All are guaranteed to capture your kindergartners' interest and make storytime special!

Are You My Mother?
Written by P. D. Eastman
Published by Random House, Inc.

Barn Dance!
Written by Bill Martin, Jr. and John Archambault
Published by Henry Holt And Company, Inc.

Bat Jamboree
Written by Kathi Appelt
Published by Morrow Junior Books

Chicken Soup With Rice
Written by Maurice Sendak
Published by Scholastic Inc.

Clap Your Hands
Written by Lorinda Bryan Cauley
Published by Putnam Publishing Group

Come Out And Play, Little Mouse
Written by Robert Kraus
Published by Mulberry Books

Five Little Monkeys Jumping On The Bed
Written by Eileen Christelow
Published by Clarion Books

Four Famished Foxes And Fosdyke
Written by Pamela Duncan Edwards
Published by HarperCollins *Publishers,* Inc.

The Gingerbread Boy
Written by Richard Egielski
Published by HarperCollins *Publishers,* Inc.

Goodnight Moon
Written by Margaret Wise Brown
Published by HarperCollins *Publishers,* Inc.

Gotcha!
Written by Gail Jorgensen
Published by Scholastic Inc.

Green Eggs & Ham
Written by Dr. Seuss
Published by Random House Books For
   Young Readers

Guess How Much I Love You
Written by Sam McBratney
Published by Candlewick Press

The Hat
Written by Jan Brett
Published by G. P. Putnam's Sons

A House Is A House For Me
Written by Mary Ann Hoberman
Published by Viking

If I Ran The Zoo
Written by Dr. Seuss
Published by Random House Books For
   Young Readers

If You Give A Mouse A Cookie
Written by Laura Joffe Numeroff
Published by Scholastic Inc.

In The Small, Small Pond
Written by Denise Fleming
Published by Henry Holt And Company, Inc.

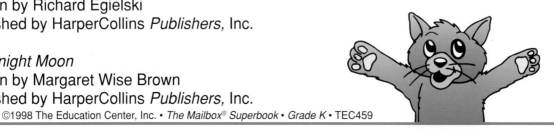

I Went Walking
By Sue Williams
Published by Harcourt Brace Jovanovich, Inc.

Ira Sleeps Over
Written by Bernard Waber
Published by Houghton Mifflin Company

Jamberry
Written by Bruce Degen
Published by HarperCollins Children's Books

Leo The Late Bloomer
Written by Robert Kraus
Published by HarperCollins Children's Books

Listen To The Rain
Written by Bill Martin, Jr. and John Archambault
Published by Henry Holt And Company, Inc.

Little Red Monkey
Written by Jonathan London
Published by Dutton Children's Books

Mama Don't Allow
Written by Thacher Hurd
Published by HarperCollins Children's Books

Mama, Do You Love Me?
Written by Barbara M. Joosse
Published by Chronicle Books

Max Found Two Sticks
Written by Brian Pinkney
Published by Simon & Schuster Books For
   Young Readers

The Napping House
Written by Audrey Wood
Published by Harcourt Brace & Company

No Jumping On The Bed!
Written by Tedd Arnold
Published by Dial Books For Young Readers

Oh, What A Noisy Farm!
Written by Harriet Ziefert
Published by Tambourine Books

Owl Moon
Written by Jane Yolen
Published by Philomel Books

Pumpkin, Pumpkin
Written by Jeanne Titherington
Published by Greenwillow Books

Quick As A Cricket
Written by Audrey Wood
Published by Child's Play (International) Ltd

Sam And The Tigers
Written by Julius Lester
Published by Dial Books For Young Readers

Snap!
Written by Marcia Vaughan
Published by Scholastic Inc.

Sun Song
Written by Jean Marzollo
Published by HarperCollins *Publishers,* Inc.

Those Can-Do Pigs
Written by David McPhail
Published by Dutton Children's Books

Where The Wild Things Are
Written by Maurice Sendak
Published by Scholastic Inc.

Who Said Moo?
Written by Harriet Ziefert
Published by HarperFestival®

Whose Mouse Are You?
Written by Robert Kraus
Published by Simon & Schuster Children's Books

cloudy

rainy

snowy

sunny

DAILY NEWS

Student Of The Day

Student Of The Day

DEVELOPING MOTOR SKILLS

In The Groove With GROSS-MOTOR SKILLS

Hop, skip, jump, or dance your way into this unit focusing on gross-motor skills. No matter how you get here, you'll find lots of energy-generating ideas to activate students' large body muscles *and* to strengthen their "mind muscles."

by Mackie Rhodes

CHORE-TIME CHARADES

Involve youngsters in the movements of routine chores with this charades-style game. To play, model a movement to simulate the performance of a particular household chore, such as vacuuming, washing windows, or scrubbing a bathtub. Ask youngsters to imitate your movements, but do not tell them which chore is being performed. After a designated time, signal for students to stop their activity; then ask them to name which chore they were doing. After all the guesses have been exhausted, tell youngsters which chore was being represented. Continue the game, modeling the actions of a different chore each time.

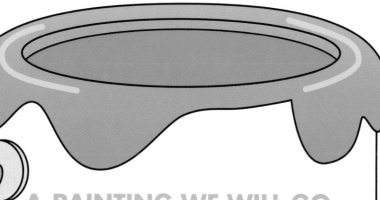

A-PAINTING WE WILL GO

Coat youngsters' imaginations with a fresh perspective when you take them into the hardworking world of a house painter. To begin, ask students to imagine they are house painters. Explain how a painter uses brushes and rollers to paint a house. Then talk students through the motions of painting a house (or a room in the house) as they perform the actions corresponding to your directions. For instance, you might have students reach high to brush-paint the top of a wall, then roll a paint roller down to paint the bottom of the wall. Or you might instruct your painters to make long left-to-right brush strokes across the middle of the wall or to create large circular strokes at eye level. As you direct your young painters, remind them to periodically dip their brushes and rollers into the paint containers. Bend, stretch, reach, roll...paint!

MARCH MADNESS

Hmmm...how does a penguin march? Find out what your students think when you create some march madness! Simply play a lively marching tune. Appoint a leader to guide a student parade around your classroom; then announce the name of an animal—such as a penguin, a duck, an elephant, a monkey, or a frog. Challenge the leader to perform a march she believes represents that animal's marching style. Then invite the other students to imitate her actions. After a designated period of time, appoint another child to be the leader; then repeat the activity, asking the leader to create a marching style for a different animal. Waddle, two, three, four.

RIBBON RIOT

Encourage youngsters to work on rhythm and muscle control with this riotous ribbon activity. To prepare a ribbon, staple a length of crepe paper to a cardboard tube for each child. Give each child a ribbon; then have her move to an area in the room so that she has plenty of personal space for free movement. On a signal, have each child control her body and ribbon in movement to the steady rhythm of a drum. You might play the rhythm fast or slow, soft or loud, or with a simple pattern. Then, at random intervals, beat the drum using an irregular, fast, and chaotic pace. At these times, youngsters will move their bodies and ribbons as if they have lost control. Return to a rhythmic drumbeat to help students regain control of their bodies and ribbons.

A WEIGHTY MATTER

Your lightweight champions will get a lift out of this fun activity. Create a set of weight-lifting dumbbells by following the directions for making the croquet mallet in "Croquet, Anyone?" up to taping over the top opening of the handle. Rather than sealing the opening, insert that end of the tube through two opposite holes cut in another chip canister; cut and tape it in place in the same manner as the other end. If desired, spray-paint the finished dumbbell. Invite student pairs to practice a series of weight-lifting routines using the dumbbells. For instance, students might lift the weights overhead from the floor. Or they might lie on their backs to perform bench presses. While youngsters exercise, be sure to emphasize positional and directional concepts, such as *high/low, up/down,* and *over/under.* Ready? Now li-i-ift!

CROQUET, ANYONE?

Introduce youngsters to the lawn game of croquet while improving their eye-hand coordination skills. To make a croquet mallet, lay a tall, lidded potato-chip can on its side; then, at the center of the can, trace around the end of a sturdy cardboard tube—such as those found in wrapping-paper rolls. Use a craft knife to cut out the resulting outline; then repeat the procedure on the opposite side of the can. Slide the end of the tube through both holes so that it extends one inch on the opposite side. Cut several slits from this end of the tube toward the can; then fold and tape the slits to the can. Cover the tube opening with tape. To keep the mallet handle from collapsing during use, pack it with sheets of twisted newspaper; then tape over the top opening of the handle. If desired, spray-paint the finished mallet. Then, to create a croquet wicket, cut off one-third of a very large plastic lid (such as one found on a large container of whipped topping or sherbet); then cut out the inside of the ring.

To play, push several wickets into the ground with adequate space between each one. Invite each player to tap his own plastic ball with a mallet, aiming it to pass through the wickets. The first player to successfully reach the designated finish line wins the game.

BUBBLES, BUBBLES, EVERYWHERE!

This imaginative bubble-blowing activity is sure to be "pop-ular" with students. To begin, invite youngsters to imagine that they are being blown into bubbles. On a signal—a swift blow into the air—have students pretend to expand into floating globes, then to drift or bounce in the air until you signal for them to pop. After a few practice sessions, divide the class into several small groups. Ask one child from each group to be the bubble blower. Have her blow through a large plastic hoop. When she blows, the other group members will become bubbles floating gently through the air. The blower must then catch each bubble with the hoop. After all the bubbles have been rounded up, invite another group member to be the bubble blower; then continue the game.

GEOMETRY ON THE GO

Students will learn about shape concepts as they figure out formations in this activity. Divide your class into a few groups; then challenge each group to cooperatively create a named shape using each member in the formation. If desired, display a picture of each shape as youngsters create. After each group forms its shape, use masking tape to outline the shape on the floor. Then assign a leader in each group to name an action—such as jump, spin, or stomp—for his group. On a signal, each group member will then perform that action, moving along the tape lines so as to maintain the shape as the group moves. Stomping squares, crawling circles, and tiptoeing triangles. Cool!

A RAINY DAY IN THE BALANCE

Keep students high and dry with this rainy-day relay. To set up the relay course, tape two lines identical in length to the floor. Divide your class into two teams. Assign each team a line; then position half of each team at one end of its line and the other half at the opposite end. Explain that the line represents a high wire similar to one seen at a circus. On a signal, the first team member uses an umbrella as a balancing pole while she walks the high wire to the opposite side. She then hands the umbrella to her awaiting team member. That student opens the umbrella and holds it overhead as she walks the high wire back to her team at the opposite end. When she arrives, she lowers the umbrella so that it can be used as a balancing pole by the next team member. Encourage each team to continue in this manner until every member has a turn. If desired, play circus music while the teams compete.

MUSICAL SQUARES

This musical game will have youngsters running—or hopping or tiptoeing—in circles. To set up, collect a set of carpet squares with one less square than there are children in your class; then arrange the squares in a circle. Invite students to stand in a circle surrounding the carpet squares. To play, name an action for youngsters to perform, such as *run, hop on one foot,* or *tiptoe;* then play a selection of lively music. Instruct youngsters to perform the action to the music as they circle around the carpet squares. After a short period of time, stop the music. Have each student step onto the nearest square so that each child is standing on a separate square. Invite the child without a carpet square to name the action to be performed for the next round. Then remove one square from the circle and play the game again. Continue play until only one child is left standing on a carpet square.

LOONY LIMBO

Here's a game that will bring some loony moves to the limbo pole. Obtain a recording of some limbo music; then set up a limbo pole. Appoint two students to control the height of the pole as the class plays. To begin, play the music, encouraging students to perform a few practice limbos under the pole. Then challenge youngsters to perform some special kinds of limbos—such as a duck-waddle limbo, a wiggle-worm limbo, and a fluttering-butterfly limbo. Continue to create as many silly limbo styles as student interest and energy dictate. You'll love the loony limbo laughter that comes with this activity!

Pass The Beanbag, Please

Give youngsters a good workout in throwing and catching skills with this activity. Instruct each child to select a partner; then give each partner a sturdy paper plate. Also give each student pair a beanbag. Explain that the partners will pass the beanbag back and forth to each other using their plates to catch *and* toss the bag. Encourage each pair to count the number of successful catches before one of the partners misses the beanbag. Then have the pair repeat the game, trying to improve the number of catches made. Increase the challenge by having the partners stand a little farther away from each other each time the game is repeated. Then, after student interest wanes, invite youngsters to throw their plates—like Frisbees®—into a box target.

GIVE THEM A HAND!

Fine-Motor Activities

Little learners will cheer for these entertaining activities that strengthen fine-motor skills.

ideas contributed by Bonnie Cave

SNACK IDEAS

"FOOD-AMENTAL" FLASH CARDS

Making edible flash cards is as easy as A, B, C. Give each child a graham cracker. Have him use a plastic knife to spread white frosting on top of it. Ask him to use one or more pieces of licorice whip to form a letter or number on the frosting. (If desired, provide clean scissors for children to use in cutting the licorice.) Invite children to eat and enjoy their creations.

PINK LEMONADE

Cool off a hot day with a pitcher of pink lemonade. Give each child in a small group a lemon half. Have him squeeze the lemon juice from his lemon half into a container. Continue until all students have squeezed their lemons. Strain out the lemon seeds. Then have youngsters help you combine 1 cup lemon juice, 1 cup sugar, 6 1/2 cups water, and 5 or 6 drops red food coloring in a pitcher. Serve chilled over ice. Aah—squeezin' is pleasin'!

COOKIE WREATH

Celebrate any special occasion with this festive cookie wreath. Give each child in a small group a butter-cookie ring. Have her use a plastic knife to spread green frosting on top of it. Invite her to decorate her cookie with sugar sprinkles and/or small candies.

MUSIC IDEAS

FEEL THE RHYTHM

Strengthen each child's pincer grasp with these super-simple rhythm instruments. Give each child two large, flat buttons (not necessarily matching). Then give her two small blobs of Sticky-Tac and have her use them to fasten one button to the tip of her index finger and the other button to the tip of her thumb. Ask youngsters to tap out the rhythm of a favorite tune, to copy your pattern of taps, or to tap out the syllables in several simple words or children's names.

KOOL KAZOO

Add these easy-to-make instruments to your class band. To prepare, gather a class supply of cardboard tubes, gift-wrap scraps, rubber bands, and five-inch circles cut from waxed paper. Give each child a cardboard tube. Have him wrap it in gift wrap and tape the covering in place. Instruct him to fold the excess paper into the ends of the tube. Show him how to place a waxed-paper circle over one end of his tube and secure it with a rubber band, so that the waxed paper is taut over the opening. Invite students to hum through the open ends of their tubes to play the kazoos.

SODA-BOTTLE MARACAS

Both making and playing these rhythm instruments will give youngsters fine-motor practice. Collect several plastic 12- or 16-ounce soda bottles with caps. Give each child two bottles. Invite students to decorate the bottles with colorful stickers or paint pens. Then have each child remove the caps and use a funnel to partially fill each bottle with rice or dried beans. Replace the caps. Show the children how to shake the bottles to create rhythmic sounds.

WATER AND SAND IDEAS

SIDEWALK PAINTING

Students will be amazed by magical masterpieces that slowly disappear! On a hot day, set out containers of water and paintbrushes in different sizes and widths—from skinny, fine-tip watercolor brushes to wide house-painting brushes. Take the class outside and invite students to water-paint on the sidewalk. Encourage them to use several different brushes, to improve wrist strength and tripod grasp. When the painting's done, youngsters can watch their creations slowly evaporate.

COLORED SAND

Have your little ones make different colors of sand, then use them for an art project that will call on their fine-motor control. Ask each student to mix together one-quarter cup of clean play sand with one teaspoon of dry tempera paint (in the color of his choice) in a container. Then place the containers of colored sand, pieces of poster board, pencils, and glue on a table. Invite each student to draw a geometric design on a piece of poster board. Next, show him how to cover a section of the drawing with a thin layer of glue and use his fingers to sprinkle on colored sand. Have him shake off the excess sand and repeat the procedure with another color. Set the finished artwork aside to dry.

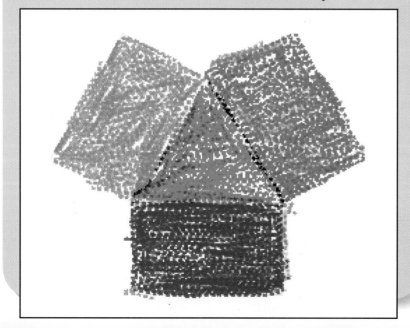

SUPER SCOOPS

These tools for playtime are quick and easy to make! Collect several plastic containers with handles, such as gallon milk jugs and syrup bottles. Use a craft knife to cut each container at an angle, and sand the cut edge to remove any rough spots. Then invite your youngsters to use the scoops at a water or sand table. Have them attempt to pass sand or water from scoop to scoop to improve eye-hand coordination and dexterity.

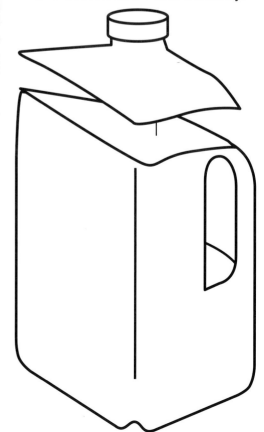

ART IDEAS

MIXING COLORS

Put a little muscle into color mixing with this activity. Give each child in a small group two balls of different-colored home-made play dough. Ask him to predict what color will be created if he kneads the two balls together. Then invite students to knead their balls of dough together to create new colors. Was anyone's prediction correct?

COLORFUL GARLAND

This festive garland will add color to your classroom *and* add to youngsters' tracing, cutting, and lacing skills. In advance, dye wagon wheel and rigatoni pasta (following the directions for "Decorative Dye" on page 198). Then invite students to trace different tagboard shapes onto bright-colored construction paper. Have each child cut out her shapes and use a hole puncher to punch a hole in the center of each one. Then have youngsters string all the cutouts and pasta pieces onto a strand of dental floss, in an alternating pattern. Tie the ends when the garland is completed.

WIRE SCULPTURE

Encourage each youngster in a small group to create a unique wire sculpture. For each student you will need a shallow container, a ball of clay, three 12-inch pieces of floral wire, and several small beads. Have her press the ball of clay into the shallow container. Next help her insert one end of a piece of floral wire into the clay. Have her thread beads onto the wire and bend it as desired. Show her how to insert the other end of the wire into the clay to secure it. Repeat the procedure with the remaining pieces of wire. Beautiful!

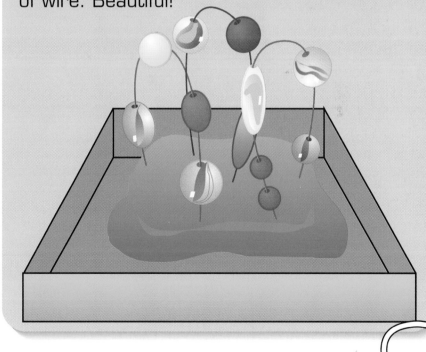

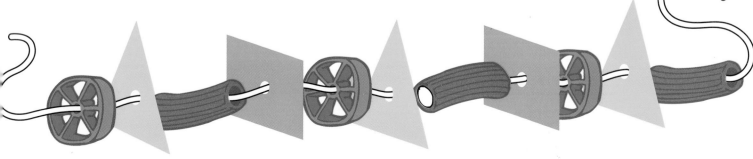

SOCK IT TO ME!

This activity reinforces sizing skills as it exercises a child's pincer grasp. String a clothesline in a learning center. Place a container of different-sized socks and a container of clothespins in the center. Challenge students to arrange the socks by size from shortest to longest. Ask them to use the clothespins to clip the socks on the clothesline in the correct order.

WRAP-'N'-STACK SCULPTURE

Wrap up dexterity and creativity with this group project. Collect several cardboard tubes and small boxes with lids. Have a small group of students wrap some boxes and tubes with wrapping-paper scraps. Then have the children stack the wrapped boxes and tubes to make a cooperative sculpture. Hot-glue the group's sculpture together.

POLISHING PENNIES

Invite students to use fine-motor control as they shake, squeeze, and manipulate small objects in this activity. Place a container of pennies, a salt shaker, a squeeze bottle of white vinegar, cotton swabs, several small bowls, and paper towels in a learning center. Ask each child to put a penny in a bowl, sprinkle it with salt, and squirt a few drops of vinegar over it. Have her use a cotton swab to scrub her penny and see it start to shine. Help the student dry the penny on a paper towel and pour out the vinegar solution. Use the clean pennies for a math activity.

FOSTERING CREATIVITY

MOVIN' THROUGH THE YEAR

Need to keep those little bodies busy? If so, then choose the ideas in this unit, and in no time at all your little ones will be movin' and groovin' through the year!

ideas contributed by Amber Weldon-Stephens

A WAKE-UP CALL

Rise and shine! Start the day with this wake-up activity that will get your little ones pumped up and primed for learning. Have students spread out in an open area of your classroom. Play some instrumental music that is slow at first, then speeds up. Instruct students to mirror your actions as you move your body in different ways, beginning slowly, then moving more quickly. For example, slowly roll your head from side to side and front to back, shrug your shoulders, and stretch high and low; then gallop, slide, or jump. Over a period of time, as students become more familiar with this activity, increase the complexity of the movements.

BODY TALK

Students will be rocking and wiggling as they move various body parts in this group activity. Play some lively music. As you name a body part, have each student move that part of his body to the beat of the music. For added fun, have students wiggle their noses, raise their eyebrows, or blink their eyes in time with the music. As children become more confident, encourage volunteers to be the leaders in this game of following directions. Let's get the beat—from our heads to our feet!

SHAKE IT UP!

You'll see giggles and grins, and a whole lot of shakin' going on when students make this tasty treat. Provide each student with a clean baby-food jar. Have each student place one table-spoon of instant pudding and one-half cup of milk into his jar; then tightly secure the lid. Play a lively rock-and-roll song, and have each student shake his jar in a variety of ways, such as high, low, to his left, to his right, etc. When the song has finished, provide each student with a plastic spoon so that he may eat this movement treat.

UNDER THE BIG TOP

Give your little ones the opportunity to perform under the big top with this movement activity. Seat your class in a group circle as you sing the song below.

As each child is named in the song, have her stand and imitate a circus animal or performer. Invite the other children to guess what animal or person she is imitating. Let the circus begin!

(sung to the tune of "Bingo")
If the circus came to town,
What would [Child's name] be?
Let's watch her/him and see,
Let's watch her/him and see,
Let's watch her/him and see,
What [Child's name] wants to be.

STEP IN TIME

Your little ones will take a step toward learning their left and right when they march to the beat of this activity. Invite students to spread out in an open area of your class-room; then place a red dot sticker on the right shoe of each child. Remind students that their right shoes have stickers on them and their left shoes do not. Play some marching music, such as Sousa's "The Stars And Stripes Forever"; then direct children to march in place. At your di-rection encourage youngsters to pivot to the right, using the stickers on their shoes as directional guides. March, two, three, four!

TRANQUIL TRANSITIONS

Calm the chaos that sometimes ensues when youngsters move from one activity to another by making a transition song tape. Record a song or instrumental piece a few times onto a cassette tape. When it is time for children to change activities, play the tape and instruct children to hop, skip, "swim," walk, or "skate" to the next activity. When the tape ends, students should be ready for the next activity. In no time at all, your students will be able to name that tune and cooperatively move to the next activity.

SHHH...QUIET

Soft sounds and soothing music are the tools your youngsters will need to discover quiet movements. Create a calming atmosphere by dimming the lights (or try this activity as a wake-up exercise after rest time). Play a soothing classical or New-Age piece of music; then have students imitate your movements as you slowly lead them in stretching various parts of their bodies.

A LONG WINTER'S NAP

Every little bear loves a long nap, but your little cubs may not be eager to do the same. Help youngsters prepare for rest time by playing soft, soothing music. Invite students to pretend to be bear cubs ready for a nap. Have students slowly crawl to their "caves" (mats). When they arrive have them settle in, let out one loud snore, and then settle down for their rest time. Nighty-night, little bears!

MOVIN' THROUGH THE SEASONS

Use the activities on the following pages to get your little ones moving in seasonal style.

○ FALL ○

APPLES ALL AROUND

This partner activity is a good pick for focusing on hand-eye coordination skills as well as giving students an opportunity to get to know each other. Prepare by making an apple beanbag for each pair of children in your class. To make one, use a funnel to partially fill a round, red balloon with birdseed. Tie off the end; then wind masking tape around the knot and attach a silk leaf so that it resembles a stem. Divide students into pairs. Provide each pair with an apple beanbag. Invite each child to toss the beanbag back and forth with her partner. At your signal, have students find new partners. Continue in the same manner until each child has met her classmates.

SEASONAL CHARADES

Give your youngsters an opportunity to explore in their own creative ways some of fall's favorite symbols. Brainstorm with your youngsters a list of fall things, such as squirrels, falling leaves, scarecrows, ghosts, and pumpkins. Draw a picture of each item on a separate index card. Invite a volunteer to choose a card, then move in a way that depicts the pictured item. Invite the remainder of the group to guess which item the child is portraying.

THE TURKEY LURKEY

Your youngsters will be struttin' their stuff in this plucky version of The Hokey-Pokey.

(sung to the tune of "The Hokey-Pokey")
You put your wing in. You put your wing out.
You put your wing in and you flap it all about.
You do the Turkey Lurkey and you turn yourself around.
That's what it's all about! Gobble, gobble!
You put your drumstick in...
You put your wattle in...
You put your tail feathers in...
You put your whole turkey in...

JINGLE ALL THE WAY

Your students will be moving to the jingle-bell beat when participating in this activity. As you play each bar on a xylophone, have students practice positioning their bodies in response to the tone, moving up for high tones and down for low tones. Then invite three or four volunteers to stand in front of the group. Provide each volunteer with a different-sized jingle bell. One at a time, have each volunteer ring her bell. Have the remaining children position their bodies in response to the tone. Jing-a-ling-a-ling!

A SNOWY DAY

What could be better on a winter's day than a fun romp in the snow? Well, if the chance of snow in your neck of the woods is slim, transform your classroom into a flurry of fun with the addition of a few props! Move all furniture from the center of the room; then spread a large quantity of packing pieces on the floor to create the feeling of snow. Group piles of packing pieces together to create snowbanks. Then have your youngsters take off their shoes—to prevent little fingers and toes from being hurt—and invite them to walk, crunch, and slide in the pretend snow. Make a snow angel by having a child lie on the floor with his hands at his sides and his legs together. Direct him in sliding his arms above his head as he spreads his legs wide. As the blizzard of fun starts to wane, supply each student with a resealable plastic bag. Have each child fill his bag with packing pieces, then seal the bag to create a snowball. Conclude the day with a snowball toss, followed by warm cups of cocoa and a snowy-day story. How delightful!

SNOWFRIENDS

Smiles and gleeful giggles will abound when your students dress a snowfriend using a real friend! Collect a variety of snowman-related items, such as a scarf, a hat, gloves, and a broom. Have students make a group circle. Invite a volunteer "snowfriend" to stand in the center of the circle. Lead students in singing the song below. Choose a student to find the named item(s) and place it on the snowfriend. Continue singing the song, each time choosing a different child to add each item of clothing, until the snowfriend is completely dressed and warm and toasty.

(sung to the tune of "Bingo")
There was a friend all made of snow,
And [Child's name] was his/her name-o!
Let's give her a [hat],
Let's give her a [hat],
Let's give her a [hat],
To keep her warm and toasty!

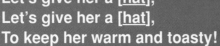

BEBOPPIN' BUNNY HOP

Your little bunnies will be shaking their little tails while reinforcing left and right concepts when you teach them the bunny hop. Make a bunny-ear headband for each child in your class. Staple a construction-paper bunny-ear shape to each side of a construction-paper band. Staple the ends of the strip together; then glue a cotton ball to the back of the band. Give each child a headband to wear.

Have students make a line. Direct each child to place her hands on the shoulders of the child in front of her. Instruct students in this modified version of the bunny hop— feet together, right heel out, feet together, left heel out, feet together, jump forward three times. Hop, hop, hop!

A DAY AT THE BEACH

Your youngsters will catch a wave of excitement when you have a Beach Day in your classroom. Prepare by gathering a large beach ball, some pool floats, and a variety of other beach-related props.

Invite a child to choose a prop, then role-play a beach activity, such as surfing, swimming, hunting for seashells, etc. Next play some "beachy" music and invite youngsters to get in shape with some aqua aerobics by twisting, "swimming," and "backstroking" to the music. Finally, end your fun in the sun with a groovy game of Beach Blanket Limbo, using a twisted beach towel as the limbo stick. Surf's up, dude!

GOIN' BUGGY

Complement a reading of Denise Fleming's *In The Tall, Tall Grass* (Henry Holt And Company, Inc.) with this nature lover's version of Follow The Leader. As a group, practice moving like the animals and insects depicted in the book. Then have students form a line. Ask the child at the front of the line to demonstrate an animal or insect movement of her choice. Have the other children copy her movement and follow along. After an appropriate length of time, ask the leader to go to the end of the line, and have the next child choose and demonstrate a new movement.

NOW INTRODUCING: DRAMATIC PLAY!

Set your youngsters' creative spirits free with these imaginative dramatic activities.

ideas contributed by Jean Feldman and Virginia Zeletzki

DOES THE SHOE FIT?

Invite your youngsters to step into someone else's shoes. In advance collect a variety of different kinds of shoes, such as work boots, high heels, and swim fins. (Or find pictures of different kinds of shoes.) Display the shoes one pair at a time. Ask a child to pretend to put on the shoes. Then ask him questions to get him thinking about the person who would wear the shoes. How would someone wearing the shoes walk? What would the person do? What would the person say? Next ask the child to get up and walk around, pretending to be the person who would wear those shoes. Continue choosing different shoes for the children to dramatize.

LIGHTS, CAMERA, ACTION!

Set the scene for dramatic action by clipping out a number of magazine pictures of people participating in a variety of activities. Choose one picture at a time, and select a child to play each person pictured. Start things rolling by saying, "Lights, camera, action!" Have the children act out the picture. Prompt players as needed by asking questions, such as, "What do you think the people in the picture are saying?", and "What do you think will happen next?"

Super Capes

Turn your little ones into super actors with these special capes. Gather one yard of fabric for each cape, along with one-inch-wide ribbon, a needle, and thread. Sew a one-inch casing along the top edge of the fabric. Thread a 14-inch piece of ribbon through the casing, gather at the neck, and sew the ribbon in place. Hem the bottom of the cape, if desired. Make capes from satin, felt, fake fur, and other specialty fabrics to encourage children to become anything they can imagine, from superheroes to royalty!

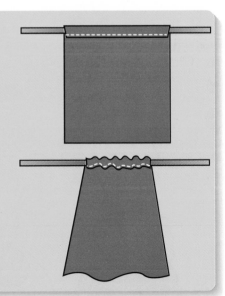

Presto! Change-O!

Wave your magic wand and turn your little ones into active learners. Paint a dowel gold or silver, then spray it with glitter spray. After the paint dries, glue colorful feathers, ribbon, and star garland to the end of the dowel; then wrap ribbon around the tip and tie it in place to cover glued areas. Have your students sit on the floor. Show them your magic wand, and introduce a game of Presto! Change-o! Wave your wand, say "Presto! Change-o! You are now [fill in the blank]!", and invite little ones to pretend to be whatever you have said. Next say, "Ready!" and instruct them to freeze. Then, with another "Presto! Change-o!" and a wave of your wand, announce the next thing they are to become.

STORY-BOX SURPRISE

Fill a decorated box with small toys, action figures, natural objects, and other interesting small items. Seat your youngsters in a circle, and pass the box around the circle. Encourage each child, in turn, to take one object from the box and use it as a prop to tell a story or act out an action.

SOUND EFFECTS

Encourage good listening skills by inviting children to make sound effects as you read aloud a poem or story. Before reading, identify several sounds that students can make. For example, a lion might growl, "GRRR!"; the wind could blow, "SHHHHH"; or a giant might stomp, "THUMP, THUMP, THUMP." As you read the poem or story, pause each time you read one of the sound effects previously identified so that students may contribute that sound. For variety, assign each sound to a small group.

SPIN A STORY

Have the children sit on the floor in a circle. Take a ball of yarn or string, and gently wrap the loose end around your hand several times as you begin telling a story. Stop the story and roll the ball of yarn to a child, keeping the wound yarn on your hand. Invite her to wrap the yarn around her hand several times and add a few sentences to the story. Instruct her to roll the yarn to another child. The game continues until all of the children have had a turn to wrap the yarn and add to the story. Once your story ends, have each child carefully slide the yarn off her hand and lay it down on the floor. Your students will enjoy the story and the giant web that they have "spun" together!

BODY TALK

Teach your students to interpret nonverbal communication by encouraging body talk. Seat your youngsters in a circle. Model body language, such as being excited, angry, or sleepy. Invite students to guess what your body is saying. Then have each child, in turn, act out a different emotion or characteristic that you name. Add more of a challenge by choosing specific parts of the body to show emotions. For example, "Make your feet be happy," or "Make your arms say 'I love you.'"

Skillful Role-Playing

Foster valuable social skills by providing opportunities for youngsters to act out some of the problems they encounter at school, at home, or in their communities. Describe a situation; then select volunteers to participate. Let the dialog unfold naturally. This can be a particularly effective way to deal with common classroom conflicts. If role-playing a situation that has happened in your class, try reversing roles so that each child has a chance to see what it feels like to be the other. Promote safety by asking students to role-play potentially dangerous situations, such as being approached by a stranger.

Animal Copycats

Have all your students snap or clap as they chant together:

Let's be animals just for fun.
Let's copy [a monkey], that's the one.
Whatever it does, we'll do the same.
That's how we play the Copycat Game!

Then have the children stand and pretend to be monkeys. Introduce the next animal by beginning the chant again. Stop and point to a student to fill in the blank with the new animal's name.

CHARACTER MASKS

Turn even the shyest youngsters into dramatic actors with these easy-to-make masks. Cut the top half off of a large paper grocery sack. Turn the sack upside down and cut a seven-inch circle from the front. Give the bag to a child, and encourage him to use markers, paints, or crayons to draw an animal's head around the circle. Invite him to use construction paper, felt, yarn, fake fur, or craft foam to add hair, ears, horns, or fur. Invite your youngsters to wear these masks as they perform plays or act out stories.

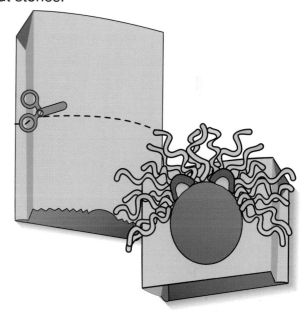

IMAGINATION BUBBLES

Cut a seven-foot piece of yarn or string for each student, and tie the ends together to make a loop. Give each child a loop and ask him to make a circle on the floor with it, then sit inside the circle. Explain that the circle is his imagination bubble. Ask him to show you how tall his bubble is, how wide it is, and what he can do in it. Begin the imaginative play by asking him to pretend his bubble is a cocoon. Invite him to pretend to turn into a butterfly, leave his cocoon, and then fly back to his seat. (Or have him pretend it is an egg and hatch from it.) On another day, play music and invite each child to dance inside his bubble.

PUPPET PLAY

Add variety to dramatic play with all kinds of puppets!

The Puppet Maker's Chest

Decorate a large box to look like a treasure chest, then fill it with puppet-making supplies. Here are some suggestions:

buttons
construction paper
fabric
fake fur
felt
craft foam
glitter
pom-poms
stickers
yarn

wiggle eyes
craft sticks
crayons
markers
miniature
hats
paint
paintbrushes
paper bags
straws

DRINKING-STRAW PUPPETS—

Provide old magazines or catalogs, and ask each child to cut out pictures of people. Tape each cutout to the end of a straw. Use these puppets in dramatic play to represent family members, community helpers, or other characters.

BURGER-BOX PUPPETS—Use

materials from the puppet maker's chest to add features to the top of a clean burger box. Cut a hole in the bottom of the box large enough for a child's hand to fit through. Staple a length of elastic inside the top of the box and a smaller length inside the bottom front. To operate the puppet, a child fits her hand through the hole, slides her fingers through the top elastic strap, and slips her thumb into the bottom strap.

PHOTO PUPPETS—Duplicate a

photograph of each child; then enlarge it on tagboard. Cut out the child's picture and glue a craft stick to the back. Hold up one child's puppet at a time as you sing this song to the tune of "Skip To My Lou":

Hello, [child's name], how are you?
Hello, [child's name], how are you?
Hello, [child's name], how are you?
How are you this
    morning?

These puppets can also be used for role-playing classroom situations.

STICKER PUPPETS—

Attach character or seasonal stickers to the tips of children's fingers for great fingerplay or storytelling fun.

POP-UP PUPPETS—

Use materials from the puppet maker's chest to turn a craft stick into an animal or a character. Cut a hole in the bottom of a paper or Styrofoam® cup. Insert the stick through the hole, entering from the top. Decorate the outside of the cup with a scene that fits the puppet.

POSTER PUPPETS—Add some fun to
sock puppets with backgrounds made from poster board. Draw a circle big enough for your fist to fit through in the middle of a section of poster board. Use a utility knife to cut out the circle. Draw a picture around the circle, such as an apple (for a worm sock puppet), a television set (the puppet becomes an actor), or a nest (for a bird puppet). The puppet possibilities are endless!

Puppet Theaters As Easy As 1-2-3!

Gather a curtain on a tension rod. Suspend the rod in a door frame for puppet performances.

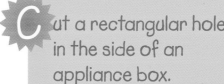

Cut a rectangular hole in the side of an appliance box.

Drape a sheet or blanket over a table.

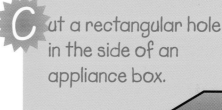

Exploratory ART

Encourage your youngsters to explore and imagine as they participate in these open-ended art experiences that focus not on finished products, but on the *process* of creating.

ideas contributed by Tricia Daughtry, Holly Dunham, and John Funk

GLOVE PAINTING

Little ones will get a new feel for fingerpainting with this activity. Gather a variety of gloves: rubber gloves, old leather gloves, garden gloves, dress gloves, loofah mitts, or surgical gloves. (Ask for donations from parents or check out your local thrift shop.) Invite youngsters to wear different pairs of gloves as they fingerpaint. Have them observe the differences in the feel of the paint, and in the strokes and textures created on the paper or tabletop.

PADDED PRINTS

Visit the foot-care aisle of the drugstore for some unique painting materials. Purchase a few packs of bunion or corn pads, or some shoe inserts. Attach the self-adhesive pads to the palm and fingers of a rubber dishwashing glove to create a random pattern of circles and ovals. Cut the pads in half or cut various shapes from the shoe inserts for variety. Invite a child to put on the glove, use a paintbrush to apply tempera paint to the pads, and then press his gloved hand onto his paper. Help him reapply the paint as necessary.

Prepare several gloves (some left-handed and some right-handed) with different patterns, as well as trays of different paint colors. Invite several children to paint at once, trading gloves as they desire.

SALTY SQUEEZE PAINT

"Please may we squeeze?" That's what your youngsters will be asking after once trying this glittery goop! Create a mixture that is one part flour, one part salt, and two parts water. Stir the ingredients together thoroughly to remove lumps; then divide the mixture and add a different shade of food coloring to each portion. Pour each color of paint into a separate squeeze bottle. The mixture will be fairly thin, so provide thick drawing paper and have little ones squeeze designs onto their papers. Set the papers aside to dry thoroughly. Then check out the sparkly results!

MORE THAN MARBLE ART

You're probably familiar with marble painting, accomplished by placing a dab of paint on a paper laid inside a shallow box or tray, then placing a marble or two on the paper and tilting the box or tray so that the marble rolls through the paint and creates designs. Try one or more of these variations for more "marble-ous" fun!

 Roll up the paper and place it inside an empty oatmeal canister. Place a marble inside and roll the canister on the tabletop.

Use nuts and bolts, jacks, or small rubber balls instead of marbles.

 Put a few magnetic marbles on a sheet of paper. Move a magnetic wand beneath the paper to make the marbles move and spread the paint.

 Cut a large circle from bulletin-board paper to fit the inside of a child's inflatable or plastic swimming pool. Roll an inflatable beach ball through the paint.

BROOM PAINTING

You may have considered your sidewalk as a canvas for chalk art, but have you considered a broom as a paintbrush? Why not? Gather several small brooms (like those from your housekeeping center) and a few buckets. Fill the buckets with water and invite youngsters to broom-paint water designs on the sidewalk. As a variation, spread long lengths of white bulletin-board paper on the sidewalk. Add some food coloring to the water, and have children broom-paint colored designs on the paper. (Caution: The food coloring may permanently discolor the broom bristles, so consider this before you proceed.) This art activity is sure to be a sweeping success!

COMBING THROUGH CREATIVITY

While you're feeling adventurous about painting tools, try using combs. Give the paint some texture for combing by thickening it with flour. Simply pour the thickened paint into squeeze bottles; then invite children to squeeze out paint onto their papers, then run combs through the paint to create designs. Try combs of various sizes, with teeth of different sizes and spacing.

SCRUBBER SCRIBBLES

For yet another paintbrush alternative, purchase (or ask parents to donate) a few nylon dish-scrubbing puffs. Clip each one inside a spring-type clothespin. Provide a different color of tempera paint for each scrubber. Encourage a youngster to hold the clothespin handle and dip a scrubber into a shallow tray of paint, then press the scrubber on her paper to create a design. Have her continue with other colors as she desires.

DRIP-DROP PAINTING

What do you get when you mix partners, pie plates, and paper? Drip-Drop Painting! To prepare, simply poke a few small holes in the bottoms of several aluminum pie plates. Pour a different color of tempera paint into each of several small pitchers. Thin the paint in each pitcher with water. Give a pie plate, a pitcher of paint, and a sheet of paper to a pair of children. Have one child slowly pour the thinned paint into the pie plate as his partner holds the pie plate over the paper. Have the child holding the pie plate rock it slowly as the children watch the paint drip through the holes. Invite them to add drips of different colors of paint to their creation if they desire.

LEAF GLITTER

When autumn leaves fall, head outdoors to collect them and make some leaf glitter. Invite youngsters to crush some dry, crinkly leaves into small bits and chunks. Sprinkle the leaf glitter over spread glue (as you would glitter) or add it to tempera paint in fall colors for a lumpy, leafy texture. If desired, add some regular glitter to the leaf glitter for a special sparkle.

DRY/WET PAINTINGS

Usually paintings start out wet, then get dry. Reverse that process with this painting technique. Provide dry tempera paint in several colors, cotton balls, and paper. Encourage each youngster to dip a cotton ball into a paint color, then brush it onto his paper. Have him continue this dry painting with as many colors as he desires. Then provide a container of water and some eyedroppers. Invite each artist to use an eyedropper to place drops of water onto his paper. Or have him dip his fingertips into the water and sprinkle water over the dry tempera, watching the colors move and meld. Then set the paintings aside to dry. A light coating of unscented hairspray will provide a finishing coat.

DRIVE 'N' DRAW

If your students love miniature cars, then they'll love this drawing activity! Use masking tape to securely attach a crayon (tip down) to the back of a toy car. Test the position of the crayon by "driving" the car over a piece of scrap paper. Adjust the position, if necessary, so that the crayon draws a line as the car moves. Prepare several car crayons in this manner, get out the paper, and steer your youngsters into a whole new art experience!

FOIL FUN

Go beyond a construction-paper picture when you provide aluminum foil instead. Give each artist a one-foot section of aluminum foil and a pair of scissors. Youngsters can strengthen cutting skills as they trim the foil into various shapes and forms of their choice. Have each child glue her foil pieces to a sheet of construction paper (black is especially striking). When the glue is dry, display the pictures. Then turn out the lights and have children take turns shining a flashlight on the pictures to observe their shiny creations.

CHEESECLOTH SCULPTURES

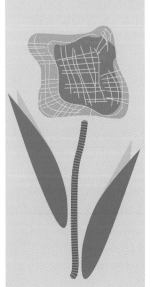

For a three-dimensional art experience, provide youngsters with squares of cheesecloth, a container of liquid starch, and various small objects for making forms (such as egg-carton sections or berry baskets). Have each young artist dip a cheesecloth square into the starch, then form it inside or around an object to create a three-dimensional shape. Allow the cheesecloth to dry thoroughly; then remove it from the form—it will maintain the shape of the object. These creations can be painted, glued onto paper, or embellished with other craft items. Invite youngsters to create abstract sculptures or to use the finished cheesecloth shapes to create realistic objects, such as a flower with a pipe-cleaner stem or a basket with a ribbon handle.

Let's Visit
THE HARDWARE STORE!

A trip to your local hardware or home-improvement store
will yield a wealth of unusual art materials. Read on....

LINOLEUM PRINTS

Purchase a few vinyl or linoleum tiles with different-textured patterns. Back in the classroom, cut large pieces of bulletin-board paper. Invite a child to paint a tile with a coat of thinned tempera, then press it onto the paper to create a print of the tile's pattern. Have her continue with other tiles and paint colors as she desires.

JOINT COMPOUND—GEE!

There are lots of things to do with a bucket of joint compound! Use the compound as is and paint children's creations after they dry, or add food coloring to the wet compound. Provide each of your young artists with a sturdy sheet of cardboard and a blob of compound. Youngsters can shape and texture the mixture with their fingers or with gadgets, such as craft sticks, forks, or combs. Lightweight items (such as birthday candles or coffee stirring sticks) can be stuck into the compound and will be embedded once a child's "sculpture" is dry.

WONDERFUL WEATHER STRIPPING

A package of foam weather stripping and a rolling pin will make for a new art experience. Cut the foam tape into various lengths and adhere them around a rolling pin. Spread a thin layer of tempera paint on a cookie sheet. Then encourage a child to roll the rolling pin over the paint, then onto a large sheet of art paper to see the design created. Provide cookie sheets with different colors of paint and a few rolling pins with different tape patterns. Your young artists will be on a roll!

RECIPES
FOR ARTS AND CRAFTS

BAKING DOUGH

2 cups flour
1 cup salt
water

Mix the dry ingredients; then add enough water to create a workable dough. Invite children to sculpt figures or roll and cut the dough with cookie cutters. Bake the dough at 300°F for 1 to 1 1/2 hours (depending on the thickness of each figure). Finished products can be painted.

MILK PAINT

evaporated milk
food coloring

Divide one or more cans of evaporated milk evenly among several containers. Add a few drops of a different color of food coloring to each container and mix until the desired shades are achieved. Have youngsters paint with this mixture on construction paper to create a creamy, pastel look.

MAGIC CRYSTALS

2 cups water
2 cups Epsom salts
food coloring (optional)

In a saucepan, combine the water and Epsom salts, and bring to a boil. Stir the mixture and allow it to cool. If desired, add a few drops of food coloring. Have students paint with this mixture on construction paper. The paint will dry to create clear or colored crystals.

DECORATIVE DYE

1 tablespoon rubbing alcohol
food coloring
rice or pasta

In a small, tightly lidded container, put one tablespoon of rubbing alcohol and a few drops of food coloring. Place rice or pasta into the mixture and seal the lid. Shake the container gently for one minute. Spread out the dyed objects on paper towels or newspaper until dry.

TEACHER-MADE PLAY DOUGH

1 cup flour
1/2 cup salt
2 teaspoons cream of tartar
1 cup water
1 teaspoon vegetable oil
food coloring

Mix the dry ingredients together. Then add the remaining ingredients and stir. In a heavy skillet, cook the mixture for two to three minutes, stirring frequently. Turn the dough onto a lightly floured surface and knead it until it becomes soft and smooth. Mix up a separate batch of dough for each color desired. Store the dough in an airtight container.

COLORED GLUE

food coloring
white glue

Add a few drops of a different color of food coloring to each of several empty squeeze bottles. Gradually add glue, using a drinking straw to stir the glue until it's evenly tinted.

EXTRA-BRIGHT TEMPERA PAINT

2 cups dry tempera paint
1 cup liquid soap (clear or
   white works best)
1 cup liquid starch

Mix the paint and soap; then add starch and stir. If the mixture becomes too thick, add more liquid soap. Store the paint in a coffee can with a plastic lid.

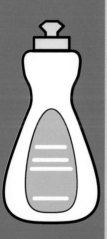

BUBBLE MIXTURE

1/4 cup dishwashing liquid
1/2 cup water
1 teaspoon sugar
food coloring (optional)

Mix the dishwashing liquid, water, and sugar together in a container. If color is desired, mix in a few drops of food coloring.

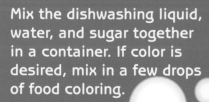

CORN SYRUP PAINT

light corn syrup
food coloring

Divide one or more bottles of corn syrup evenly among several containers. Add a few drops of a different color of food coloring to each container and mix until the desired shades are achieved. This paint requires a few days of drying time.

NUTTY PUTTY

3 1/2 cups peanut butter
4 cups powdered sugar
3 1/2 cups corn syrup or honey
4 cups powdered milk
chocolate chips (optional)

Mix all ingredients except chocolate chips. Divide mixture into 15 to 20 portions, place into plastic bags, and refrigerate. After students wash their hands, have them mold and shape the dough on waxed paper. Use chocolate chips as decorations if desired. Students may eat their creations.

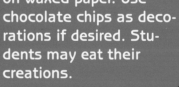

KOOL-AID® DOUGH

2 1/2–3 cups flour
1/2 cup salt
1 package unsweetened Kool-Aid®
1 tablespoon alum
2 cups boiling water
3 tablespoons corn oil
1 cup additional flour

Mix the first six ingredients into a dough. Using some or all of the additional flour, knead the dough until it reaches the desired consistency. Store the dough in an airtight container.

EASY PAPIER-MÂCHÉ

liquid starch
cold water
newspaper torn into strips

Mix equal parts of liquid starch and cold water. Dip the newspaper strips into the mixture before applying to a form of chicken wire or rolled newspaper.

SALT PAINT

2 teaspoons salt
1 teaspoon liquid starch
a few drops of tempera paint

Mix the ingredients together. The salt gives a frosted appearance to the paint.

COLORED GRITS

liquid tempera paint
grits

In a large bowl, mix the ingredients, being careful not to let the grits get too wet. Spread the mixture onto cookie sheets to dry for a day or two, stirring occasionally. Use as you would colored sand.

SHINY PAINT

1 part white liquid glue
1 part liquid tempera paint

Mix the ingredients. This paint will retain a wet look after it has dried.

EXPLORATIONS

SUPER SCIENCE SAMPLER

Engage youngsters in some scientific thinking with this collection of activities designed to promote their skills in observation, communication, data collection, measurement, making inferences and predictions, and estimating.

ideas contributed by Suzanne Moore

SENSORY SLIME

Activate all the senses of your youngsters with this glorious goo! To begin, invite each student to mix an individual portion of slime following the recipe shown. As students measure, mix, and manipulate the slime, encourage them to discuss their sensory observations. (Yes, they can safely take small tastes of this harmless substance.) Record their statements on chart paper under the appropriate category for each of the five senses. Then have each child store his slime in a zippered plastic bag to take home at the end of the day.

Sensory Slime

6 tablespoons cornstarch
1 teaspoon flavored gelatin mix
3–4 tablespoons water

Using a spoon or hands, mix ingredients together in a plastic bowl until a doughlike substance is achieved. Mold and manipulate the mix as desired.

Weather-Watcher Journals

Weather is wonderful—and always a reliable source of observation for this idea. To prepare, duplicate and cut out a week's supply of the journal page (page 206) for each student. Stack each child's set of pages between construction-paper covers; then staple the booklet together along the left edge. Each day during the week, invite youngsters to step outside to observe the weather. Encourage them to discuss how the weather affects the sights, sounds, smells, and feeling of their surroundings. After returning to the classroom, have each student write/dictate a completion to the statement on her journal page for the day; then ask her to illustrate her statement. At the end of the week, invite each child to share her weather journal during circle time.

_____Outside_____ is where I'd like to stay

Because it is a _____sunny_____ day!

A TASTY DOUBLE TAKE

This experiment will prompt youngsters to take a second look at a delicious, nutritious treat—raisins! To begin, have each child pour half the contents of a snack-sized box of raisins onto a napkin and describe his raisins by sight, smell, touch, and taste. Next have him drop one or two raisins into a paper cup half-filled with water and then cover his cup with a foil square. Have him place his half-full box of raisins on top of the foil. Then set the cups aside, and invite each child to eat the remaining raisins on his napkin. Leave the cups undisturbed overnight.

The next day, have each youngster empty his raisin box onto a napkin. Then ask him to uncover his cup and remove the raisins from the water. Prompt him to again use his senses—sight, smell, touch, and taste—to describe the raisins, this time comparing the boxed raisins to the waterlogged raisins. After the experiment, invite each child to illustrate both the dried and the waterlogged raisins on a sheet of paper. Have him write/dictate this sentence formation to describe his observations: "Yesterday my raisin was _____, but today it is _____!" Invite each child to share his illustrations with classmates as they snack away on the rest of their raisins.

What Color Is Your Door?

When you do this data-collection activity, you'll be making your home-school connection right at your students' front doors. In advance, duplicate the parent note on page 206 to send home with each child. When your students return their completed notes, label a large graph so that each child's door color is represented. Then have each child cut out his door pattern. During group time, sing the song below. As each child's door color is mentioned in the song, invite her to tape her door cutout in the appropriate column on the graph. Repeat the song as often as necessary, filling in a different color name each time, until every child has attached her cutout to the graph. Discuss the results, and open the door to science!

What Color Is Your Door?
(sung to the tune of "The Farmer In The Dell")

What color is your door?
What color is your door?
Heigh-ho, at home, you know.
What color is your door?

Is your front door [color name]?
Is your front door [color name]?
Heigh-ho, at home, you know.
Is your front door [color name]?

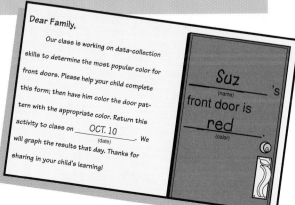

Dear Family,

Our class is working on data-collection skills to determine the most popular color for front doors. Please help your child complete this form; then have him color the door pattern with the appropriate color. Return this activity to class on ___OCT. 10___ . We
(date)
will graph the results that day. Thanks for sharing in your child's learning!

____Suz____'s
(name)
front door is
____red____.
(color)

Just Rollin' Along

Youngsters will roll right into this data-collection activity while learning some basic shapes along the way. In advance, convert a cube-shaped, empty tissue box into a large die by covering it with a piece of bulletin-board paper. Glue a different shape cutout (from the form on page 207) onto each side of the die; then cover the die with clear Con-Tact® paper. Make a copy of page 207 for every two students in your class. Then divide your class into pairs, appointing a roller and a recorder for each pair. Give each pair a copy of the recording form. In turn have each roller roll the die. His recorder will then color a graph square corresponding to the shape rolled. After several rounds, ask the partners to count the number of colored squares in each column. Which shape was rolled most often by each pair? Total the number of squares for each shape to determine which shape was rolled most frequently by the class as a whole. Then, if desired, give each pair a new recording form, have the partners switch duties, and roll forward with another round of this activity.

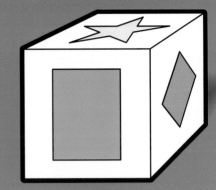

Measuring Up

How do your youngsters measure up to one another—physically, that is? With this activity students can measure, then compare, the length of specific body parts. To begin, invite each student to find a partner. Then have both partners illustrate a designated body part—such as a leg, an arm, or a foot—on the same sheet of paper. Instruct the partners to help each other cut a piece of yarn the length of each of their illustrated body parts. Then have each child use a sticky dot to attach her piece of yarn to the bottom edge of the pair's paper (near her own illustration). Encourage the partners to compare the lengths of each piece of yarn. Which child has the longer body part? Continue in this manner, designating a different body part for children to measure.

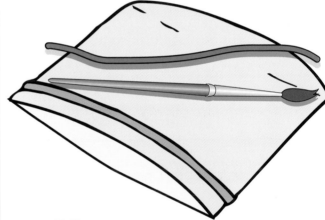

Measurement Match

With this game, youngsters will use critical skills in measuring, comparing, and matching lengths of objects. To prepare, collect a number of items that vary in length and will fit easily into a large zippered plastic bag. You might select common items such as a pencil, a craft stick, a book, and a paintbrush, or toys such as a small car and a block. Measure and cut a length of yarn to match the length of each item; then place the items and pieces of yarn into a large zippered plastic bag. To use, invite a youngster to remove each object from the bag and find the piece of yarn that matches its length.

What Comes Next?

Promote students' skills in making inferences with this pattern-building activity. To begin, create a simple pattern using a set of building or pattern blocks. Ask youngsters to study the pattern and to secretly guess—or infer—which block will continue the pattern. Then sing the song below, naming a different child each time you repeat it. Invite the named child to add his block choice to the pattern. After the supply of appropriate blocks is exhausted, create a new pattern and begin again. If desired, periodically repeat this activity using other materials such as a collection of pasta, coins, attribute blocks, or plastic counters.

What Comes Next?
(sung to the tune of "Are You Sleeping?")
Pattern pieces, pattern pieces,
In a row, in a row.
Show me what comes next.
Show me what comes next.
Do you know? Do you know?

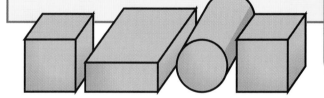

Meltdown Marathon

Try this icy investigation to discover how different colors influence the speed at which ice melts. To prepare, select several different colors of construction paper. Place one ice cube in a separate zippered plastic bag for each color. Use tape to secure each sheet of paper around a bagged cube; then set all the wrapped ice cubes outdoors in direct sunlight or on a windowsill. Give each child a sticky note and have him write the color of the paper in which he believes the ice will melt first. Invite students to post their predictions on a graph labeled with all the colors. Ask each child to give his reasons for his prediction; then total the number of predictions for each color. After 30 minutes, unwrap the ice cubes to see which cube has melted the most. Did any students predict correctly? If desired, rewrap the cubes and allow them to continue to melt, checking them every ten minutes. Which cube is the slowest melter?

A Handful Of Peanuts

Here's an estimating activity that packs a handful of learning opportunities. Have each child fold a large sheet of construction paper in half; then ask her to trace one hand on each half of the paper. Show students a container of foam packing peanuts. Challenge each youngster to guess the number of peanuts she thinks she can pick up in one hand. Help her to label the top left side of her paper "I guessed…"; then have her write her guess on the hand outline. Invite her to actually grab a handful of peanuts and count them. Have her write "I counted…" on the top right side of her paper, and the actual number of peanuts that she picked up below that hand outline. Then have her glue the peanuts to the second hand outline. Was her "guess-timate" accurate?

Journal Page
Use with "Weather Watcher Journals" on page 202.

_____ **is where I'd like to stay**

Because it is a _____ **day!**

Parent Note
Use with "What Color Is Your Door?" on page 203.

Dear Family,

    Our class is working on data-collection skills to determine the most popular color for front doors. Please help your child complete this form; then have him color the door pattern with the appropriate color. Return this activity to class on _____. We

(date)

will graph the results that day. Thanks for sharing in your child's learning!

_____'s
(name)

front door is

_____.
(color)

Name _____

Note To The Teacher: Use with "Just Rollin' Along" on page 204.

The Great Outdoors

Your little learners will be eager to explore, conserve, and observe with this collection of nature and outdoor activities. From collecting trash to bird watching to making mud pies, your youngsters are sure to discover it's not such a jungle out there!

ideas contributed by Jean Feldman

Hiking-Trail Treasures

Encourage creativity and outdoor exploration with these simple nature bracelets. Place a piece of wide masking tape or clear packing tape around each child's wrist with the sticky side out; then take the children on a nature walk. Invite them to stick small leaves, flowers, or berries onto their bracelets. Remind them to use only objects found loose on the ground instead of pulling leaves or flowers off plants. When you return to the classroom, encourage youngsters to compare bracelets and talk about the items they have found.

Let The Sun Shine In

Spruce up your classroom by bringing a little bit of nature inside. On a short nature hike, ask your little explorers to collect fall leaves or spring flowers they find on the ground. Back in the classroom, give each child a square of clear Con-Tact® paper. Ask the child to arrange her nature finds on the sticky side of the paper to make pretty designs. Cover each design with another square of clear Con-Tact® paper. Label each design with the child's name. Tape the squares to your classroom windows to make suncatchers.

Talk About A Walkabout

Nature is the perfect setting to practice sorting, counting, letters, shapes, and other skills. Take your little nature lovers on a "green walk." Instruct them to find as many different green things as possible. Collect the items in a bag or basket. In the classroom, invite small groups of students to sort the objects by various attributes. Or encourage them to count the number of items in the collection. On your next walk, ask students to find items that begin with a certain letter or resemble a certain shape.

On The Texture Trail

Explore shapes and textures with this fun and artistic activity. Provide each student with some blank paper and an old crayon with the paper torn off. Demonstrate how to lay a piece of paper over an object, such as a coin, and rub gently with the side of the crayon to make an impression. Then head outdoors in search of textures in nature. Challenge youngsters to make rubbings of items they find from the list below. After a set amount of time, return to the classroom. Invite students to share their rubbings and identify them.

Textures To Find:
tree bark
leaves
rocks
pinecones
blades of grass
feathers

Animals All Around

Animals love the great outdoors as much as children do—maybe more! After all, it's their home! Discuss with youngsters the many types of animal homes they might see outdoors, such as a spider web, an anthill, a nest, and a tree stump. Then give each child a copy of page 213 and a crayon. Take the children on a walk to hunt for animal homes. Invite each child to draw an animal home that she spots and to write or dictate the name of the animal that she thinks lives there. When you return to the classroom, have youngsters share their findings with the class.

Name Jamie
Home Hunting
Who lives here?
a spider

For The Birds

Little explorers will enjoy searching for birds in the wilds surrounding your school. Give each child two bathroom-tissue rolls to decorate with crayons, paints, or markers. Staple the two rolls together; then punch a hole near one end on both sides. Thread the ends of a length of string or yarn through the holes and tie them in place to make a strap so the "bird-watcher" can be worn around the neck. Invite youngsters to take their bird-watchers on a nature walk. Using a bird identification book, such as *Crinkleroot's Guide To Knowing The Birds* by Jim Arnosky (Aladdin Paperbacks), challenge the children to find the names of the birds they see with their binoculars. On future nature walks, encourage students to identify plants, rocks, or insects they find on the playground using other nature guides.

Drawn To Nature

Students will be inspired by the world around them when they create art in a natural setting. Take clipboards, scratch paper, crayons, chalk, colored pencils, pens, and markers outside. Invite your young Monets to draw pictures of plants, trees, or other natural objects. Encourage them to make sketches of the clouds and the sky, copy environmental print, or try their hands at creative writing. When you return to the classroom, invite students to share their creations with the class. Mount the drawings and writings on construction paper, and post them on a class bulletin board. Or make a book of the designs to share with parents.

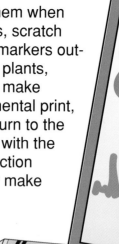

Earth Rangers

Your young Earth Rangers can help clean up the earth with these portable trash-collection boxes. Prepare for this activity by discussing the importance of picking up litter. Then suggest that each child make a trash-collection box so he can be an Earth Ranger. For each child, cut off the top of an empty cereal box. Punch a hole near the top of each short side of the box. Create a shoulder strap with a length of string or yarn. Line the box with a plastic grocery bag.

Invite youngsters to take some walks around your school grounds, stashing trash in their boxes as they go. Have youngsters wear plastic or rubber gloves, and caution them against picking up glass and other sharp objects. Empty the boxes into the class trash can when you return to the room. If the students have collected any recyclable materials, place those in your recycling bin. Invite students to take their trash-collection boxes home for use in their families' cars.

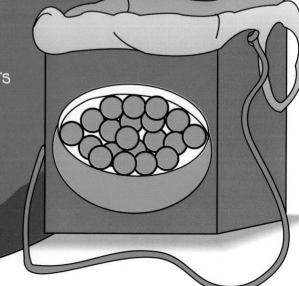

On A Sunny Day...

What's childhood without the sensory pleasure of making mud pies? Ask the children to wear old clothes to school or to bring in a smock or an apron. Then set up the Mud Pie Bakery on your playground, complete with aluminum pie pans and muffin tins and an area where the muddy creations can be left undisturbed to "bake." Mix four parts dirt with one part flour. Add just enough water to make the mud easy to mold. Invite the children to make mud pies or other mud creations from the mixture. Encourage youngsters to use natural items such as leaves, twigs, or rocks for decoration. While the students are working, ask them to describe how the mud feels. Allow the mud pies to dry in a warm, sunny spot. When the creations are dry, invite the children to touch them and describe how the mud feels. What happens to the mud pies as children handle them?

On A Snowy Day...

Students will warm up to these freezing winter activities. Fill some plastic spray bottles with water and add a few drops of food coloring to each one. Take the class outside when there is some snow on the ground. Invite youngsters to use the water bottles to spray colorful designs and patterns on the snow.

Then put some colored water in buckets. Set the containers outdoors. Invite students to check the buckets periodically to see how long it takes the water to freeze. When the water is frozen, dump out the "icebergs." Invite youngsters to check the icebergs occasionally to see how much time passes before the ice completely melts. If the icebergs take several days to melt, ask students if they melted more on one day than another. Encourage them to discuss why this happened.

On A Windy Day...

Create an outdoor symphony with this unique musical activity. Ask students to bring in old bells, wind chimes, and pie pans from home. Use string to tie these items to the branches of a tree on the playground. When the wind blows, the tree will make music. As days go by, ask the children if they notice the music more on some days than others. Encourage them to discuss why this may be.

You can also use your musical tree for an outdoor version of Musical Chairs. Students walk in a circle while the tree music is playing. When it stops, they all sit down. (If necessary, give the music a helping hand by thumping one of the pie pans with a stick.) The last student to sit down moves to the middle of the circle. When the music starts again, youngsters stand and continue walking in a circle. The game is over when all the students are in the center of the circle.

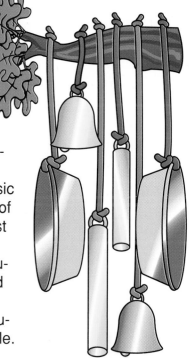

Great Nature Books For Children

Books by Jim Arnosky:

Deer At The Brook (Lothrop, Lee & Shepard Books)

Raccoons And Ripe Corn (William Morrow And Company, Inc.)

Watching Foxes (Lothrop, Lee & Shepard Books)

All Night Near The Water
Every Autumn Comes The Bear

(both published by The Putnam Publishing Group)

Books by Jane Burton:

Animals At Night
Animals At Rest
Animals At Work
Animals Eating

(all published by Newington Press)

Books by Lois Ehlert:

Feathers For Lunch
Growing Vegetable Soup
Planting A Rainbow
Red Leaf, Yellow Leaf

(all published by Harcourt Brace & Company)

Books by Donald M. Silver:

One Small Square: Backyard
One Small Square: Pond
One Small Square: Seashore

(all published by W. H. Freeman & Company)

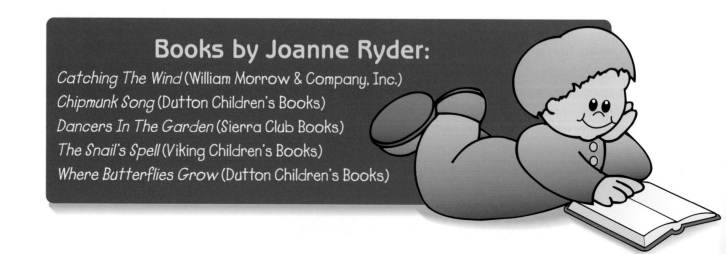

Books by Joanne Ryder:

Catching The Wind (William Morrow & Company, Inc.)

Chipmunk Song (Dutton Children's Books)

Dancers In The Garden (Sierra Club Books)

The Snail's Spell (Viking Children's Books)

Where Butterflies Grow (Dutton Children's Books)

Name _____

Home Hunting

Who lives here?

_____

Note To The Teacher: Use with "Animals All Around" on page 209.

Mad About Manipulatives

From crayons to craft sticks, this unit is packed with ideas to transform ordinary classroom items into terrific teaching tools in the blink of an eye!

ideas contributed by Rachel Castro, Diane Gilliam, and Lori Kent

LINKING CUBES

- Ordinal numbers are as easy as 1, 2, 3 when you use linking cubes. Position five different-colored linking cubes in a row. Ask a student to tell you which color is first, second, and so on. For a variation, ask a student to place the colored cubes in a specific order.

- Challenge youngsters to create geometric art by repeatedly pressing the bottom of a cube onto a colored ink pad and then onto a sheet of paper to create buildings, animals, and people.

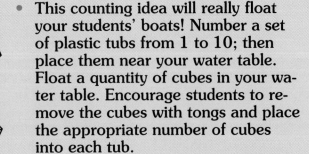

- This counting idea will really float your students' boats! Number a set of plastic tubs from 1 to 10; then place them near your water table. Float a quantity of cubes in your water table. Encourage students to remove the cubes with tongs and place the appropriate number of cubes into each tub.

- Your youngsters will enjoy making these pattern cards. Provide a child with two colors of linking cubes. Have him connect his cubes to make a color pattern. Next have him reproduce the pattern by dipping cubes into matching colors of paint and pressing them onto a sheet of newsprint.

- Concentrate on patterning skills as well as hand-eye coordination by having a child string linking cubes onto a shoestring in a pattern. Tie the ends of the string together to create a nifty necklace.

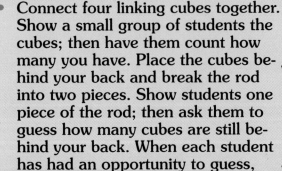

- Have students snap ten cubes together. Challenge each student to find objects in your classroom that are shorter than, longer than, or the same size as their rod of linking cubes.

- Connect four linking cubes together. Show a small group of students the cubes; then have them count how many you have. Place the cubes behind your back and break the rod into two pieces. Show students one piece of the rod; then ask them to guess how many cubes are still behind your back. When each student has had an opportunity to guess, show them the remainder of the cubes.

PATTERN BLOCKS

- Recycle plastic lids into pattern-block stencils. To make one, cut the rim off a plastic lid. Trace a pattern-block shape onto the lid; then use an X-acto® knife to cut around the resulting outline. Place the stencils in a math center along with a supply of pattern blocks, paper strips, pencils, and crayons. Have a child create a pattern with blocks and then use the stencils to reproduce the pattern onto paper.

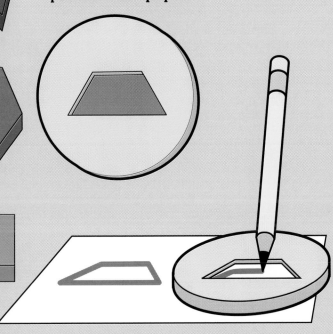

- Invite children to use pattern blocks to create designs that relate to your thematic unit, such as animals, dinosaurs, or vehicles.

- Fill a jar with pattern blocks; then invite students to estimate the number of blocks in the jar. When each child has estimated, count the blocks. Compare the estimates to the actual number of blocks. How many estimates were high? Low? Exactly right? Vary the difficulty of this activity by using smaller or larger jars.

- Use your overhead projector and some pattern blocks for this visual discrimination activity. Provide students with a variety of pattern blocks. Use pattern blocks to create a simple design on the stage of an unlit overhead projector. Turn the projector light on; then ask children to try to reproduce the projected design with their own sets of blocks. As students become more confident, increase the difficulty of the design.

- Provide a pair of students with a tic-tac-toe grid and a set of different-shaped pattern blocks. Encourage them to play tic-tac-toe using the blocks as markers.

- Provide small groups of students with a tub of same-shaped pattern blocks and a tub of small classroom items—such as a ruler, a pencil, and crayon. Encourage youngsters to measure the items using the pattern blocks. When each group has measured the items in their tub, rotate the groups.

- Write a letter or numeral on a sheet of construction paper. Invite a student to place pattern blocks along the lines. For added challenge, have a student reproduce the letter or numeral on a separate sheet of paper.

CRAYONS

- Send your little ones out on a colorful scavenger hunt. Divide students into groups of three or four. Give each group a different color of crayon. Send the groups off to hunt for classroom items that match their crayons.

- Your youngsters will have bundles of fun coloring with these crayons. Tape a few similar-colored crayons into a bundle, making sure the tips of the crayons are even. Stock an art center with several crayon bundles and large sheets of paper. Invite a child to use the crayon bundles to create a multi-colored drawing.

- Have students work in small groups to sort crayons into color families, such as reds, greens, and yellows. When the crayons have been sorted, instruct each group to count the crayons in each family and lay them end-to-end to create a bar graph. Which color family has the most? Which has the least? Are any equal?

- Provide students with a supply of crayons in varying lengths. Name a shape; then have students arrange the crayons into the appropriate shape. For a variation, have youngsters form letters or numerals.

- Stock a center with a balance scale, small classroom items, and a supply of crayons. To use the center, a student weighs each object using the crayons as a non-standard unit of measure.

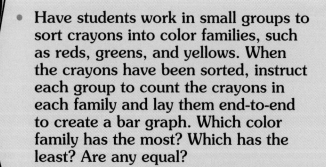

- Trace the outline of a child onto a large sheet of bulletin-board paper. Have the student cut out his outline, then use crayons to measure his height.

- Make pattern cards by hot-gluing crayons in a pattern onto a strip of tagboard. Place the pattern strips and some crayons in a center. Encourage a child to choose a strip and use crayons to reproduce or extend the pattern.

BUTTONS

- Place a small container of assorted buttons in a center. Challenge a student to sort the buttons by size, color, or number of holes.

- Place a quantity of buttons into a resealable plastic bag. Close the bag; then secure it with tape. Make at least two more buttonbags in this manner. Position three boxes of graduated sizes in a line from smallest to largest. Invite students to stand at a distance and toss a buttonbag into each box.

- Practice patterning skills with this high-fashion idea. Cut out large shirt, dress, and coat shapes from construction paper. Provide each child with a cutout and a quantity of buttons. Encourage each student to create a button pattern on her cutout. When she is satisfied with her pattern, have her glue the buttons onto the cutout.

- Make musical instruments by placing a few buttons into each of several empty film containers. Snap on the lids; then invite students to shake the containers to some lively instrumental music.

- Here's a center activity you can count on! Locate ten flavored-coffee tins. Cover each tin with Con-Tact® paper; then label them from 1 to 10. Cut a slot in each tin's plastic lid. Place the tins and a supply of buttons in a center. To use the center, a child counts the correct number of buttons into each tin.

- Invite your little ones to make a button bracelet by stringing a variety of buttons onto a pipe cleaner. When a child is finished, have him twist the ends of his pipe cleaner together to make a bracelet.

- Place a few different-colored buttons on a paper plate. Ask a small group of students to study the buttons. After a few minutes hide the plate from the students' view by shielding it with a file folder. Remove one button from the plate; then reveal the plate. Ask students to tell you which button is missing. To make the game more challenging, increase the number of buttons.

CRAFT STICKS

- Introduce the concept of keeping a tally. Give each child a craft stick and ask everyone to sit in a semi-circle. Pose a yes/no question; then lay tagboard cards that read "Yes" and "No" on the floor to form two headings. Ask each child, in turn, to come forward and place his craft stick under the heading for his response. Help the children arrange the sticks in tally fashion. Then count the sticks under each heading.

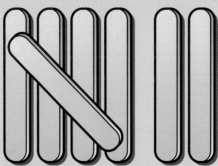

- Have children use craft sticks for spreading and cutting in your cooking center. When each child is finished with his stick, he may simply throw it away. Safe and sanitary!

- Students will find it delightful to use this snowman bookmark. To make one, have a child paint a wide craft stick white. When the paint is dry, have him use a black marker to draw eyes, a mouth, and buttons. Have him glue on a construction-paper top hat and carrot-shaped nose, and add a short length of ribbon for a scarf.

- Have students measure classroom items using craft sticks as a non-standard unit of measure.

- Create a ribbon wand by taping several long pieces of curling ribbon to the end of a craft stick. Invite a child to use the wand to point out a suggested letter or word when using a pocket chart.

- Your little ones will be eager to practice spelling their names when they piece together a puzzle. Write each letter in a child's name on a separate craft stick. Place the sticks in a personalized resealable bag. Place the bags in a center or have children practice with their puzzles during free time.

- Numeral sequencing is a snap with these magnetic number sticks. Program each of 20 craft sticks with a different numeral from 1 to 20. Stick a piece of magnetic tape to the back of each stick. Place the sticks and a cookie sheet in a center. To use the center, a child orders the sticks on the cookie sheet.

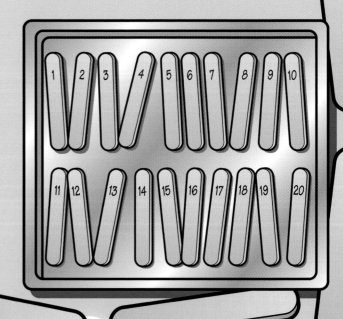

PASTA

- Supply each child in your class with a handful of different pasta pieces. Encourage her to sort the pieces. Then have her identify her most common pasta shape and glue it onto a class graph. Discuss which shape is most common and which is least common. Are any shapes equal?

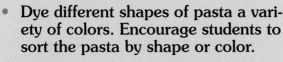

- Dye different shapes of pasta a variety of colors. Encourage students to sort the pasta by shape or color.

- You'll be stirring up lots of letter-recognition skills when you use alphabet pasta. Provide each child with a handful of alphabet pasta. Show the class a letter. Ask a volunteer to identify the letter, then have youngsters search through their pasta pieces to find a matching letter.

- Practice seriation skills with spaghetti! Provide each child with a long piece of spaghetti. Have him break his spaghetti into pieces, then seriate the pieces from longest to shortest.

- Create spaghetti art using overcooked spaghetti. Provide each child with a bowl full of sticky spaghetti. Invite her to arrange the spaghetti onto a sheet of construction paper to create a design. When the spaghetti dries, it will stick to the paper.

- Fill your sensory table with a quantity of dyed pasta and a variety of spoons, scoops, and tubs. Encourage students to scoop, fill, and pour the pasta.

- Fill a bowl with various pasta shapes; then mix them thoroughly. Give a child a piece of pasta. Have him close his eyes and find a matching shape in the bowl.

- Have each child make his own treasure box by gluing a variety of pasta pieces onto a shoebox or another lidded container. Spray-paint the boxes gold or silver. Invite youngsters to place keepsake "treasures" in their boxes.

PIPE CLEANERS

- Try this twist on the traditional bar graph. Create a three-dimensional column graph by inserting pipe cleaners into balls of clay. Press the balls onto a shoebox lid as shown; then label each pipe cleaner with a graphing category. Provide each child with one Unifix® cube. To record his vote, a child slides his cube onto the appropriate pipe cleaner.

Chocolate | Vanilla | Peach | Strawberry

- Try this slinky chain to count down the days until a holiday or special event. Bend a supply of pipe cleaners into S shapes. Link the appropriate number of pipe cleaners together. Each day invite a child to remove one link and count the remaining links.

- Invite each student to shape pipe cleaners into the letters of his name. Have him glue the letters onto a tagboard rectangle to make a tactile name card.

- Have each student make a friendship bracelet by lacing pieces of drinking straws, small beads, and sequins onto a pipe cleaner. Twist the ends together to form a bracelet. Encourage each child to exchange bracelets with a friend.

- Provide plenty of pipe-cleaner patterning practice with this center. Cut a supply of different-colored pipe cleaners in half; then place them in a center. To use the center, a child creates a color pattern with the pipe cleaners. When she has finished her pattern, show her how to twist the ends of a pipe cleaner together to form a circle, thread the next pipe cleaner through that loop, twist its ends together to form a circle, and so on to make a chain. Have each child share her pattern chain with the class. If desired, fasten the ends together to make a necklace, bracelet, or belt.

- Invite your youngsters to string O-shaped cereal onto a pipe cleaner. Twist the ends of the pipe cleaner together to create a bracelet. Have students wear their bracelets on a nature walk or field trip for a quick and easy snack.

- Gather several pipe cleaners into a bundle; then bend them in half. Bind the bent ends together with a separate pipe cleaner to form a handle. Fan the cut ends out to resemble a broom. Invite youngsters to use their pipe-cleaner brooms to paint.

POM-POMS

- This center is a pinch above the rest for practicing fine-motor skills! Fill one bucket with pom-poms and a pair of tongs. Have a child use the tongs to move the pom-poms one by one to an empty bucket.

- Program sheets of construction paper with different dot sets from one to ten. Encourage a child to place a pom-pom on each dot, then count the number of pom-poms on each sheet.

- Your youngsters will enjoy playing this counting game. Provide each child in a small group with an egg carton and a supply of pom-poms. To play, a child rolls a die and then places the corresponding number of pom-poms into his egg carton. Play then passes to the next child. Continue playing until a child fills each cup in his carton.

- Invite a child to create a color pattern by gluing pom-poms onto a sentence strip. Fit the strip to the child's head; then staple the ends of the strip together to make a headband.

- Place various sizes of same-colored pom-poms into a basket. Encourage a child to sort the pom-poms by size.

- Scatter a large quantity of pom-poms around your classroom. Provide each child with a length of masking tape. Direct her to stick as many pom-poms onto her tape as she can. When she has filled her tape, have her count the number of pom-poms she collected.

- Hot-glue sparkle pom-poms to the end of an unsharpened pencil. Have students use this pretty pointer to identify letters or words during pocket-chart or shared-reading lessons.

ANIMAL FIGURES

- Label each of several inverted berry baskets with a different numeral from 1 to 10. Place a tub of zoo animals next to the baskets. Encourage a child to place the appropriate number of animals in each "cage."

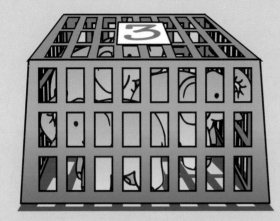

- Place an assortment of plastic animals in a bag. During a group time, invite a student to select an animal from the bag. Encourage him to tell you what he knows about the selected animal.

- Conduct an animal "race." Have each child in a small group select an animal figure and place it at one end of a floor graph with marked spaces. Ask each child, in turn, a question about the beginning letter in an animal name. For example, you might ask, "What does *gorilla* begin with?" If a child answers correctly, he may move his animal ahead one space, and wait for his next turn. First one to the end of the graph wins!

- Students will love this animal pantomime game. Invite three or four volunteers to stand in front of the class. Secretly show the standing group a plastic animal. In turn, direct each child standing to act out the actions of the suggested animal. When each child has had a turn, ask the remainder of the class to guess the name of the depicted animal. When the animal has been named or after several guesses, ask each standing child to choose a new person to be an actor.

- There are all sorts of ways to sort animals! Invite your students to sort a quantity of animals by color, number of legs, markings, habitat, and size. Or encourage students to find other ways to sort the animals.

- Provide youngsters with ordinal-number practice using animal figures. Position five different animals in a line. Ask a student to tell you which animal is first, second, and so on. Further challenge students by mixing up the animals or adding more animals to the line.

PENNIES

- Cut out coupons ranging in value from 10¢ to 50¢. Place them in a center along with a supply of pennies. Challenge a youngster to select a coupon, and then count out the number of pennies equal to the value of the coupon.

- Students will flip for this tallying activity. Provide each student with a recording sheet and a penny. Direct each student to flip his penny, and then tally whether it shows heads or tails. After a designated number of times, have each child share his results with the rest of the class.

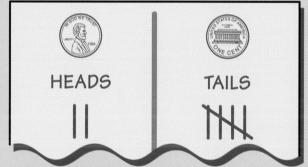

HEADS   TAILS

- Place a supply of pennies and an empty jar near your classroom door. Each day, as a child enters the classroom, have him place a penny in the jar. During a group time, count the pennies and return them to the jar. At the end of the week, count the total number of pennies. Then divide them into groups of 5¢, 10¢, or 25¢.

- Your little ones will go hog-wild over this counting activity! Purchase several small plastic piggy banks. Label each bank with a monetary value ranging from 5¢ to 50¢. Place the banks in a center along with a few rolls of pennies. Encourage a child to place the appropriate number of pennies in each bank.

- Provide a pair of students with a tic-tac-toe grid and a supply of pennies. Have them use the pennies as markers: heads for *X*s and tails for *O*s.

- Turn your dramatic-play area into a grocery store. Label empty boxes of food products with monetary values. Have a child pretend to purchase food by counting out the appropriate number of pennies for each item she wishes to purchase.

- Invite students to go on a seasonal shopping spree! Clip pictures of items in newspaper flyers during seasonal sales, such as Christmas items in December or beach-related items in June. Glue each picture to a small tagboard card and print an imaginary price (from 1¢ to 25¢) on the back of each card. Give each child in a small group a stash of pennies and let the buying begin! Have each child choose a specified number of items and count out her pennies to "pay" for them. Gotta stay within your budget!

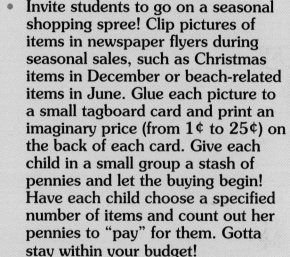

5¢

More Manipulatives

Here's a handy reference guide listing additional manipulatives you may want to consider using in your classroom. Busy hands are happy hands!

- beanbags
- dominoes
- novelty erasers
- greeting cards
- drinking straws
- plastic eating utensils
- die-cut shapes
- paper bags
- keys
- yarn lengths
- rocks
- dried beans
- artificial flowers
- plastic eggs
- balls
- scarves

- jumbo paper clips
- cookie cutters
- assorted candles
- colored candies
- magnets
- paper cups
- assorted gift boxes
- seashells
- clothespins
- nuts and bolts
- playing cards
- hats
- shoes
- tile and countertop samples
- assorted bells
- toy jewelry
- leaves
- whole fruits

SOCIAL SKILLS

Full Esteem Ahead!

Get on the right track to building youngsters' self-esteem by showing them what makes each of them a special individual. Just "choo-choo-choose" any of these activities!

ideas contributed by Lisa Cowman

A Song About YOU!

Celebrate the special traits of each student with this sing-along song. Have the class stand in a circle, and invite students to take turns standing in the middle. Begin the song, announcing the center student's name and a personality trait. Encourage the other children to skip around the youngster in the middle as you sing the song together. Continue until every student has had a chance to stand in the middle.

You Are Special
(sung to the tune of "The Wheels On The Bus")
The [Lucy] in our class is [very kind, very kind, very kind].
The [Lucy] in our class is [very kind] all through the day.

Your Laugh Is Like A Fingerprint

Students will have a good chuckle over this laughable contest. Tell students that a laugh is like a fingerprint—no two are exactly alike. Bring in a tape recorder and record each child's laughter. Write down the names of the children in the order in which you recorded them. Then play back the tape and see if students can recognize the laughs.

Youngsters will delight in discovering what makes their names special. Bring in a baby-name book and tell each child what his name means. Or, if desired, ask parents to share why children were given their particular names. Then whip up a batch of the baking dough recipe on page 198 for children to use in making nameplates. Have each student roll a portion of dough into thick snakes, then form the snakes into the letters of her name. Help her slightly overlap and press together the letters so they form nameplates. Use a straw to poke two holes in the top of each name (where convenient). Bake the nameplates in a 200˚ oven for four to five hours until they harden.

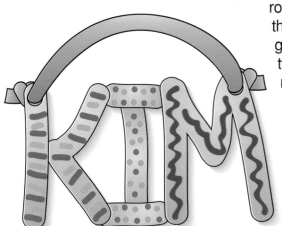

When the nameplates are cool, have children decorate their creations with fabric paints. Insert a ribbon through the holes at the top of each name, and knot the ends to create a hanger. (Hint: Use hot glue to repair any broken letters.) Encourage students to take their nameplates home to show their parents.

You're Creative!

Compare the unique beauty of a flower to the unique beauty of a child with this activity. Bring in several different flowers, and ask children to describe their shapes, colors, and leaves. Explain that just like people, each flower is different from the next. Then invite youngsters to create these flowers that will reflect their individual creativity.

Cover the work area with newspaper. Give each child a large shredded-wheat biscuit and three tablespoons of glue in a paper cup with wax coating. Have each child mix his choice of food coloring into his glue. Instruct him to break his biscuit into little pieces and mix the pieces together with the colored glue. Then have him form the mixture into a flower shape of his choice. Using fabric paint, write each child's name in the center of his flower. Invite students to decorate their flowers with other colors of fabric paint. Let the flowers dry for at least two hours.

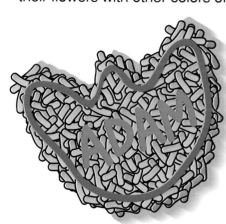

You Know What You Like

A week filled with favorite things will help students enjoy their differences and similarities. Listen to the song "My Favorite Things" from the musical *The Sound Of Music.* Explain to the class that since each of us is different, we like different games, toys, foods, etc. Ask students to discuss some of their favorite things. Then plan a Favorites Week.

Send a note home to parents asking that each child bring in his favorite toy on Monday, his favorite game on Tuesday, a picture of his favorite people on Wednesday, a favorite book on Thursday, and a favorite food on Friday. Each day set aside some time for students to play with or discuss their favorite objects. On Friday celebrate with a feast of favorite foods.

And The Winner Is...YOU!

Remind your students how truly amazing they are and how no one else is like them. Ask each student to name one thing she is good at. Remind children that they don't have to name a sport or skill. Who thinks she's talented at giving hugs? Or smiling? Or remembering to wear her safety belt in the car?

After the discussion, make these "Best At Being ME" medals for students to wear proudly. Give each child one large York® Peppermint Pattie and one yard of wide ribbon. Have her fold her ribbon in half and glue the loose ends to the back of her wrapped candy. Using an ink pad or thin paint, have each student stamp her thumbprint on a piece of white paper. Help students cut out around their thumbprints and glue them to the fronts of their wrapped candies. Then use a fabric pen to write "Best At Being ME" on each child's ribbon. Encourage students to wear their medals throughout the day.

Books About Being Special

Dandelion
Written by Don Freeman
Published by Puffin Books

Horton Hears A Who!
Written by Dr. Seuss
Published by Random House, Inc.

I'm Terrific
Written by Marjorie Weinman Sharmat
Published by Holiday House, Inc.

Love You Forever
Written by Robert Munsch
Published by Firefly Books Ltd.

Oh, The Thinks You Can Think!
Written by Dr. Seuss
Published by
Random House, Inc.

It Means A Lot, Coming From You

Help children build one another's self-esteem with these activities that encourage them to compliment classmates and pay attention to others.

Have You Heard It's Your Birthday?

Birthdays are special days! Celebrate with a special birthday present from the whole class. At some point during the day on a child's birthday, arrange for her to be out of the classroom—on an errand or at the library. While she is gone, place an empty cassette tape in a tape recorder and ask the class to sing "Happy Birthday" while you record it. After the song, invite children to shout out compliments to the birthday child as you record them. Complete the tape by stating your school name, grade, class, and year. When the birthday child returns, shout, "Surprise!" and play the recording. Present the child with the tape to keep as a special remembrance of this year's birthday. This is a birthday tradition your little ones will love!

Huggin' Hands

This extraspecial necklace will encourage children to attend to others' feelings. Lead a discussion about hugs. When do your youngsters give them? When do they need them? Then suggest the class make a special Hug Necklace.

To prepare, cut a two-foot length of yarn, and wrap tape around one end for easy lacing. Cut a few plastic drinking straws into half-inch pieces. Then ask each child to trace her hand on a piece of construction paper. Help each child cut out her hand shape, punch a hole in the bottom of the palm, and write her name in the center. Invite each child to string her hand shape and a straw piece onto the yarn. When all the hand shapes are in place, tie the ends of the yarn together to create a necklace.

Hang the Hug Necklace in a designated spot in your classroom. Tell your class to be on the lookout for someone who needs a hug. When a student sees someone in need, she can give the necklace to that person to wear.

ALL ABOUT me

Your little ones will find learning their full names, addresses, birthdays, and phone numbers is a snap with these games, puzzles, and songs.

ideas contributed by Rachel Castro

Personal Pocket Chart

Give students daily practice in identifying their names. Write each student's first and last names on a sentence strip. Make a puzzlelike cut between the first and last names of each child. Hang a large pocket chart where students can reach it. Place the first names in a column down the left side of the chart, leaving enough space after each name for the last name to follow. Place the last names (in the wrong order) in a column down the right side of the chart. Each morning, have each student find her last name and place it next to her first name. She'll know she's done it correctly

if the puzzle pieces fit. Once students can easily match their first and last names, change the puzzle cards to have students match their names with addresses, phone numbers, or birthdates.

Letter Seek

Students won't hide during this name-spelling game. Before playing, prepare a supply of letter cards. Write one letter on each card, until you have enough for each child to spell her first and last names. (If your class is large, try this as a small-group activity.) Then program letter-sized envelopes with the first and last names of each child. Hide all the letter cards around your classroom.

To play the game, distribute each envelope to the appropriate child along with a pencil or crayon. Challenge your little ones to find the letters in their names hidden around the room. As each child finds a letter, she should cross it off on the front of the envelope and put the letter inside her envelope. The first child to find all her letters wins the game. After everyone has found her letters, ask the children to return to their seats and unscramble the letters to form their names.

Pass The Phone

911

If full names and addresses don't ring a bell with students, try calling on this group activity. Explain to students that if they need to call for help, they should dial 9-1-1; then tell them they need to know their full names and addresses when they do this. Review each child's full name and address. Then ask students to sit in a circle and pass around a plastic phone (as they would in the game Hot Potato). Periodically, make a sound that signifies a smoke alarm. The student holding the phone must pick up the phone receiver, dial 9-1-1, and say his full name and address. Continue this activity until all students have had a chance to recite their names and addresses.

Pizza-Delivery Dilemma

Pizza adds pizzazz when learning personal information. Beforehand, cut out several ten-inch tan construction-paper circles and several seven-inch red construction-paper circles. Glue the red circles on top of the tan ones to make pizzas. Put them inside a pizza box donated from a local restaurant. Tell the class you have a number of pizzas that need to be delivered, but you are not sure who gets each one. As the delivery person, you say, "I have a pizza for_____" and use the last name or address of one of the students. The student whose name or address you called out should say, "That's my pizza!" If that child is correct, give him a pizza. Otherwise say, "I'm sorry, I have the wrong house." Continue playing until all children have had two turns or the pizzas run out. To extend the activity, challenge students to use a play phone to order their own pizzas, giving the correct names and addresses to the pizzeria.

Congratulations! You've won a prize!

Hello.

PHONE 'PHUN'

For phone number practice, duplicate a class supply of the pattern on page 233. Give each student a copy of the pattern, a 12-inch piece of yarn, tape, and a pair of scissors. Have each student color her phone and copy her name and phone number on the line. Have her cut out the phone and receiver shapes on the boldfaced lines. Then have her tape one end of the yarn to her receiver and the other end to her phone.

To play the game, call out a student's phone number. When a child hears her number, she should pick up her telephone receiver and say, "Hello." If she has correctly identified her number say, "Congratulations! You've won a prize!" and award her a candy treat. If the number identified by the child is incorrect, simply say, "I'm sorry. I must have the wrong number. I was calling_____."

Present Sense

Presents always get children excited about birthdays, so try this idea for birthdate recognition. Wrap the top and bottom of a gift box separately and decorate the top with a bow. Fill the box with an assortment of treats. Sit in front of your class with the box and call out one student's birthdate. When that child hears her birthdate, she comes to the front of the class and picks out a treat from the box. Continue until every student identifies her birthdate and receives a goodie gift.

The Birthday Song

Students will quickly tune into their birthdates with this little ditty sung to the tune of "The More We Get Together."

CLASS:
What day is your birthday,
Your birthday, your birthday?
What day is your birthday?

STUDENT'S RESPONSE:
It's _____.

Name/Number _____

Sharing

When each child shares a little, everyone gains a lot. Try these activities to help promote sharing—not only with friends and family, but also with your community and the world.

ideas contributed by Barbara Spilman Lawson

Jenni Can Share A Jump Rope

Incorporate sharing with letter recognition to double the learning fun! Write each child's first name on your chalkboard or a chart, and add the words *can share* after each name. Ask each child to think of an item she could share that starts with the same letter as her name. Extend this activity by having your students think of things to share starting with each letter of the alphabet; list them on a chart called "Things We Can Share From A To Z."

Things We Can Share

Angie can share apples.

Lori can share Lincoln logs.

Nick can share neon crayons.

Mary can share markers.

Beth can share books.

Paul can share puzzle pieces.

Sarah can share scissors.

Eddie can share erasers.

Sharing Buddies

Pick a time once a week for Sharing Buddies. Have each child choose a game or book to share. Put everyone's name in a bag; then draw two names at a time. Encourage each pair of children to share with each other during this special time. For a slightly different twist, play Sharing Buddies Switch-A-Roo. Put all the names back in the bag every ten minutes or so, and draw new buddies.

The Art Of Sharing

Teach youngsters the art of sharing with some fun art materials. In advance cut out a paper heart for each of your kindergartners. Fill a plastic bag for each child with a different type of collage item, such as buttons, glitter, sequins, yarn, or colorful paper scraps. Put the plastic bags in a large grocery bag. Invite each student to reach into the grocery bag (without looking) and take one plastic bag. Then provide glue and invite students to decorate their paper hearts collage-style. By sharing art materials, each child will have a variety of materials with which to decorate his heart.

Group Soup

Cook up a little fun by reading *Stone Soup* told by Marcia Brown (Simon & Schuster Children's Books) and then make your own Group Soup. Discuss how the townspeople in the story hide their food and do not share for fear of not having enough. Then ask students to recall what happens when everyone shares just a little food. Afterward prepare your little chefs to make their own Group Soup. Send home a note asking each child to bring in a quart-sized zippered plastic bag filled with washed and cubed or sliced vegetables. Let each little cook dump her own vegetables into a large pot. Add water, broth, and some mild spices. As the soup cooks, record your recipe in a class book by having each child write or dictate and then illustrate what she added to the soup. Soon you'll be sharing your own special version of Group Soup!

Dare To Share

Divide your class into groups of four. Give each child a zippered plastic bag containing four different types of small manipulatives, such as counting bears, Unifix® Cubes, paper clips, and wooden beads. Tell students that the object of this Dare To Share game is for each group to put the items into categories by sharing, not taking. Invite each group to begin when you say, "Dare to share." First each group decides which group member will collect each type of manipulative. Then the children start sharing! On each child's turn, he may give another team member the material he needs. Remind students that no one may take an item he needs from someone else. Each child must wait for it to be given to him. If all team members share what they have, the entire team will succeed in grouping the materials. When each child has his set of like manipulatives, he puts them into his bag to complete the game.

The Sharing Chair

Your children will become more aware of *all* the ways they share with others when you transform your rocking chair or another comfy chair into a Sharing Chair once a week. Model the procedure first, by sitting in the chair and telling about how you have shared your possessions, time, or talents with others that week. Invite your principal or another staff member to share next. Then invite each child, in turn, to sit in the chair and tell about how he has shared with others. To promote further awareness, have each child tell how someone else has shared with him.

Share A Story

Invite your youngsters to share a story with friends and families by compiling this class book. Collect a story "written" and illustrated by each of your kindergarten authors to include in the book. Add your own story, as well as a few blank pages. Then bind the pages between construction-paper covers. Let everyone have a turn taking the book home to share with his family. Invite parents to share stories, if they like, by writing on the blank pages provided.

If your students like this book, continue the fun with additional books, such as *Share A Rhyme*, *Share A Picture*, and *Share A Happy Thought*. Your students may come up with ideas for more shared books.

The Together Tower

Show your budding architects how they can create something together by sharing ideas. Invite each student to select a block from the block center. Have the children sit in a circle, and explain that they will be working together to build a tower one block at a time. Choose a student to begin the tower, and recite the following poem; then repeat the poem each time you choose another builder.

> Look at the idea [child's name] has got!
> If we all build together, we all gain a lot.

Have the first child place his block somewhere in the open area inside the circle. Invite the second student to place his block on or near the first block. Remind your construction crew that each person's building idea is special and that no one knows what the tower will look like until every block has been placed. Label your finished product "The Together Tower," and leave it standing for a while for all to appreciate.

Give Yourselves A Hand

Show everyone how much your little ones share with a "We Share, We Care" bulletin board. Have your students trace and cut out hand shapes from bright, colorful construction paper. Each time someone shares, write down what was shared on a hand cutout and staple it to the board. Remind youngsters that sharing includes not only sharing toys and games with their classmates, but also sharing posses-sions, time, or talents with others in your school, com-munity—even the world! If your class collects canned goods for charity, partici-pates in a recycling project, or performs a skit for the class next door, be sure to record it!

Arrange the hand shapes randomly, or section off the board like a learning web, with areas for sharing with friends, family, your school, the community, and the world. If there's room, add a section for how others have shared with your students.

Share Fair

Let your community in on the fun of sharing by holding a Share Fair. Have your students write stories and poems about sharing. Invite them to draw pictures and make up skits about sharing. Put up displays including your decorated sharing hearts (page 234); con-tinue to fill up your "We Share, We Care" bulle-tin board (above); and build a Together Tower (page 236) for the occasion. Then in-vite representatives from local businesses or clubs to visit with your class and share infor-mation about the ways they share with your community. Conclude this event by sharing some student-made refreshments—perhaps a pot of Group Soup (page 235)!

We Are ALIKE, We Are DIFFERENT

Alike and different at the same time? You bet! Use these activities to help your little ones discover that because of our similarities we have plenty in common, and because of our differences we have a lot to offer each other.

ideas contributed by Lucia Kemp Henry

My Body, Your Body

Youngsters will recognize basic similarities with this introductory activity. Trace the outline of each child's body onto a separate length of bulletin-board paper. Display several of the outlines on a wall near your group area. To point out how the outlines are alike, ask youngsters to name the outlined body parts. Record the parts on separate sentence strips; then put them in a writing center. Have each child visit the center with his body outline. Direct him to refer to the cards as he uses a marker to label his outline. Set the labeled outlines aside for later use with "Who Am I?" on page 241.

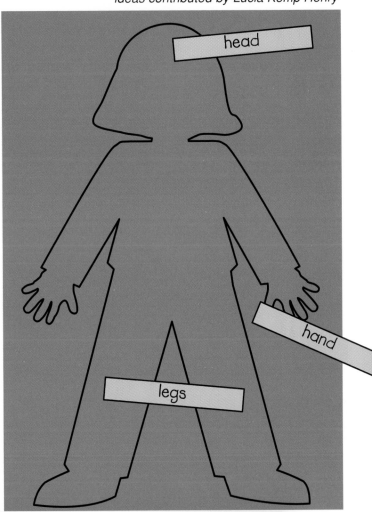

Physical Similarities

Reinforce youngsters' observations of their physical similarities by teaching them this action rhyme.

We are alike. We all have heads.	*Point to head.*
We rest them when it's time for bed.	*Fold hands under head.*
We are alike. We all have eyes.	*Point to eyes.*
We all have noses, girls and guys.	*Point to nose.*
We are alike. We all have feet.	*Point to feet.*
We like to move them to the beat.	*Dance by moving feet.*
We are alike. Oh, yes I know.	*Nod head.*
We all have bodies that move and grow.	*Stand on toes and reach arms up.*

We All Have Feelings

Now that your little ones understand their similarities on the outside, explain that we have many similarities on the inside, too. As a group, make a list of feelings. Next record behaviors associated with each emotion. Sing the following song to remind youngsters that we all have feelings.

The More We Are Together

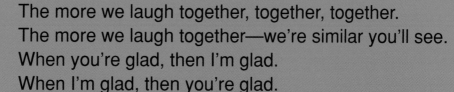

(sung to the tune of "The More We Get Together")

The more we laugh together, together, together.
The more we laugh together—we're similar you'll see.
When you're glad, then I'm glad.
When I'm glad, then you're glad.
The more we laugh together—we're similar you'll see.

The more we cry together, together, together.
The more we cry together—we're similar you'll see.
When you're sad, then I'm sad.
When I'm sad, then you're sad.
The more we cry together—we're similar you'll see.

The more we frown together, together, together.
The more we frown together—we're similar you'll see.
When you're mad, then I'm mad.
When I'm mad, then you're mad.
The more we frown together—we're similar you'll see.

The more we scream together, together, together.
The more we scream together—we're similar you'll see.
When you're scared, then I'm scared.
When I'm scared, then you're scared.
The more we scream together—we're similar you'll see.

The more we grin together, together, together.
The more we grin together—we're similar you'll see.
When you're proud, then I'm proud.
When I'm proud, then you're proud.
The more we grin together—we're similar you'll see.

We're All Smiles

Life would certainly lack color and interest if everyone looked the same! Ask your children what might happen if everyone had the same face. Then visually demonstrate the idea with these masks. For each child, duplicate a smiling face pattern onto yellow construction paper. Direct each child to cut out the circle, and then glue it to the bottom of a paper plate. Cut around the yellow circle again, through the bottom of the plate, leaving an inch above the smiling face to create a flap. When each child has a completed mask, have the group stand together. Direct the children to hold the masks in front of their faces; then take an instant picture of the temporarily nondiverse group. Next have the children lift and hold up the smiling faces to reveal their own special faces. Take another picture of your group as it appears in all its radiant diversity. Display the photos in a location that will prompt discussion among your little ones.

A Rainbow Of Faces

Put a colorful rainbow of faces into an art project that will brighten any display. Ask each child to choose a shade of People Colors® tempera paint to paint a portrait onto a large piece of paper. When the paint is dry, have her paint facial features. When this paint is dry, lay the portrait on top of another sheet of paper; then cut around the face through both layers. Glue the edges together, leaving an opening at the top of the face. Stuff the face with tissues; then glue the top closed. Ask the artist to help you add yarn hair to the face. Display the portraits on a bulletin board titled "A Rainbow Of Colorful Faces."

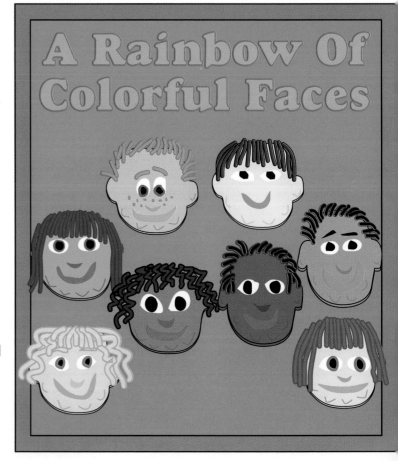

We Are Different

(sung to the tune of "This Old Man")

Me and you, you and me,
We are different, as you see.
With our different faces, eyes
  and noses, too,
We are different, me and you.

Me and you, you and me,
We are different as can be.
With our different names and
  different families, too,
We are different, me and you.

Who Am I?

Once youngsters have labeled their body outlines as described in "My Body, Your Body" on page 238, personalize their outlines with descriptions of the physical and inward characteristics that make them unique. Around the outline write the child's height, descriptions of her appearance, and several unique character traits. Display the outlines along a wall with the question "Who Are We?"

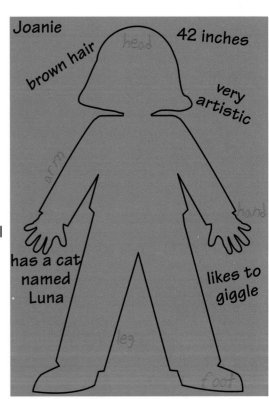

Colorful Books About Colorful People

Use these books to further discuss equity and diversity.

All The Colors Of The Earth
Written by Sheila Hamanaka
Published by Morrow Junior Books

Two Eyes, A Nose And A Mouth:
  A Book Of Many Faces, Many Races
Written by Roberta Grobel Intrater
Published by Scholastic Inc.

All About You
Written by Laurence Anholt
Published by Puffin Books

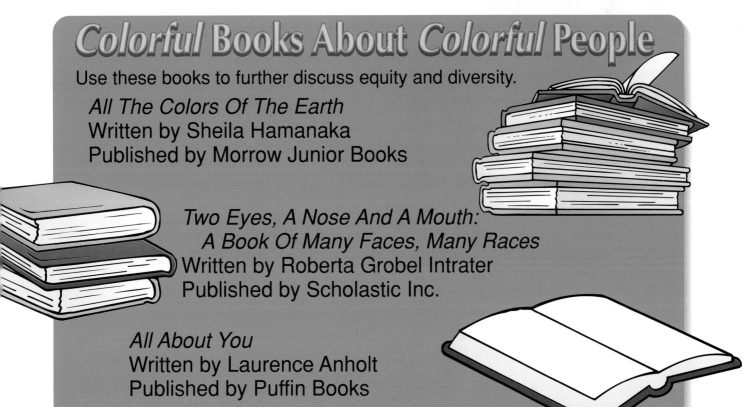

I CAN DO IT!

These words are music to a teacher's ears. And these activities provide just the practice needed for youngsters to develop their independence skills so that they can sing their own praises. Oh, beautiful music!

by Mackie Rhodes

Pipe-Cleaner Ties

Try this idea to help youngsters learn to tie laces into bows. Create a tying board by punching two holes two inches apart in the center of a 4" x 5" piece of sturdy cardboard. Attach hole reinforcers to each hole on both the front and back of the board. Then tightly twist the ends of two pipe cleaners together. Lace one end of the long pipe cleaner through one hole in the back of the board and the other end through the other hole; then secure the pipe cleaner to the back with a piece of masking tape. To use, have a child tie traditional or bunny-ear bows with the pipe-cleaner laces.

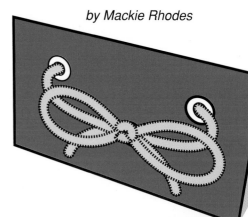

Bozo Button-Ons

Youngsters will enjoy clowning around with buttoning to create these clown faces. To make a clown head, cut a large felt oval; then sew a separate button onto the felt head where you might find the nose, mouth, and each eye on a clown's face. Also sew a button near the top of each side of the head. From different felt colors, cut out different shapes to represent a clown's eyes, nose, mouth, and hat. For example, you might cut a yellow diamond for each eye, a red circle for the nose, a pink half-moon for the mouth, and an orange triangle for the hat. Then cut out several more sets of features, varying the shapes and colors in each set. Cut a buttonhole in the center of each piece to correspond to the width of the appropriate button on the felt head; then place all the felt pieces in a center. To use, invite a child to create a clown face by buttoning his choice of facial features onto the felt head.

Shoe Shuffle

As youngsters sort through this cooperative matching game, they will get valuable practice in putting on and fastening their shoes. To begin, ask each child to remove her shoes; then fasten one of each child's shoes to that of another child's. Place the mismatched sets of shoes into a large box. Then invite a volunteer to find one of her shoes in the box. Ask her to unfasten the attached shoe, then give that shoe to its owner. Have both children put on and fasten their own shoes. Then invite the second child to find her shoe's mate in the box. She will then unfasten the attached shoe and pass it on to its rightful owner. Proceed in this manner until each shoe and its mate are reunited on the correct feet. Students are "shoe" to enjoy this game!

Giant Belt Loops

Round up some spare belts to use with this "fasten-ating" activity. To prepare, collect an assortment of buckle-style belts in different widths and lengths. Invite members of a small group of students to connect the belts together to create a giant loop. Encourage them to plan how to arrange and fasten the belts together so that as many belts as possible can be used. Place the group's completed loop on the floor; then have a volunteer lead the class in a rambunctious round of The Hokey-Pokey around the loop. Then have the group unfasten all the belts so that another group can take a turn creating a giant loop. Youngsters will enthusiastically belt out a song and dance with this idea.

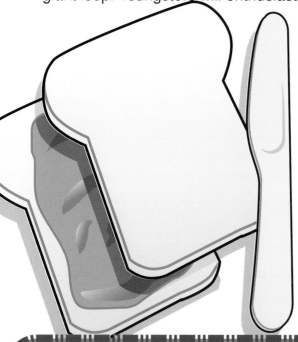

Foam Finger Sandwiches

While youngsters hone their spreading and cutting skills in this activity, be sure to sandwich in some dramatic play, too. To begin, cut two bread slices per child from thick, disposable Styrofoam® plates or meat trays. Then give each child a serrated plastic knife and a portion of brown play dough to represent peanut butter. Instruct him to spread the play-dough peanut butter on one bread slice, then place the other slice on top to create a sandwich. Then ask each child to cut his sandwich in half or into quarters. After the finger sandwiches are prepared, invite youngsters to use them as pretend food in the housekeeping center. Spread the peanut butter; then spread the news—the kitchen is open!

Designer's Delight

The highest form of flattery is imitation— and that's just what youngsters will engage in during this patterning game involving button closures. Collect a quantity of front-buttoning shirts; then divide the class into student pairs. To begin, invite one child in each pair to select a shirt from the collection, then create a pattern with the button closures. For instance, she might button every other button on a shirt, leaving the remaining buttons unfastened. Have her partner duplicate the buttoning pattern on another shirt with the same number of button closures. Then invite the partners to switch roles. After several rounds, you might increase the difficulty level by having a child create a pattern using two different shirts, then challenging her partner to imitate the pattern on another set of shirts.

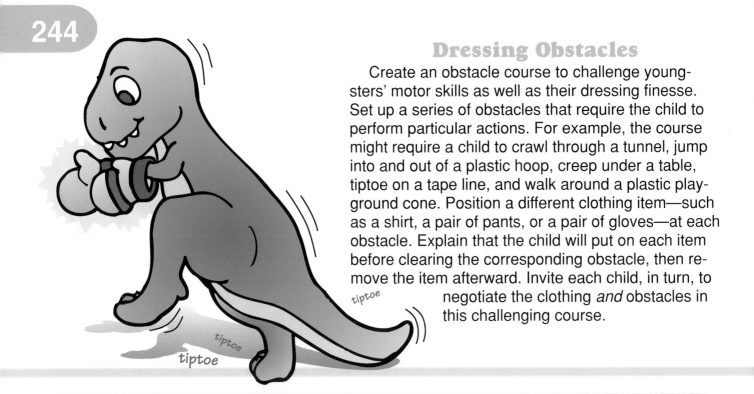

Dressing Obstacles

Create an obstacle course to challenge youngsters' motor skills as well as their dressing finesse. Set up a series of obstacles that require the child to perform particular actions. For example, the course might require a child to crawl through a tunnel, jump into and out of a plastic hoop, creep under a table, tiptoe on a tape line, and walk around a plastic playground cone. Position a different clothing item—such as a shirt, a pair of pants, or a pair of gloves—at each obstacle. Explain that the child will put on each item before clearing the corresponding obstacle, then remove the item afterward. Invite each child, in turn, to negotiate the clothing *and* obstacles in this challenging course.

Career Wear

Students will dress for success in this activity that highlights different careers while providing dressing practice. Gather and display a variety of clothing articles associated with different types of careers, such as jobs in the medical profession, fire fighting, and construction work. Ask a volunteer to be your career model; then shine a flashlight on an article that might be worn by a person in a particular career (do not tell the child the name of the career). Have the child put on that article; then shine the light on another career-related item for the child to don. Continue in this manner until the child is completely outfitted. Ask him to name the career that his outfit represents. Then have him return the articles to the display. Invite that child to shine the light on career articles while another student assumes the model role.

Serve Up A Sensory Delight

Dish out some skill development in self-service with this "sense-ible" idea. Fill each of several plastic serving dishes with one of the following: rice, playdough balls, shaving cream, or packing peanuts. Or select any of your preferred sensory materials to put in the dishes. Set an appropriate serving utensil—such as a fork, a spoon, or tongs—inside each dish; then give each child a Styrofoam® plate. Have youngsters pass each serving dish and its utensil from child to child so each child can carefully serve herself a portion of each item. Encourage students to try not to spill anything over the dish edges or off the serving utensils. After everyone has been served, invite each youngster to create a sensational mix of materials on her plate, using either plastic tableware or her hands. What a delight!

Rhythmic Warm-Up

Youngsters will warm up quickly to this hand-clapping, toe-tapping rhythm activity. To play, gather a pair of gloves and oversized socks for each child. Have each child put on his socks, positioning them correctly on his heels and toes. Then challenge him to independently put his gloves on his hands. When students are properly "socked" and "gloved," challenge them to repeat the rhythm patterns that you create with your own covered hands and feet. Begin with simple clapping or stomping patterns. Then add more beats to lengthen the rhythms, or increase the speed of the patterns. Or, if desired, mix the clapping and stomping to create interesting sounds and patterns. What a cool warm-up!

Pastry Party

Invite students to show off their table skills during this special play-dough pastry party. Give each child in a small group a set of plastic tableware and a portion of play dough. Ask her to form her play dough into some type of pastry, such as a pie, cake, or bread loaf. Then have her place her pastry on a foam plate. Encourage her to use her plastic knife to cut her play-dough pastry into serving portions. Then have her use her fork to pierce a pastry portion and serve it to each of her groupmates. Invite youngsters to then pretend to eat their pastries with their personal utensils. Be sure to use your manners—and your napkin.

WACKY WEATHER WARDROBE

It's time to dress for the weather! But just what is the day's weather? In this wacky dressing activity, the answer could be anything...or everything! Prepare for this activity by collecting an assortment of wardrobe items designed for as many different weather conditions as possible. For example, you might include swimsuits, fur-lined boots, raincoats, sweaters, sunglasses, earmuffs, gloves, shorts, knit caps, and heavy coats in your collection. To play, invite each student, in turn, to be your weather-wear model. Set a kitchen timer for a designated amount of time, such as one or two minutes. Then announce a weather condition to the model. Instruct him to don as many appropriate articles as possible that are suited to that weather condition. Then, when the timer rings, pretend to check the weather again. Announce at that time that the weather conditions have suddenly changed! Name the new weather conditions, reset the timer, and have the child adjust his wardrobe to suit the changed weather. What a wacky weather day!

Snap To It!

Try this snappy idea to give students practice in fastening snaps on their clothes. Provide a variety of clothing articles with snap fasteners, such as jackets, vests, raincoats, and pants. Then divide your class into small groups. Working with one group at a time, invite each child to put on an item with snap closures. On a signal, have each youngster fasten one snap at a time, pausing to snap his fingers between each successful attempt. How many snaps did he snap? After several practice rounds, give each child a snack—a gingersnap!

Tie-On Skates

Here's a cool idea to help youngsters glide into shoe-tying practice. To make a skate, obtain two shoebox lids identical in size; then follow the steps in the diagram. To use, have a child slip each foot into a skate. Instruct her to tie each skate lace so that the skate fits as snugly as possible around her foot. Then play some flowing music, inviting students to sli-i-ide and gli-i-ide to the rhythm.

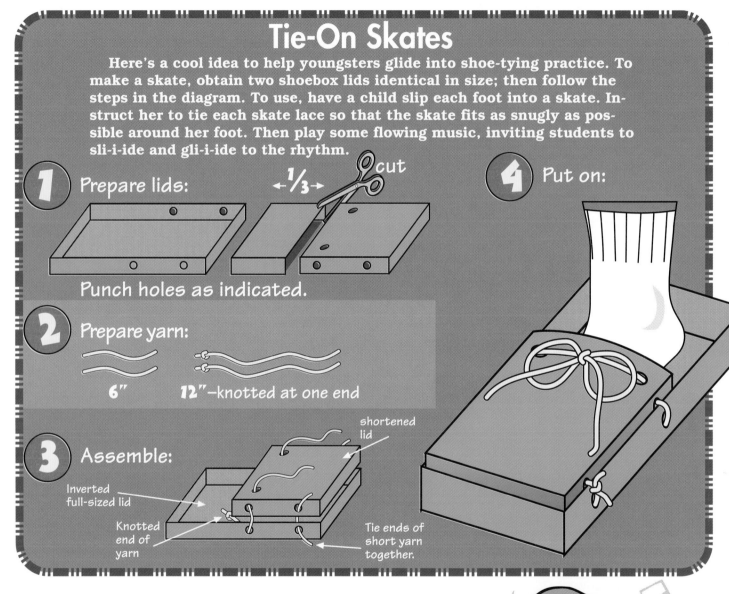

1 Prepare lids: ←1/3→ cut

Punch holes as indicated.

2 Prepare yarn:

6"   12"–knotted at one end

3 Assemble:

shortened lid

Inverted full-sized lid

Knotted end of yarn

Tie ends of short yarn together.

4 Put on:

A Bubbly Scrub

Students will bubble with enthusiasm when they sing this little hand-washing reminder.

(sung to the tune of "If You're Happy And You Know It")

Make some soapy, sudsy bubbles with your hands.
Make some soapy, sudsy bubbles with your hands.
Make some soapy, sudsy bubbles—
Give your hands a good, clean "scrub-ble."
Make some soapy, sudsy bubbles with your hands!

RECYCLE & REUSE

PLAY IT AGAIN, SAM!

A teacher's trash really is a classroom's treasure. Use these nifty ideas to recycle and re-use common objects in unusual ways.

ideas contributed by Suzanne Moore

CARDBOARD TUBES

Totally Tubular Printing

Save cardboard tubes to use as handy tools for printing.
— To make circles, simply dip one end of the tube into paint and print.
— For flower prints, use a rubber band to secure two-inch strips of tagboard to one end of a tube. Bend the two-inch strips back. Dip that end of the tube into paint and print. If students twist their wrists while printing, they can create even flashier designs.
— To print waves, glue yarn in a wave pattern to the side of a toilet-tissue tube. Stuff the tube with newspaper for reinforcement. When the glue is dry, dip the side of the tube into paint and press lightly against paper. Wavy prints make good backgrounds for ocean scenes.

Let The Fun Rain Down On Me

Paper-towel tubes are the perfect size for making rain sticks. Cover one end of a tube with a 4" x 4" square of waxed paper; secure the paper with a rubber band. Insert brad fasteners (the more the better) into the tube in random spots. Put some rice, unpopped popcorn, or dried beans into the tube. Then cover the other end of the tube with another square of waxed paper. Tilt the tube to listen to the rhythm of the falling rain!

Broomstick Math

Reinforce number sequencing with this spiffy activity. Cover toilet-tissue-tube rings with Con-Tact® paper or clear packing tape. Label each tube with a number from one to ten. Then grab a broom or mop from your house-keeping center, and challenge students to slide the tubes onto the handle in numerical order.

More Ideas For Cardboard Tubes...

• Decorate toilet-tissue tubes to make finger puppets. Use yarn to make hair, buttons for eyes, and fabric scraps or paint for clothes.
• To reinforce size-sequencing skills, cut tubes to varying lengths. Challenge students to order them from shortest to longest.
• Keep take-home assignments and notes from getting crushed or lost by rolling and sliding papers into paper-towel tubes labeled with children's names.

Totem Poles

Your little ones will be eager to build their own totem poles after you share *Totem Pole,* written by Diane Hoyt-Goldsmith (Holiday House, Inc.). Paraphrase text and share selected photographs from this book, which shows how a modern-day totem pole is made.

Prior to reading aloud, partially fill a number of boxes with sand (for weighting) and tape the box flaps shut. Enlist parent volunteers to cover the boxes with bulletin-board paper. Have students use construction paper and glue to make a face on one side of each box. For a three-dimensional effect, show students how to add paper features such as fins, wings, or noses. Stack three or four boxes, largest to smallest, into a totem-pole shape. Have your class work cooperatively to make one or two totem poles; or divide your class into small groups and have each group make one.

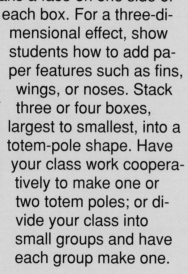

A Sound Sensation

Empty boxes can become unique new rhythm instruments. Fill small cereal boxes with pebbles, sand, dried beans, unpopped popcorn, or rice. To reinforce the boxes, cover them with Con-Tact® paper.

Or fill pairs of small cereal boxes with matching fillings for a sound-matching activity. Again, cover the boxes with Con-Tact® paper for durability. Instruct students to shake each box and match it with its mate. Number or letter the bottoms of the boxes to make this center self-checking.

Won't You Be Mine?

Students will love the idea of individual valentine mailboxes. Ask each student to bring in one large cereal box. Remove the top flaps. Recruit parents or your assistant to help cover each box with pink or white bulletin-board paper. Gather an assortment of doilies, valentine stickers, construction-paper hearts, and other scrap items for your students to use to decorate the boxes. Label each box with the child's name and a photocopy of her school picture. On Valentine's Day, place the boxes around your room within reach of your students. Invite small groups of children to take turns delivering their valentines. At the end of the day, these decorative boxes make taking home valentines easy!

More Ideas For Boxes...

- Decorate boxes to make hand puppets, and invite children to act out their favorite stories.
- Cut out panels from cereal boxes to make student clipboards. Cover each panel with Con-Tact® paper; then staple or paper-clip several sheets of paper to the panel along the top edge.
- Cover cereal-box panels with Con-Tact® paper to make front and back covers for student-made books.

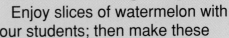

PLASTIC LIDS

Rolling, Rolling, Rolling

Collect plastic lids to use as wheels on these fun transportation pictures. In advance, use brads to attach pairs of plastic lids to sheets of 12" x 18" construction paper. Then let students incorporate the lids as wheels in illustrations of various modes of air and land transportation. Have each student write or dictate where he is going in his vehicle. If desired, compile the pictures into big books. (Because of the thickness of the plastic lids, you'll probably have to make more than one book.) Add a front cover to each book with the title "Where Are You Going?" Include a cover illustration with lid wheels, if desired. Have each child share his page with the class, and then place the books in your library center.

I'm going to a fire!

J.T.

Put A Lid On It!

Count on plastic lids for a class math lesson or learning-center activity. Gather 20 plastic lids. On each of ten lids, write a different numeral from one to ten. In each of the remaining lids, punch a different number of holes from one to ten. Place one of the hole-punched lids on an overhead projector. Ask children to count the number of holes in the lid. When a volunteer gives the correct number, invite her to come up and find the corresponding numeral lid and show it to the class. Continue using the other lids. Or place both sets of lids at a learning center. Ask students to match the numeral lids with the hole-punched lids. Check students' work or illustrate an answer card for self-checking.

Mouthwatering Magnets

Enjoy slices of watermelon with your students; then make these adorable watermelon magnets. Rinse the watermelon seeds from your snack and let them dry. For every two students, cut a plastic lid in half. Give each student one half and instruct him to paint the outer portion with a mixture of green tempera paint and glue. Let the paint dry. Then have each child paint the rest of his lid half with a mixture of red tempera paint and glue. After the paint dries, invite him to glue some real watermelon seeds to the red area. Attach a magnetic strip to the back of each lid. Parents will love receiving this handy craft!

More Ideas For Plastic Lids...

- Small lids may be glued to student illustrations to make eyes.
- Use lids to make handheld streamers. Cut centers out of plastic lids, leaving a half-inch margin all the way around. Tie strips of crepe paper around the plastic ring.
- Make easy mobiles. Invite students to decorate several lids with paint, glitter, paper scraps, etc. Punch a hole at the top of each decorated lid and use yarn or string to tie the lids to a plastic hanger.

PLASTIC BOTTLES

Weighty Decision

Students get hands-on practice with weight estimation in this activity. Fill several 20-ounce soda bottles with varying amounts of sand. To seal, line the caps with hot glue and screw them in place. Then invite students to order the bottles from the lightest to the heaviest. Make this activity self-checking by numbering the bottoms of the bottles. You can also have students weigh the bottles using balance scales.

Making Waves

Immerse your students in the study of insolubles by creating some waves. Using a funnel, pour 3/4 cup of water into a 20-ounce plastic bottle. Add several drops of blue food coloring to the water. Swirl the water around in the bottle to mix. Then add 1/2 cup of baby oil to the water. Line the bottle cap with hot glue and screw it in place tightly. Tip and swirl the bottle to watch the waves. No, oil and water won't mix—they *are* insoluble—but your little scientists will certainly enjoy trying!

Sink A Bottle

How many pebbles will it take to sink a bottle at the water table? Challenge your little ones to use problem-solving skills to find out! Ask students to gather pebbles small enough to fit into 20-ounce plastic bottles. When they've made a pile of pebbles, ask them to predict how many pebbles will be needed to sink one bottle. Record their predictions. Place the pebbles in a bucket near the water table, and encourage students to test their predictions. To extend this activity, provide measuring cups and invite students to discover exactly how much water it will take to sink a bottle.

More Ideas For Plastic Bottles...

- Create a fountain for your water table by poking random holes in a 20-ounce bottle.
- Cut plastic bottles of any size in half. Use the top portions as funnels and the bottoms as planters.
- Fill several 20-ounce bottles with 1/4 to 1/2 cup of sand each, provide a playground ball, and set up a bowling center.

BERRY BASKETS

Blowing In The Wind

On a windy day, take your class outside and ask students to watch how the wind moves objects. Inside the classroom, discuss what students observed about the wind. Explain how windsocks indicate which way the wind is blowing. Then help students make simple windsocks. Lace three-foot strips of crepe paper (or strips cut from gallon-sized plastic bags) through the holes located at the top of a berry basket. Invert the basket, and thread an 18-inch piece of yarn through the center bottom of the basket. Tie the yarn into a loop for hanging. Then invite your students to test the wind direction with their berry-basket windsocks.

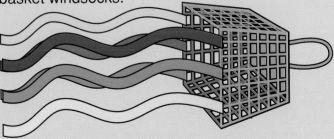

A "Berry" Nice Village

Give your block or sand center homey appeal with these berry-basket houses. Build each house from two baskets. Turn the first basket upside down and cut a door out of one of the panels. For the roof, cut two side panels from a second berry basket. Pinch the remaining two sides together and secure them at the top with pipe cleaners. Use pipe cleaners to attach the triangular roof to the first basket, as shown. Have students arrange the basket houses to create a village at your sand table or block center.

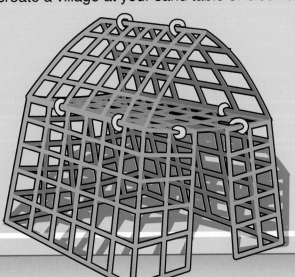

A Basketful Of Drawings

Panels from berry baskets can enhance student illustrations. Try one or more of these ideas:

— Glue the panels from the sides of a berry basket onto a drawing to represent a fence.
— Glue on the panels to represent cages for zoo pictures.
— Try making skyscraper pictures. Cut panels into building shapes, and glue them to blue or black construction paper to make cityscapes.

More Ideas For Berry Baskets...

- Use berry baskets as strainers at your sand table.
- Dip berry baskets into bubble solution to use as bubble blowers.
- Use berry baskets as organizers in your centers; they can hold puzzle and game pieces, flash cards, or small items in your housekeeping center.

Paper-Bag Band

Lunch sacks can make a symphony of sounds! Enhance your students' sensory and rhythmic skills with this activity. Give each child a lunch sack and have her experiment with making these sounds:

— Rub a closed bag back and forth; it makes a sand-block sound.

— Clap hands with the closed paper bag between; this makes a snapping sound.

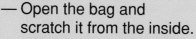

— Open the bag and scratch it from the inside.

— Make a fist and gently punch the sides of an open bag from the inside.

Have students try making each of these sounds slowly, then quickly. Then form a paper-bag rhythm band! Assign small groups to make sounds while your class sings their favorite songs.

Crowned Head Of The Classroom

Need crowns for your little kings and queens? To make one, open a large lunch bag and fold the edges down until the sack is about five inches tall. Then cut the bottom out of the bag and make a cut from top to bottom in the remaining loop so the crown will lie flat. Snip zigzags all the way across the unrolled edge of the flattened crown. To size the crown, insert a brad fastener in the two bottom (folded) corners of the bag and loop one end of a rubber band around each brad. Decorate the crowns with sequins, plastic gems, and glitter.

Go, Team, Go!

Practice scissor skills and create pom-poms to cheer on a favorite team! Give each child a large paper bag. Help students to snip half-inch-wide strips in the closed bags up to where the bottoms are folded. Roll each bag bottom into a tight tube and secure it with tape. (Note: You can also use these pom-poms to make a swishing sound for your "Paper-Bag Band.")

More Ideas For Paper Bags...

- Need big brushes for a mural? Cut half-inch fringe around the top of a lunch sack; then roll it into a tight tube. Secure the roll with tape.
- Fill lunch bags with 1/2 cup unpopped popcorn each, and twist the top of the bags to close. Secure with colorful yarn, and you'll have noisy maracas.
- Decorate paper lunch sacks with crayons, markers, glitter, yarn, and construction paper to make hand puppets.

PACKING PEANUTS

Styrofoam® Structures

Have your little architects create structures with packing peanuts. Invite them to connect the peanuts into three-dimensional designs with toothpicks. Encourage students to build structures with wide bases and narrow tops, as these will be the most sturdy. Small designs will float in water or move when gently blown.

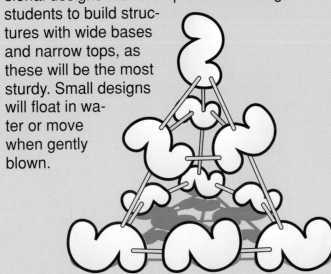

Peanut Printing

Add to your art center or a group mural with packing-peanut printing. Glue packing peanuts to the tops of several large plastic lids. For handles, hot-glue a plastic film canister to the other side of each lid. Have a student dip a peanut-covered lid into paint, then print onto paper. The resulting prints make good ocean or grass backgrounds.

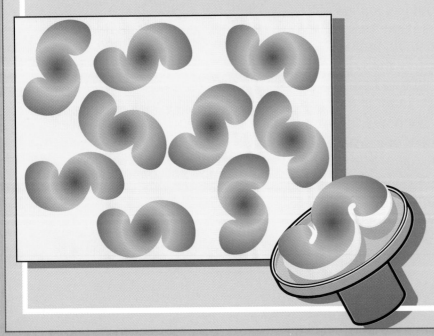

Dissolving Peanuts

Invite little ones to experiment with those environmentally friendly, dissolving packing peanuts. You know they dissolve in water, but have students predict whether they will dissolve in paint, baby oil, hairspray, shampoo, or other liquids. Then test out their theories.

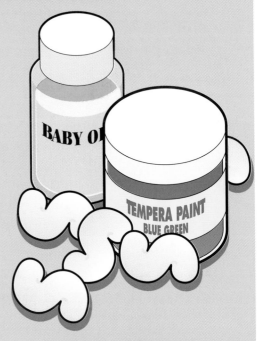

BABY OIL

TEMPERA PAINT
BLUE GREEN

More Ideas For Packing Peanuts...

- Collect packing peanuts in various colors. Ask a small group of students to sort the peanuts by color and create a graph showing the results.
- Use packing peanuts as stuffing in paper bags to make 3-D sculptures.
- Replace a messy sand or water table with packing peanuts.

SEASONAL & HOLIDAY

Seasonal & Holiday Displays

ideas contributed by Kimberli Carrier

Fall Is All Around Us

Fill a bulletin board with fall colors and photos. Have each child brush a coffee filter with water and then squeeze a few drops of red and yellow food coloring onto the filter. Provide tagboard templates of leaves (page 261). Have each child trace a leaf onto her dried filter and then cut it out. Arrange the leaves as a border and add the title to your display. Then mount photos of your youngsters participating in autumn activities.

Our Wacky Witch's Brew

Brew up a pot of beginning-sounds practice. Enlarge, color, and cut out the witch (page 262). Cut a large pot from black poster board. Attach the witch and pot to the board; then add green cotton for the brew. Cut the first letter of each child's name from construction paper. Ask each youngster to choose a food that begins with the same letter as her name. Staple a card with the name and food next to each large letter to top off this wild, wacky brew!

Have each child make a gorgeous gobbler for this Thanksgiving display. To make one, staple together two 5-inch circles cut from a brown paper bag, stuffing shredded newspaper between the layers before stapling around them completely. Cut a red head and orange beak and feet from construction paper, then glue them in place. Add two wiggle eyes. Then trace one hand onto four different colors of construction paper, then cut out the hand shapes. Glue the hand cutouts onto the turkey's body. Attach all the turkeys and the title to the bulletin board.

Turn your classroom into a winter wonderland! Use paper plates to create two snowpeople. Add construction-paper faces and arms. Enlarge, duplicate, and cut out the animals (pages 262 and 263), and have student volunteers color them. Staple or glue the animal cutouts, along with real (lightweight) articles of clothing, onto the board. Add some student-made snowflakes and a title and...let it snow!

Festival Of Lights

Celebrate Hanukkah with this festive bulletin board. To create the menorah, wrap tubes from paper towels or wrapping paper in shiny paper or cellophane. Staple the tubes to the board in the shape of a menorah (as shown). Use construction paper and glitter to make the candles' flames. "Light" the middle candle first; then add one flame to the bulletin board for each of the eight nights of Hanukkah. Invite students to draw pictures of Hanukkah celebrations; then display their artwork around the menorah.

Oh, Christmas Tree

Ask students to give you a hand with Christmas decorating. Trace each child's two hands and help him cut out the shapes. Place the pairs of hands so that one hand slightly overlaps the other; then glue them in place. Have each child use construction paper and glue to make a glittered star for the top and a brown trunk for the bottom of his tree. Have students use different colors of ink pads to make fingerprint ornaments for their trees. Display these "hand-y" trees with a Christmas-lights border.

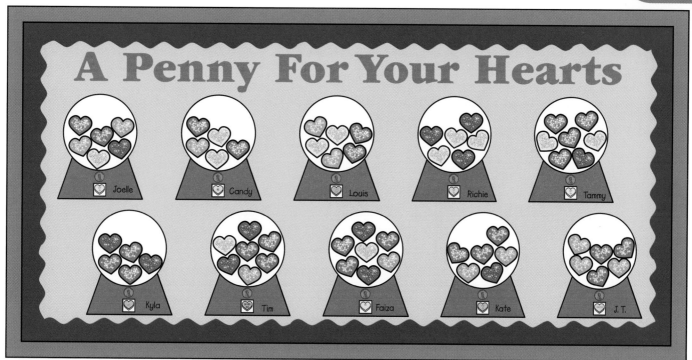

Everyone will love this sweet Valentine's Day bulletin board. Provide each child with a large white circle, a small white square, a red trapezoid, and several small hearts cut from construction paper. Have each student decorate her hearts with glitter and then glue them onto her circle. Have her glue the square to the trapezoid (as shown) and then glue the trapezoid below the circle to resemble the base of a gumball machine. Use hot glue to attach a real penny and a candy conversation heart as shown. Mount the designs and title on a bulletin board for a delicious display!

Invite youngsters to create springtime crafts for this display. To create a butterfly, paint a coffee filter with watercolors. Pinch the center with a clothespin and add pipe-cleaner antennae. To make a bee, add gold-glitter stripes, a pipe-cleaner stinger, waxed-paper wings, and wiggle eyes to a black construction-paper circle. To make a kite, decorate a construction-paper diamond with glitter; then add a yarn-and-ribbon tail. Look…up in the air…it's spring!

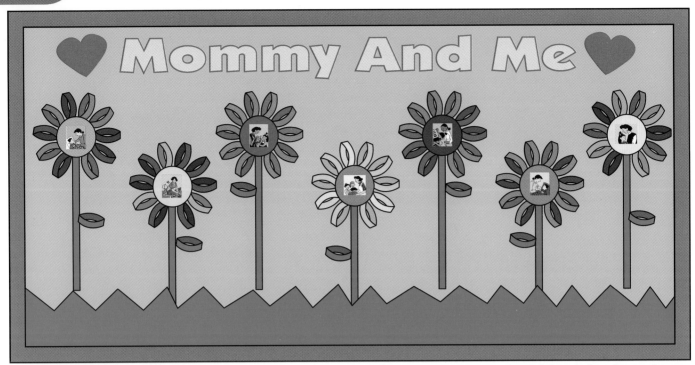

Love is in bloom with this special Mother's Day bulletin board. Ask each child to bring in a picture of herself with her mother. Then have her create a flower by making ten loops from 12-inch strips of construction paper. Have her glue the loops around a six-inch construction-paper circle and then add a green stem and loop leaf. Invite her to glue her special photo to the center of her flower. Display the finished flowers and title where moms can see them, and watch their smiles blossom!

Show off your youngsters' sunny smiles on this sunflower display. Provide each child with a six-inch brown circle and several yellow triangles cut from construction paper. Have each student glue his triangles around his circle. Have him add a personalized green stem and a leaf, then glue a photo of himself to the center of his flower. Invite him to glue on some real sunflower seeds to complete his project. Display the flowers and title, and enjoy your little ones' gorgeous grins!

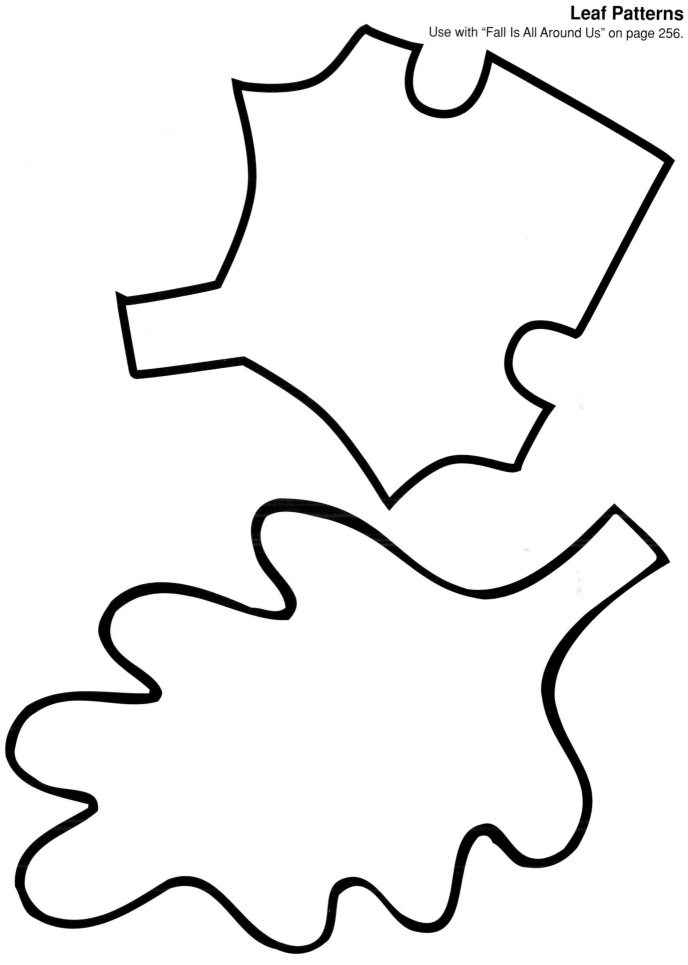

Witch Pattern
Use with "Our Wacky Witch's Brew" on page 256.

Animal Patterns
Use with "Let It Snow!" on page 257.

SPRING

Spring will be bursting out all over your class-room when your students create these special crafts.

Shy Sheep

These shy sheep are a "shear" delight! To make one, glue cotton balls onto a paper doily, making sure the frilly edge remains exposed. Glue two 1" x 2" black construction-paper strips to the lower edge of the doily to resemble legs. Make a face by folding down two points of a three-inch black construction-paper triangle as shown. Glue it to the center of the sheep's body. Glue wiggle eyes, a cotton-ball tuft of hair, and a pink pom-pom nose to the sheep's face. Glue a small bell just below the sheep's nose. Baaaah!

Monarch Magnets

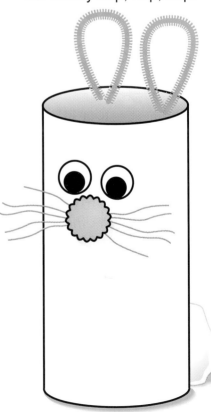

Happy, Mother's Day!

Each child's handprints will make this butterfly magnet an extraspecial gift for Mother's or Father's Day. Invite a child to press her hand into paint, then onto a sheet of tagboard twice. When the paint is dry, cut out the two handprints. Have the child embellish the handprints with faux jewels and sequins. Next direct him to use a marker to color a clothespin.

To assemble the butterfly, hot-glue the handprints to either side of the clothespin body to resemble wings. Hot-glue wiggle eyes and pipe-cleaner antennae to the clothespin. Complete the butterfly by gluing a magnet to the back of the clothespin. Finally, clip a greeting to the butterfly. Parents are sure to admire this fancy way of displaying their child's handiwork.

Bunny Puppet

Your little ones will be hopping down the bunny trail with this sweet puppet. Cover a toilet-tissue tube with white construction paper. Cut a pink pipe cleaner in half; then bend each piece into a loop to resemble a bunny ear. Glue the ears to the inside of one end of the tube. Make a face by gluing wiggle eyes, string whiskers, and a pink pom-pom nose onto the tube. Complete the bunny by gluing a cotton-ball tail to the back of the tube.

To use the puppet, have a child insert two fingers inside the tube and make her bunny hop, hop, hop!

A SEASONAL SAMPLER

Craft your way through the school year with this sampling of seasonal and holiday crafts.
ideas contributed by Bonnie Cave, Lori Kent, and Linda Ludlow

FALL

Jump right into fall festivities when you take your pick from this tasty crop of ideas.

Johnny Appleseed Headbands

Your youngsters will love wearing these headbands for Johnny Appleseed's birthday (September 26). To make one, staple two 6" x 12" black construction-paper strips end-to-end. Glue an apple cutout to the center of the band. Staple the band to fit a child's head. Round one end of a 9" x 3" construction-paper rectangle to resemble a pot handle. Use a round or apple-shaped hole puncher to punch a hole in the rounded end of the handle. Fold the opposite end of the handle, creating a tab for gluing. Glue the handle to the headband as shown.

Apple Wreaths

Fall-colored apple prints are the inspiration for these student-made wreaths. To make a wreath, have a child repeatedly press an apple half into thinned tempera paint, then onto a sheet of paper. When the paint is dry, have her add brown stems with a thin marker, then cut around the apple prints. Cut out the center from a paper plate; then direct the child to glue her apple-print cutouts onto the remaining rim of the plate. Glue a picture of the child to another apple-print cutout; then use yarn and tape to suspend this apple from the rim of the plate, so that it hangs in the center opening. Add a bow to complete the wreath. Hey, sweetie pie, you're the apple of my eye!

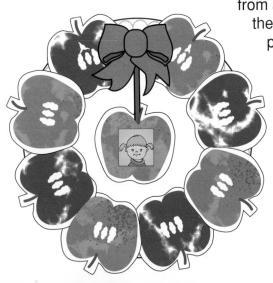

BLOWIN' IN THE WIND

Take a nature walk to collect some fall leaves; then head back to the classroom to make these windsocks. To make one, place a leaf—vein-side-up—under a sheet of construction paper. Rub the paper with the side of an unwrapped crayon. Repeat this process, overlapping the leaves and using different crayon colors and different leaves. Then cut fall-colored crepe paper into 14-inch strips. Glue a few construction-paper leaves onto each strip; then glue the strips to the bottom edge of the paper with the rubbings. Roll the paper into a cylinder and staple it in place. Punch holes near the top; then lace a length of yarn through the holes and tie the ends together. Suspend the windsocks from the ceiling of your classroom for a fabulous fall display.

Pumpkin Pumpkin

Make these pumpkins as a follow-up to a reading of *Pumpkin Pumpkin* by Jeanne Titherington (Greenwillow Books), and your youngsters will have seeds for planting in the spring. Paint the backs of two paper plates orange. When the paint is dry, paint the inside of each plate yellow. Glue a green construction-paper stem to the top of each plate. Punch two holes in each plate; then use green curling ribbon to hinge the plates together as shown. Glue black construction-paper shapes to the front of the pumpkin to create a jack-o'-lantern face. Place six pumpkin seeds inside a resealable plastic bag; then tape the bag inside the pumpkin. Finish the project by attaching a copy of the poem shown to the pumpkin stem.

Here is my jack-o'-lantern,
Smiling at you and me.
And when you open up his lid,
You're sure to shout, "Yippee!"
'Cause what you'll find tucked inside,
Are six little seeds to sow.
Just plant them in the spring sunshine
And watch a pumpkin grow!

WEB WALKERS

These eerie web walkers will create a creepy-crawly atmosphere in your classroom this Halloween. Begin by cutting white cotton string into varying lengths. Dip the string into a mixture of two parts glue and one part water; then arrange the string onto a piece of waxed paper so that it resembles a web. Sprinkle the web with silver glitter if desired. When the glue is dry, gently peel the web from the paper.

To make a spider, hot-glue black pipe-cleaner legs and wiggle eyes to a black pom-pom. Hot-glue the spider to the web. Use fishing line to suspend the webs from the ceiling of your classroom. Ooooh, spooky!

Turkeys On Top!

Your little ones are sure to strut their stuff when wearing these turkey hats. To make one, paint a cone-shaped birthday hat brown. Glue construction-paper tail feathers to one side of the hat. Glue wiggle eyes to the front of the hat just below the point. Complete the hat by gluing a construction-paper beak and wattle to the face. Gobble, gobble!

Slide into the winter months in a flurry with this cool collection of ideas!

WINTER

Spice Boys

These delightful spice boys will fill your classroom with the delicious aroma of gingerbread. Have a child paint a gingerbread-boy shape with brown tempera paint. When it is completely covered, have him sprinkle the wet paint with pumpkin-pie spice or cinnamon. When the paint is dry, have each child decorate his cutout with a variety of craft supplies, such as glitter, ribbon, fabric scraps, buttons, and stickers. To display your spice boys, punch holes in the hands of each cutout; then lace them together as shown.

Jolly Ol' Santa Claus

Your little elves are sure to feel jolly and bright when wearing this adorable holiday pin. To make one, use skin-colored paint to paint the metal top from a frozen-juice can. When the paint is dry, glue a length of white Christmas-tree garland to the lower half of the lid to resemble a beard. Glue a red felt triangle to the top of the lid to create a hat. Embellish the hat with a piece of silver pipe cleaner and a white pom-pom. Use black dimensional paint to make eyes; then glue on a red pom-pom nose. Complete the Santa by hot-gluing a bar pin to the back of the lid. Ho, ho, ho!

Annette Thompson and Kimberly Clayton—
    Preschool
Leading Edge Preschool
Rigby, ID

Frosty Snowmen

These cute little snowmen are sure to warm hearts. Duplicate a copy of the snowman pattern (page 270) on tagboard; then cut it out. Trace the snowman pattern onto white felt; then cut around the resulting outline. Decorate the snowman with felt scraps, ribbon, buttons, and other craft supplies. Cut two slits in the center of the snowman; then insert a peppermint or cinnamon stick through the slits to resemble arms. Personalize each snowman; then punch a hole in the top. Thread a length of ribbon through the hole and tie the ends together. Hang these frosty friends in your classroom for a display that is "snow" cool!

Spoolin' Around With Snowflakes

Create a blizzard of excitement in your classroom with these icy wonders! For each child duplicate a copy of the snowflake pattern (page 271) on blue construction paper. Have each child cut out his snowflake. Then have him repeatedly press one end of a spool into paint and onto his snowflake. While the paint is still wet, have him sprinkle the entire snowflake with iridescent glitter. When the paint is dry, use clear fishing line to suspend the snowflakes from the ceiling of your classroom. Let it snow, let it snow, let it snow!

A Handsome Gift

Your youngsters will give this handy Valentine's Day gift the high five! Place a red or pink jelly bean in each finger and in the thumb of a disposable latex glove to resemble painted fingernails. Stuff the remaining portion of the glove with cooled popcorn. Insert an unsharpened valentine pencil into the bottom of the glove. Gather the wrist of the glove around the pencil; then secure it with red curling ribbon. Complete the project by sticking a heart sticker to a finger to resemble a ring. What a sweet treat!

Hundredth-Day Spectacles

Your little ones will go loopy over these spectacular Hundredth-Day spectacles. For each child duplicate a copy of the spectacles pattern (page 270) onto tagboard. Invite a child to decorate his spectacles using construction-paper scraps, stickers, and markers. Fold the side pieces on the dotted lines; then glue each piece to the front of the glasses as shown. Punch a hole in the end of each side piece. Next have the child string 100 pieces of fruit-flavored O-shaped cereal onto a length of yarn. Tie the ends of the yarn to the side pieces of the spectacles to resemble a glasses chain. These spectacles are out of sight!

SPRING

Spring will be bursting out all over your classroom when your students create these special crafts.

Shy Sheep

These shy sheep are a "shear" delight! To make one, glue cotton balls onto a paper doily, making sure the frilly edge remains exposed. Glue two 1" x 2" black construction-paper strips to the lower edge of the doily to resemble legs. Make a face by folding down two points of a three-inch black construction-paper triangle as shown. Glue it to the center of the sheep's body. Glue wiggle eyes, a cotton-ball tuft of hair, and a pink pom-pom nose to the sheep's face. Glue a small bell just below the sheep's nose. Baaaah!

Monarch Magnets

Happy Mother's Day!

Each child's handprints will make this butterfly magnet an extraspecial gift for Mother's or Father's Day. Invite a child to press her hand into paint; then onto a sheet of tagboard twice. When the paint is dry, cut out the two handprints. Have the child embellish the handprints with faux jewels and sequins. Next direct him to use a marker to color a clothespin.

To assemble the butterfly, hot-glue the handprints to either side of the clothespin body to resemble wings. Hot-glue wiggle eyes and pipe-cleaner antennae to the clothespin. Complete the butterfly by gluing a magnet to the back of the clothespin. Finally, clip a greeting to the butterfly. Parents are sure to admire this fancy way of displaying their child's handiwork.

Bunny Puppet

Your little ones will be hopping down the bunny trail with this sweet puppet. Cover a toilet-tissue tube with white construction paper. Cut a pink pipe cleaner in half; then bend each piece into a loop to resemble a bunny ear. Glue the ears to the inside of one end of the tube. Make a face by gluing wiggle eyes, string whiskers, and a pink pom-pom nose onto the tube. Complete the bunny by gluing a cotton-ball tail to the back of the tube.

To use the puppet, have a child insert two fingers inside the tube and make her bunny hop, hop, hop!

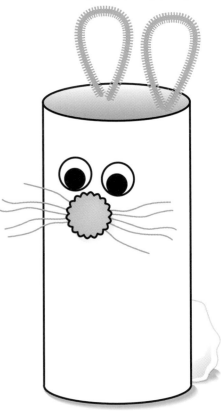

Mr. Frog

Your youngsters are sure to find these little hoppers "toad-ally" awesome! Begin by painting the back of a red paper plate green. When the paint is dry, fold the plate in half, so that the green side is facing out. Glue wiggle eyes to the top of two large green pom-poms; then glue the pom-poms to the plate. Create back legs by accordion-folding two 2" x 12" green construction-paper strips. Glue the strips to the back of the plate as shown. Accordion-fold two 2" x 6" green construction-paper strips; then glue them in place to create front legs. Trim all the legs at the ends as shown. To complete the frog, roll a narrow strip of red construction paper around a pencil; then glue it to the inside rim to create a tongue.

Encourage each student to use his frog to retell a frog-related story or use it as a prop for a favorite song or fingerplay. Ribbet, ribbet!

Thumb Buggies In A Jar

Got the springtime bug? If so, then this project will get you buzzin'! For each child, outline a simple jar shape on a sheet of white construction paper. Have a child repeatedly press a thumb into paint, then onto her paper. When the paint is dry, have her use a marker to add wings, eyes, legs, and other buggy features to each thumbprint. Use the completed picture as a page in a number book or as a booklet cover. Bugs near, bugs far. How many bugs in your bug jar?

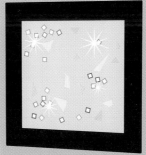

Sunny Suncatchers

Fill your classroom with the warm glow of summer colors when you hang these "sun-sational" catchers in your windows. To make one, press a variety of craft materials—such as foil pieces, tissue-paper scraps, and glitter—onto the adhesive side of a piece of clear Con-Tact® covering. Cover the collage with another sheet of Con-Tact® covering, so that the adhesive sides are together. Trim the edges; then tape it into a black construction-paper frame. Tape the suncatchers to your classroom window to create a stained-glass effect.

Snowman Pattern
Use with "Frosty Snowmen" on page 266.

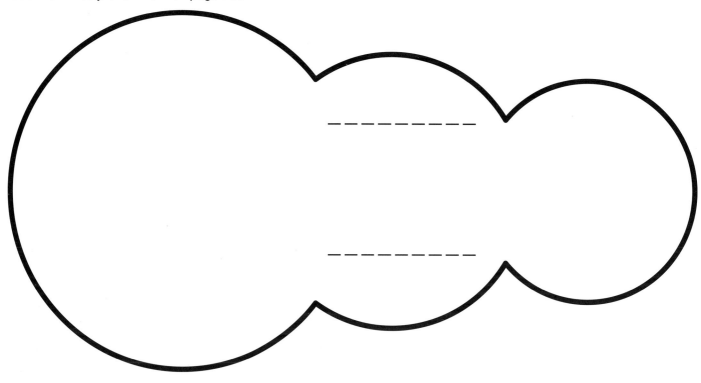

Spectacles Pattern
Use with "Hundredth-Day Spectacles" on page 267.

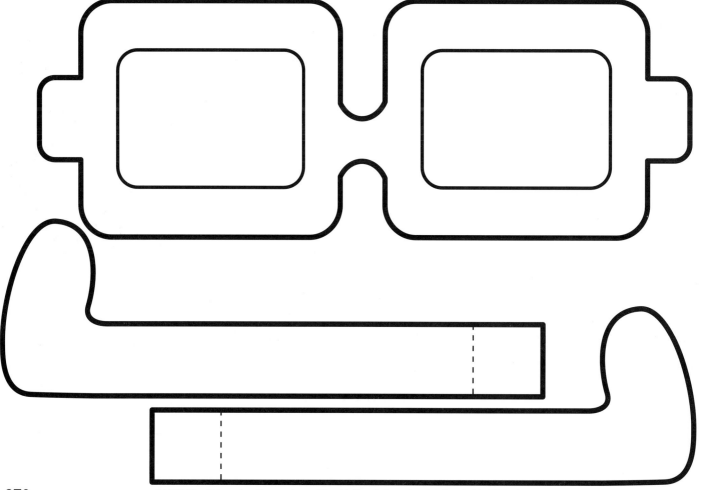

©1998 The Education Center, Inc. • *The Mailbox® Superbook • Grade K* • TEC459

A YEAR'S WORTH OF SONGS, POEMS, AND FINGERPLAYS

Is it time for a Thanksgiving rhyme? Need to sing about spring? Here's a collection of original seasonal and holiday songs, poems, and fingerplays to keep youngsters' hands clappin' and toes tappin'!

contributed by Lisa Cowman, Lucia Kemp Henry, and Angie Kutzer

WELCOME TO KINDERGARTEN!

(sung to the tune of "Deck The Halls")
Welcome to our kindergarten.
We will learn a lot of things today.
Here we are in kindergarten.
We will have a lot of time to play.
We will learn the alphabet and
We will learn how to write numbers, too.
We'll have fun in kindergarten,
'Cause there are so many things to do!

MAKING NEW FRIENDS

After teaching this counting poem to your little ones, arrange five volunteers in a row. Assign each child in the group a different number from one to five. As the class recites the poem again, direct each child to stand when his number is called; have the standing children perform the corresponding motions.

Here is **one** friend,	(Hold up one finger.)
Turning around.	(Turn a circle in place.)
Here are **two** friends,	(Hold up two fingers.)
Jumping up and down.	(Jump.)
Here are **three** friends,	(Hold up three fingers.)
Reading a book.	(Pretend to be holding a book open.)
Here are **four** friends,	(Hold up four fingers.)
Learning to cook.	(Make stirring motions in a pretend bowl.)
Here are **five** friends,	(Hold up five fingers.)
On the go.	(Jog in place.)
We are **all** friends here, you know!	
	(Open arms out wide.)

Trick or treat! This poem is sure to spark lively discussions about dressing up for Halloween. Invite your students to act out the characters in the poem. Or extend the poem into a math activity by having each child draw his favorite character from the poem; then graph the drawings to see which character is the class favorite.

Let's pretend. It's lots of fun!
Pretend to be most anyone.
Pretend to be a furry cat,
Or a dog in a silly hat.
Pretend to be a funny clown,
Or a ghost with a scary frown.
Pretend to be a king or queen,
Pretending is fun on Halloween!

IT'S FALL!

Fall is all around you.
Yes, it's time for fall.
Feel fall with your senses—
Five senses in all.

See fall with your two eyes,
In the leaves so bright.
Red and orange and brown leaves,
Such a pretty sight.

Hear fall with your two ears,
As the birds fly by.
Squawking, honking, loud geese,
Calling way up high.

Smell fall with your nose,
In the chilly air.
Cool and damp and wet rain,
Falling everywhere.

Feel fall with your two hands,
On the clothes you wear.
Warm and snuggly, soft coat,
Like a fuzzy bear.

Taste fall with your tongue now,
In an apple sweet.
Juicy, crunchy apple—
What a yummy treat!

Fall is all around you.
Yes, it's time for fall.
Feel fall with your senses—
Five senses in all.

WE'RE THANKFUL

Bring a little Christmas spirit into Thanksgiving with this adaptation of "O Christmas Tree."

It's Thanksgiving, it's Thanksgiving,
Let's count our many blessings.
It's Thanksgiving, it's Thanksgiving,
Let's count our many blessings.
A place to live, and clothes to wear,
Our families' love, and friends who care.
It's Thanksgiving, it's Thanksgiving,
Let's count our many blessings.

MITTEN MELODY

Brrr! It's getting colder! Sing this song as your youngsters bundle up for outdoor fun. Can your little ones think of other adjectives to substitute for the boldfaced words?

(sung to the tune of
"We Wish You A Merry Christmas")
Let's put on our **winter** mittens.
Let's put on our **winter** mittens.
Let's put on our **winter** mittens.
It's so cold outside!

Let's put on our **fuzzy** mittens.
Let's put on our **fuzzy** mittens.
Let's put on our **fuzzy** mittens.
It's so cold outside!

HOLIDAY LIGHTS

Light up the holidays with these verses that represent Christmas, Hanukkah, and Kwanzaa. No matter what the reason, this song is in season!

(sung to the tune of "This Little Light Of Mine")
These **colored lights so** bright,
Are such a pretty sight.
These **colored lights so** bright,
Are such a pretty sight.
These **colored lights so** bright,
Are such a pretty sight.
Let them shine! Let them shine!
Let them shine!

Sing the song twice more,
substituting "little candles"
and "little stars so" for
the boldfaced words.

FIVE LITTLE SNOWMEN

Five little snowmen shivering in the ice.
The first one said, "This isn't very nice."
The second one said, "I can hardly wait for spring."
The third one said, "Then birds will sing!"
The fourth one said, "Here comes the bright, warm sun!"
The fifth one said, "This is our last day of fun!"
"Aah," said the snow as warm breezes blew.
Five little snowmen know winter is through.

CHEER FOR THE NEW YEAR

(sung to the tune of "Row, Row, Row Your Boat")

Cheer, cheer, let's all cheer.
January's here!
Hip, hip, hooray! The very first day,
Of a brand new year.

100TH-DAY FINGERPLAY

Two, four, six, eight, what do we appreciate? The 100th day of school, of course! Chant this rhyme to celebrate the 100th day and also to practice skip-counting by tens.

(chanted to the rhythm of "Bubble Gum, Bubble Gum")

We deserve, we deserve a lot of praise.
We've been at school one hundred days!
10, 20, 30, 40, 50, 60, 70, 80, 90, 100.
Hooray, hooray, hooray!

A VALENTINE IS...

(sung to the tune of
"My Bonnie Lies Over The Ocean")
A valentine is very special.
A valentine is very sweet.
A valentine is very friendly.
A true valentine can't be beat.

Will you, will you,
Oh, will you be my valentine? Be mine!
Will you, will you,
Oh, will you be my valentine?

SPRING IS HERE!

Time to shed those heavy coats and furry mittens! Take your spring chicks outside to breathe the fresh spring air and feel the warm sun. Then use this poem as a springboard for discussing and anticipating lots of spring fun.

Spring is here! Let's all cheer!
Time for bikes and nature hikes.
Time for skates and picnic dates.
Time for the park and games at dark.
Time for friends and tent weekends.
Time to cheer—new life is here!

A WINDY DAY

What do paper, hats, leaves, and hair have in common? "The answer, my friend, is blowing in the wind" in this March melody. Once youngsters are familiar with the song, encourage each child to name something else that the wind blows to substitute for the boldfaced word. Whoosh!

(sung to the tune of
"Row, Row, Row Your Boat")
What does the March wind blow,
On a windy day?
Tumbling, tumbling, **paper** is tumbling.
Watch it blow away!

What does the March wind blow,
On a windy day?
Tumbling, tumbling, **leaves** are tumbling.
Watch them blow away!

BEAUTIFUL SPRING

Here's April rain that drizzles down.
> *(Hold arms up and wiggle fingers as arms lower.)*

Here is the sun that warms the ground.
> *(Form circle above head with arms.)*

Here is the seed, so very small.
> *(Press thumb and pointer finger together.)*

Here is the plant, so strong and tall.
> *(Hold arms up straight, above head.)*

Here is the bud that blooms one day.
> *(Clasp hands together, above head.)*

Here's the pretty flower. It must be May!
> *(Open hands and spread fingers wide to form a flower.)*

SUMMER SUNSHINE

(sung to the tune of "Daisy, Daisy")

Summer sunshine,
We are so glad you're here!
Summertime is our favorite time of year.
Oh, summer's just right for playing.
Dear sun, say you'll be staying!
In summer sun,
We'll have some fun.
Summer sunshine, we sure love you!

I LOVE MY MOMMY AND MY DADDY

Here's a quick tune to honor mothers and/or fathers everywhere on their special days in May and June. Simply insert the appropriate word—mommy or daddy—and its pronoun to complete a very loving verse. If desired, record solos of this song on separate cassettes and send them home as treasured keepsakes.

(sung to the tune of "My Country 'Tis Of Thee")
My [mommy] is so sweet.
You know, [she]'s really neat.
[She] loves me so!

With me [she]'ll laugh and play.
[She]'s with me every day.
And so I have to say,
I love [her] so!

Four Seasons Of Fun

Celebrate the seasons with these group and center activities that will both challenge and entertain your little learners.

ideas contributed by Bonnie Cave and Patricia A. Staino

Leave It To Autumn

Discover your students' favorite fall colors with this group graphing activity. Make a large graph with drawings of a yellow leaf, a red leaf, an orange leaf, and a brown leaf down the left side. Cut construction paper in those same four colors into squares. Ask each child to choose the leaf color she likes best and write her name on a construction-paper square of that color. Have each child use tape to attach her square to the graph beside the appropriate leaf. Have students count the squares in each row and determine which leaf color is the class favorite.

To extend the activity, take students outside and ask each child to find a leaf of her favorite color. Back in the classroom, help each child cover her leaf with Con-Tact® paper to preserve it; then mount all the leaves around the graph.

AN APPLE TODAY

An abundant apple harvest lends itself to exploring our senses. Give each child in a small group an apple. Invite students to observe, touch, smell, and taste their apples. Ask them to describe the apples. Make a list of the descriptive words they use on your chalkboard or on a sheet of poster board. Then give each youngster a four-ounce container of applesauce and a spoon. Invite them to use their senses to explore the applesauce; then record their observations. Encourage them to compare and contrast the apple and the applesauce. To end this lip-smacking activity, invite students to finish feasting on their apples and applesauce.

Hungry Jack

Little ones will be hungry for knowledge when you add this activity to your October circle time. To prepare, draw a large, simple jack-o'-lantern on a piece of orange poster board. Cut out the design and then cut an opening for the mouth. Attach the cutout to a large shoebox so the box sits below the mouth opening. Then program a set of index cards for a basic skill you'd like to reinforce, such as letters, numerals, or shapes.

Each day during circle time, bring out the cards and "Hungry Jack." Present a card and ask a volunteer to identify the symbol shown. If the child is correct, he may "feed" the card to Hungry Jack. Continue as time permits and add cards for other skills as desired. Mmmm…what a smart idea!

Great Pumpkin Seeds!

Add fall flair to your math center to help youngsters practice fine-motor and counting skills. To prepare, create miniature jack-o'-lanterns by painting ten baby-food jars orange. When the paint is dry, use a black permanent marker to make facial features on one side of each jar. On the opposite side of each jar, write a numeral from 1 to 10. Place the jars in your math center, along with a pair of tweezers and a supply of dried pumpkin seeds in a small plastic jack-o'-lantern bucket. Invite youngsters who visit the center to pour some seeds onto the tabletop and use the tweezers to pick up the seeds and place the corresponding number into each jack-o'-lantern jar.

COMPARISON SHOPPING

Identifying similarities and differences is in the bag—the grocery bag, that is! Gather several typical Thanksgiving meal items, such as a potato, a sweet potato, a box of stuffing mix, a small bottle of apple cider, a small pumpkin, and a can of green beans (or other food items that may reflect your students' cultures). Place the items on a table, along with a large grocery bag. Gather a small group of students and tell them that they are going to pretend to shop for the groceries needed to make a Thanksgiving meal. Select two items. Ask volunteers to describe how the items are the same and how they are different. Each time a child successfully tells a likeness or difference, invite him to "buy" one of the two items and place it in the grocery bag. Repeat the activity with other pairs of items until the group has completed its Thanksgiving shopping.

The ABC Tree

The alphabet becomes a holiday decoration in this letter game, which is perfect for a small group or as a circle-time activity. To prepare, cut a large Christmas tree shape from a piece of green felt. Select several letters you'd like to review with your students. Cut these letters—upper- and lowercase—from colorful felt. Place the tree on your flannelboard. Decorate the tree with the uppercase letters. Then distribute the lowercase letters to children in the group. Ask each child, in turn, to replace the correct uppercase letter with her lowercase version. On another day, try the reverse: have students replace lowercase letters with uppercase ones.

LIGHT UP YOUR LESSONS

Holiday lights glow with learning possibilities. Hang a string of large outdoor Christmas lights in your classroom and watch students' eyes light up!

 Have children count how many bulbs are on the string. (Vary the number of bulbs from day to day.)

 Ask children to name the color of each bulb on the string or tell how many lights are a certain color.

 Insert the bulbs on the string in a specific color pattern, leaving a few open sockets. Ask children which colors are needed to complete the pattern; then insert them.

Having A (Snow) Ball!

To prepare for this art activity, trace a few large snowman shapes onto sheets of white poster board. Cut out the snowmen and attach them to a bulletin board. Then read aloud Lois Ehlert's *Snowballs* (Harcourt Brace & Company). Discuss the many objects used to create the snowpeople pictured in the book. Tell youngsters that they'll be using "found" items to decorate the paper snowpeople, and point out that any items used must be lightweight so they'll stay in place when stapled or glued to the paper. Ask youngsters to bring in appropriate items from home on a subsequent day. Use the students' items to create unique snowpeople. To extend the fun, have students name each snowman or "snowmiss."

Snow...Snow...Snowflake!

Students will warm up to this fun, active game. In advance prepare a supply of faux snow. Have youngsters help you cut white tissue paper into small bits of confetti. Then use the faux snow to play a game similar to the traditional Duck, Duck, Goose. Seat your youngsters in a circle. Choose a child to be It and give him a small handful of faux snow. Have him walk around the outside of the circle, tapping each child lightly as he says, "Snow." When he reaches the child he wishes to be the chaser, he yells, "Snowflake!" and sprinkles the faux snow over the child's head. That child then jumps up and chases It around the circle, attempting to tag him before he reaches the chaser's empty spot. Whether It is caught or not, have the chaser become It for the next round, and supply him with a handful of fresh snow.

Secret Valentines

These secret valentine messages will be a treat for your class—and someone else's! Get together with another teacher (perhaps the teacher of your reading buddies or the class next door) and arrange for her class to create valentines for your students and vice versa. To prepare each secret valentine, cut a heart shape from white construction paper. Have each child dictate a Valentine's Day message as you use a white crayon to write it; then have the child use the same crayon to sign her name. Send the valentines to the other class. When your children's valentines arrive, have each child brush watercolor paint over the heart to reveal the secret message.

DANDY CANDY HEARTS

Students will love this "heart-y" hands-on math activity. On a sheet of pink construction paper, draw four grids like the one shown. Cut the grids apart and laminate them for durability. Place the grids, a pair of dice, and a container of candy conversation hearts in a learning center. To play, each child, in turn, rolls the dice and places a candy heart on the corresponding box on his grid. If a child rolls a number that he has already covered, play goes to the next person. Continue until one child fills his grid.

To extend the activity, challenge students to roll the dice and remove the candy hearts from their grids. The first child to remove all his hearts is the winner. But everyone wins when you invite students to eat the candy hearts after completing this activity!

| 2 | 3 | 4 | Be Mine | 6 | 7 | 8 | 9 | 10 | 11 | 12 |

Alphabet Egg Hunt

This egg hunt ends with an alphabetical discovery! To prepare, purchase 26 plastic eggs. Place a different felt alphabet letter inside each one. Then hide the eggs in your classroom. Invite a small group of children to find the eggs. Ask them to open the eggs and identify the letters they find inside. Challenge students to place the letters in alphabetical order on a flannelboard. They'll know that they've located all the eggs when the alphabet is complete. Youngsters will enjoy replacing the letters in the eggs and hiding them for the next group of children.

It's A Breeze

A warm and breezy spring day is the perfect setting for a lesson on air power. Place several small objects—such as a feather, a key, a cotton ball, a piece of paper, a wood block, a toy car, and a Ping-Pong® ball—on a table. Ask your students to sort the items according to which are easy to move with air and which are not. Take students outside and place the items on the ground. Watch what happens as the wind blows. Were their predictions correct?

If the weather is not cooperative, have your children provide the wind power. Invite a child to blow through a drinking straw to create a "gust" of wind directed at each object. Ask students to compare their predictions with what really happened.

BUGS IN A BOX

Students will go buggy over this guessing game. To prepare for this activity, collect several small shoeboxes with lids. Put a different number of plastic bugs in each box. Then invite a small group to listen as you read *How Many Bugs In A Box?* by David A. Carter (Simon & Schuster Books For Young Readers). Afterward, invite each child in the group to shake one box and estimate the number of bugs inside. Record all the guesses on a sheet of chart paper. Then open the box and count together the actual number of plastic bugs to determine whose guess was closest to the actual number. Repeat the activity with the remaining boxes. To extend the lesson, have students use the bugs in the boxes for sorting or patterning.

PEEKABOO CARDS

Get a glimpse of spring or summer with this fun activity. First ask each child to find a picture in a magazine that reminds her of spring or summer. Tell students not to show their pictures to anyone else. For each child, fold a sheet of white construction paper in half. Unfold the paper and cut a square anywhere on the left-hand side of the paper. Guide each child in gluing her magazine picture to the right-hand side of the paper so that a portion of the picture shows through the hole when the paper is folded again. Ask each student to hold up her folded card while the others guess what is shown in the picture. After a few guesses, unfold the card to show the whole picture. If desired, collect the cards and compile them into a peekaboo class book with the title "Peekaboo Spring" or "Peekaboo Summer."

Flower Petals

Make counting skills blossom at your math center! Cut four 1-inch circles from yellow construction paper. Cut 32 petal shapes from red construction paper. Laminate all the pieces. Place the flower pieces and a die in a zippered plastic bag at your math center. Invite two to four children at a time to use the activity. Each child takes a yellow circle (a flower center). Instruct the players to take turns rolling the die and adding the corresponding number of petals to their flowers. The first child to add eight petals to his flower is the winner. If desired, when all the players have eight petals on their flowers, have them roll the die and remove the corresponding number of petals, replacing them in the plastic bag. There you go—counted, recounted, and cleaned up!

CELEBRATE!

When it's time to celebrate the seasons and holidays, the books in this handy list will make it easy to introduce a unit, follow up an activity, or settle into storytime.

compiled by Kim Griswell

FALL

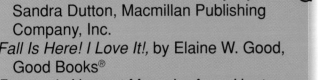

The Cinnamon Hen's Autumn Day, by Sandra Dutton, Macmillan Publishing Company, Inc.

Fall Is Here! I Love It!, by Elaine W. Good, Good Books®

Possum's Harvest Moon, by Anne Hunter, Houghton Mifflin Company

Red Leaf, Yellow Leaf, by Lois Ehlert, Harcourt Brace Jovanovich, Publishers

Too Many Pumpkins, by Linda White, Holiday House, Inc.

WINTER

Boot Weather, by Judith Vigna, Albert Whitman & Company

F-Freezing ABC, by Posy Simmonds, Alfred A. Knopf, Inc.

Ice Cream Is Falling!, by Shigeo Watanabe, Philomel Books

Sadie And The Snowman, by Allen Morgan, Scholastic Inc.

Snowballs, by Lois Ehlert, Harcourt Brace & Company

SPRING

April Showers, by George Shannon, Greenwillow Books

Max And Maggie In Spring, by Janet Craig, Troll Associates

Spring, by Ron Hirschi, Puffin Unicorn Books

Spring Green, by Valrie M. Selkowe, Lothrop, Lee & Shepard Books

That's What Happens When It's Spring!, by Elaine W. Good, Good Books®

SUMMER

It's Summertime!, by Elaine W. Good, Good Books®

One Hot Summer Day, by Nina Crews, Greenwillow Books

Summer Legs, by Anita Hakkinen, Henry Holt And Company, Inc.

Those Summers, by Aliki, HarperCollins Publishers, Inc.

Watermelon Day, by Kathi Appelt, Henry Holt And Company, Inc.

HALLOWEEN

Big Pumpkin, by Erica Silverman, Scholastic Inc.

The Hallo-Wiener, by Dav Pilkey, The Blue Sky Press

Pumpkin Pumpkin, by Jeanne Titherington, Greenwillow Books

Two Little Witches, by Harriet Ziefert, Candlewick Press

The Vanishing Pumpkin, by Tony Johnston, The Putnam & Grosset Group

THANKSGIVING

Gracias The Thanksgiving Turkey, by Joy Cowley, Scholastic Press

Sometimes It's Turkey—Sometimes It's Feathers, by Lorna Balian, Abingdon Press

Thanksgiving At The Tappletons', by Eileen Spinelli, HarperTrophy

Turkey Pox, by Laurie Halse Anderson, Albert Whitman & Company

A Visit To Grandma's, by Nancy Carlson, Viking

HANUKKAH

Beni's First Chanukah, by Jane Breskin Zalben, Henry Holt And Company, Inc.
By The Hanukkah Light, by Sheldon Oberman, Boyds Mills Press, Inc.
The Gift, by Aliana Brodmann, Simon & Schuster Books For Young Readers
Inside-Out Grandma: A Hanukkah Story, by Joan Rothenberg, Hyperion Books
    For Children
The Ugly Menorah, by Marissa Moss, Farrar Straus & Giroux, Inc.

CHRISTMAS

Happy Christmas Gemma, by Sarah
    Hayes, Lothrop, Lee & Shepard Books
*Morris's Disappearing Bag: A Christmas
    Story,* by Rosemary Wells, Dial Books
    For Young Readers
Santa's Secret Helper, by Andrew
    Clements, Picture Book Studio
Shhh!, by Julie Sykes, Little Tiger Press
Wombat Divine, by Mem Fox,
    Harcourt Brace & Company

KWANZAA

The Gifts Of Kwanzaa, by Synthia Saint
    James, Albert Whitman & Company
Kente Colors, by Debbi Chocolate,
    Walker Publishing Company, Inc.
Kwanzaa, by Janet Riehecky,
    Childrens Press®, Inc.
A Kwanzaa Celebration: Pop-Up Book, by
    Nancy Williams, Little Simon
Seven Candles For Kwanzaa, by Andrea Davis
    Pinkney, Dial Books For Young Readers

VALENTINE'S DAY

The Best Valentine In The World, by
    Marjorie Weinman Sharmat,
    Holiday House, Inc.
Four Valentines In A Rainstorm, by Felicia
    Bond, HarperCollins Children's Books
Little Mouse's Big Valentine, by Thacher
    Hurd, HarperCollins Children's Books
One Zillion Valentines, by Frank Modell,
    Greenwillow Books
A Village Full Of Valentines, by James
    Stevenson, Greenwillow Books

EASTER

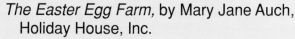

The Easter Egg Farm, by Mary Jane Auch,
    Holiday House, Inc.
*The Great Big Especially Beautiful Easter
    Egg,* by James Stevenson,
    Greenwillow Books
Max's Chocolate Chicken, by Rosemary
    Wells, Dial Books For Young Readers
The Spring Hat, by Madelaine Gill, Simon
    & Schuster Books For Young Readers
Where Is It?, by Tana Hoban,
    Macmillan Publishing Company, Inc.

MOTHER'S DAY

Flowers For Mommy, by Susan Anderson,
    Africa World Press, Inc.
Happy Mother's Day, by Steven Kroll,
    Holiday House, Inc.
The Mother's Day Mice, by Eve Bunting,
    Clarion Books
The Mother's Day Sandwich, by
    Jillian Wynot, Orchard Books
My Very Own Mother's Day, by
    Robin West, Carolrhoda Books, Inc.

FATHER'S DAY

Happy Father's Day, by Steven Kroll,
    Holiday House, Inc.
Hooray For Father's Day!, by Marjorie
    Weinman Sharmat, Holiday House, Inc.
My Father's Hands, by Joanne Ryder,
    Morrow Junior Books
My Ol' Man, by Patricia Polacco,
    Philomel Books
A Perfect Father's Day, by Eve Bunting,
    Clarion Books

SPECIAL SONGS FOR SPECIAL DAYS

Here's a list of seasonal musical selections to add to the flavor, fun, and fancy of holiday and special days celebrations.

compiled by Mackie Rhodes

SEASONS

"Snowflake"
Rockin' Down The Road (winter)

"The Garden Song"
10 Carrot Diamond (spring)

"Star Sun"
Bahamas Pajamas (summer)

"Hello Winter"
Diamonds & Dragons (all seasons)

HALLOWEEN

Halloween Fun (entire album)

"Halloween Night" *Bahamas Pajamas*

"Halloween On Parade" *Holidays And Special Times*

"Have A Good Time On Halloween Night"
Holiday Songs & Rhythms

"Jack-O-Lantern" *Dinosaur Ride*

"Looking For Dracula" *10 Carrot Diamond*

"Monster" *Can You Sound Just Like Me?*

"Scared As I Can Be"
Mr. Al Sings Friends And Feelings

THANKSGIVING

"Happy Thanksgiving To All"
Holidays And Special Times

"Things I'm Thankful For"
Holiday Songs & Rhythms and
Holiday Magic

WINTER CELEBRATIONS
CHRISTMAS, HANUKKAH, KWANZAA

These recordings include Christmas songs, in addition to the following selections for the special days indicated.

Holiday Magic
"Chanukah, Oh Chanukah"

Holiday Songs & Rhythms
"Hanukkah"

Tis The Season
"Hanukkah Medley: Hanuk-kah, Oh Hanukkah Ha-nukkah"

Holiday Times
"Dreidel, Dreidel, Dreidel"
"Harmonica For Hanukkah"
"My Little Blue Dreidel"
"Kwanza Time"

The Christmas Gift
"Little Dreydl Spin"

VALENTINE'S DAY

"If Apples Were Pears" *Imagine That!*

"Love Is..."
Holidays And Special Times

"Valentines Song"
Holiday Songs & Rhythms

MOTHER'S DAY AND FATHER'S DAY

"A Mother Is Forever" and "Hush Little Baby"
Diamonds & Daydreams

"May There Always Be Sunshine" (multilingual) *10 Carrot Diamond*

EASTER

"Peter Cottontail"
Holidays And Special Times

"Easter Time Is Here Again"
Holiday Songs & Rhythms

For more information or to order the listed recordings, contact:

10 Carrot Diamond, Charlotte Diamond,
Hug Bug Records
([604] 931-7375)

Bahamas Pajamas, Joe Scruggs,
Shadow Play Records
(1-800-274-8804)

Can You Sound Just Like Me?,
Red Grammer,
Red Note Records
([315] 676-5516)

Diamonds & Daydreams,
Charlotte Diamond,
Hug Bug Records
([604] 931-7375)

Diamonds & Dragons, Charlotte Diamond,
Hug Bug Records
([604] 931-7375)

Dinosaur Ride, Jim Valley And Friends,
Rainbow Planet Records And Tapes
(1-800-523-2371)

Halloween Fun,
KIMBO® Educational
(1-800-631-2187)

Holiday Magic, Hap Palmer,
Hap-Pal Music Inc.
(1-800-645-3739)

Holiday Songs & Rhythms, Hap Palmer,
Educational Activities, Inc.
(1-800-645-3739)

Holiday Times, Ella Jenkins,
Smithsonian Folkways Recordings
(1-800-410-9815)

Holidays And Special Times, Greg & Steve,
Youngheart Music
(1-800-444-4287)

Imagine That!, Jim Valley And Friends,
Rainbow Planet Records And Tapes
(1-800-523-2371)

Mr. Al Sings Friends And Feelings, Mr. Al,
Melody House
(1-800-234-9228)

Rockin' Down The Road, Greg & Steve,
Youngheart Music
(1-800-444-4287)

The Christmas Gift, Charlotte Diamond,
Hug Bug Records
([604] 931-7375)

Tis The Season, Fred Koch,
Melody House, Inc.
(1-800-234-9228)

NO TRICK...JUST A TREAT!

Happy
Halloween!

From Your Teacher

©1998 The Education Center, Inc. • *The Mailbox® Superbook* • *Grade K* • TEC459

Have a
gobblin'-good
Thanksgiving!

From
Your Teacher

©1998 The Education Center, Inc. • *The Mailbox® Superbook* • *Grade K* • TEC459

Note To The Teacher: Duplicate a class supply of each card. Color the cards; then use an X-acto®
knife to cut slits along the bold lines on each card. Complete the cards by inserting lollipops through
the slits. Secure lollipops with tape, if necessary.

Have a sweet holiday!

From Your Teacher

©1998 The Education Center, Inc. • *The Mailbox® Superbook • Grade K • TEC459*

finished sample

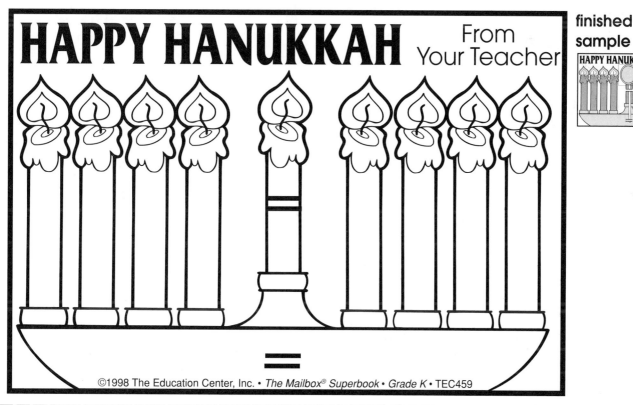

HAPPY HANUKKAH

From Your Teacher

©1998 The Education Center, Inc. • *The Mailbox® Superbook • Grade K • TEC459*

finished sample

Note To The Teacher: Duplicate a class supply of each card. Color the cards; then use an X-acto® knife to cut slits along the four bold lines on each card. Complete the cards by inserting lollipops through the slits. Secure lollipops with tape, if necessary.

THAT'S WHAT FRIENDS ARE FOR!

Happy
Valentine's
Day

From Your
Teacher

Note To The Teacher: Duplicate a class supply of each card. Color the cards; then use an X-acto® knife to cut slits along the four bold lines on each card. Complete the cards by inserting lollipops through the slits. Secure lollipops with tape, if necessary.

finished
sample

A-tisket, a-tasket, Here's something for your basket!

From Your Teacher

©1998 The Education Center, Inc. • *The Mailbox® Superbook* • *Grade K* • TEC459

finished
sample

HIP, HIP, HOORAY!
You're Going To First Grade!

GOOD JOB!

Way to Go!

HI!

©1998 The Education Center, Inc. • *The Mailbox® Superbook* • *Grade K* • TEC459

Note To The Teacher: Duplicate a class supply of each card. Color the cards; then use an X-acto® knife to cut slits along the four bold lines on each card. Complete the cards by inserting lollipops through the slits. Secure lollipops with tape, if necessary.

- -

Programming Suggestions: Use a copy of this page for a newsletter, a parent note, a booklist, or a student's
creative writing.

Programming Suggestions: Use a copy of this page for a newsletter, a parent note, a booklist, or a student's creative writing.

Programming Suggestions: Use a copy of this page for a newsletter, a parent note, a booklist, or a student's creative writing.

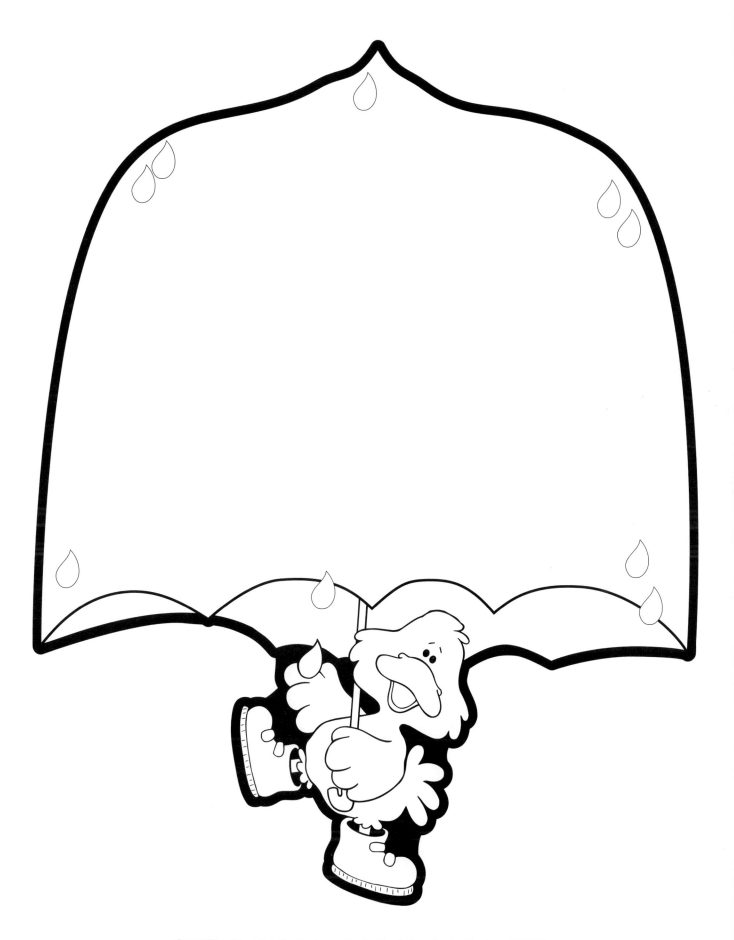

Programming Suggestions: Use a copy of this page for a newsletter, a parent note, a booklist, or a student's creative writing.

Programming Suggestions: Use a copy of this page for a newsletter, a parent note, a booklist, or a student's creative writing.

Programming Suggestions: Use a copy of this page for a newsletter, a parent note, a booklist, or a student's creative writing.

Programming Suggestions: Use a copy of this page for a newsletter, a parent note, a booklist, or a student's creative writing.

Programming Suggestions: Use a copy of this page for a newsletter, a parent note, a booklist, or a student's creative writing.

Programming Suggestions: Use a copy of this page for a newsletter, a parent note, a booklist, or a student's creative writing.

Programming Suggestions: Use a copy of this page for a newsletter, a parent note, a booklist, or a student's creative writing.

Programming Suggestions: Use a copy of this page for a newsletter, a parent note, a booklist, or a student's creative writing.

Programming Suggestions: Use a copy of this page for a newsletter, a parent note, a booklist, or a student's creative writing.

Sunday	Monday	Tuesday	Wednesday	Thursday	Friday	Saturday

FEBRUARY

Sunday	Monday	Tuesday	Wednesday	Thursday	Friday	Saturday

MARCH

Sunday	Monday	Tuesday	Wednesday	Thursday	Friday	Saturday

APRIL

Sunday	Monday	Tuesday	Wednesday	Thursday	Friday	Saturday

MAY

Sunday	Monday	Tuesday	Wednesday	Thursday	Friday	Saturday

JUNE

Sunday	Monday	Tuesday	Wednesday	Thursday	Friday	Saturday

Sunday	Monday	Tuesday	Wednesday	Thursday	Friday	Saturday

Sunday	Monday	Tuesday	Wednesday	Thursday	Friday	Saturday

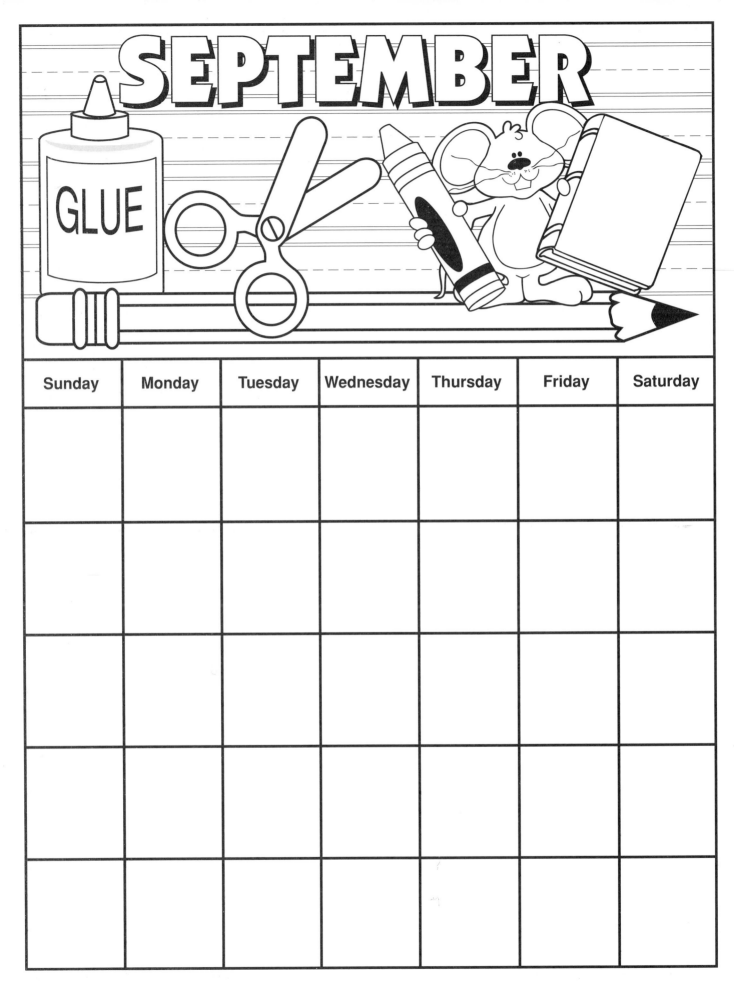

SEPTEMBER

Sunday	Monday	Tuesday	Wednesday	Thursday	Friday	Saturday

OCTOBER

Sunday	Monday	Tuesday	Wednesday	Thursday	Friday	Saturday

NOVEMBER

Sunday	Monday	Tuesday	Wednesday	Thursday	Friday	Saturday

DECEMBER

Sunday	Monday	Tuesday	Wednesday	Thursday	Friday	Saturday